JEWISH VOICES, GERMAN WORDS

Growing Up Jewish in Postwar Germany and Austria

Edited and with an introduction by Elena Lappin

Translated from the German by Krishna Winston

CATBIRD PRESS

First edition

CATBIRD PRESS
16 Windsor Road, North Haven, CT 06473
Our books are distributed to the trade by
Independent Publishers Group.

The publisher wishes to thank Mary Steinberg for doing early drafts of some
of the translations and for coming up with the title; Elena Lappin for all her
editorial help; Maxim Biller for his scouting efforts; and Richard Edelson for
his technical help. The editor is grateful to The Writers Room in New York City
for the use of its facilities and for the help and friendship which the staff and
members provided during the preparation of this anthology.

The publisher also wishes to acknowledge permission to include in this
book English translations of the following German-language copyright
material (English translations are used for selections, but not for books):

KATJA BEHRENS: "Perfectly Normal" from *Salomo und die anderen: Jüdische
Geschichten*, by permission of S. Fischer Verlag. Copyright © 1993
S. Fischer Verlag GmbH, Frankfurt am Main. "Crows of God"
by permission of the author, © 1993 Katja Behrens.
Acknowledgments continued at the back of the book.

Library of Congress Cataloging-in-Publication Data

Jewish Voices, German words :
growing up Jewish in postwar Germany and Austria /
edited and with an introduction by Elena Lappin ;
translated from the German by Krishna Winston. -- 1st ed.
p. cm.
ISBN 0-945774-23-0 : $23.95
1. Authors, Jewish--Europe, German-speaking--Biography. 2. Authors,
German--20th century--Biography. 3. Authors, Austrian--20th century
--Biography. 4. German prose literature--20th century. 5. Austrian
prose literature--20th century. 6. Germany--History--1945-
7. Austria--History--20th century. I. Lappin, Elena.
PT405.J48 1994
830.9'8924043--dc20 93-39950 CIP
[B]

CONTENTS

ELENA LAPPIN

Introduction

I OWE MY CONNECTION WITH GERMANY to the fact that
my parents emigrated there from Czechoslovakia after the Soviet
invasion of 1968. It was an accidental choice, made on the basis
of such arbitrary factors as a job in Hamburg for my father and
contacts with a few emigré friends. However, I quickly
discovered that there are significant consequences when a Jew
chooses to live in post-Holocaust Germany.

On my very first day in a German high school, our class
received a distinguished visitor: a well-known Israeli journalist
who was interested in German teenagers' knowledge of their
country's past. He asked a simple question: what did they know
about Hitler? My new classmates answered that Hitler was a
dictator who was very good for the German economy because
he built the Autobahn and solved the unemployment problem.
They were critical of his nationalism and militarism, but did not
mention the Holocaust. The Israeli visitor seemed amused, but
the school principal, who was present during the discussion,
looked horrified and embarrassed. This was 1970, twenty-five
years after the end of World War II.

In Germany I did not have any obvious reason to feel
discriminated against or ostracized in any way. But after a while,
certain experiences began to leave an unpleasant aftertaste.
German reactions to my Jewishness would range from awkward
philo-Semitism to cautious anti-Semitism, depending not so
much on the person I was dealing with as on the circumstances
of our encounter. Thus, the same teacher would ask me solici-

tous questions about my family's past, and on a different occasion mutter something concerning "all those lies about the camps."

As a Jew in Germany, one develops a sort of divided vision: suspect all the older people, don't blame the young ones. It doesn't always help. From the moment I realized that the sense of history of the Germans—including those of my generation—did not exactly match my own, I no longer saw Germany as a country like any other. I saw myself as a polite visitor who was trying hard to ignore the fact that her (equally, if not more) polite host was a child molester. Once, I dozed off on an express train from Hamburg to Munich; when I opened my eyes, we were passing Dachau. The station signs—Dachau-Dachau-Dachau—triggered an emotional turmoil I can describe only as a flash of collective memory. To the German friends traveling with me, Dachau was just another town.

Yet, thanks to a very knowledgeable and demanding teacher in high school, I immersed myself in German language and literature. I studied German classics, German contemporary writing, German translations of world literature from the ancient Greeks to Marcel Proust. This teacher was very surprised, and sorry, when I later informed her that I felt myself to be incompatible with the German language. As an aspiring writer, I experienced a strong conflict between my desire to write and my reluctance to do so in German. So I moved away, in search of a more compatible adopted home and language. My brother (Maxim Biller), however, surprised me some years later by becoming a German writer. The idea for this anthology emerged when I discovered that he was only one of many young Jewish authors writing in German.

New generations of Germans have grown up with hardly a notion of the evil that happened under Hitler. On the other hand, young Jews raised in postwar Germany or Austria by parents who had either returned from exile or had survived the concentration camps, were brought up on the (often very immediate) memories of that evil, as if the Holocaust had happened only yesterday.

In this collection, fourteen young Jewish authors write about their experience of growing up in post-Holocaust Germany and Austria. There are 40,000 Jews living in Germany and 10,000 in Austria today, a mere shadow of their pre-Holocaust presence. Yet, less than fifty years after the virtual annihilation of their communities by the Nazi regime, Jewish writers are, once again, a distinctive and important voice on the German and Austrian cultural scene.

To be a young German Jewish writer takes more than talent and the desire to write. It requires, at the very least, the writer's acceptance of his or her parents' decision to make or remake Germany their home, however transitory. And it means writing in the language of those who committed genocide against the Jewish people. It is a conscious choice one makes, and it is not an easy one, as one can see from my own experiences.

The writers whose work is presented here have all made this choice. A few are very close to the experience of surviving the Holocaust, most quite remote from it. None can ignore the issue, and some have tried (more or less successfully) to remove themselves physically, though not culturally, from the country where they feel both rootless and comfortable.

Their books and articles are of great interest to the German reading public. They are widely read and reviewed. In fact, it is tempting to think that to be demonstratively Jewish is a definite asset for a young writer in Germany today. Observed with curiosity as exotic representatives of an almost extinct species, they attract a great deal of critical attention, which sometimes lacks literary objectivity. The German cultural establishment looks upon the very existence of young Jewish authors with self-satisfaction, as it suggests that Germany and Austria are, once again, "ordinary" European countries.

If this were actually the case, we would expect contemporary

German literature to reflect a deep recognition of these countries' recent history of brutality. As it is, however, the discrepancy is quite blatant: for most young German writers, the past appears to have been deleted, whereas for their Jewish counterparts it is an indelible part of their consciousness of the present. In Germany there seems to be a significant gap between the way in which the Holocaust is approached in scholarly works and historical documentaries, and the capacity of German writers to cope with their past on an emotional level.

It should be noted that young Jewish authors writing in German do not produce what has come to be known as "Holocaust literature." They do not dwell on the horror and the suffering of the Holocaust, nor do they, for the most part, reach into their own family history for their material. On the contrary: some are eager to show how tired they are of constantly having to deal with the past, of being singled out as interesting, unusual specimens. They realize their anomalous position, and they are fed up with its implications.

The official Jewish community in Germany, if it is mentioned at all, is depicted in unflattering terms by its literary offspring, and is not seen as a source of support by those who feel isolated as Jews. Their resentment of their parents' choice to ignore all they lived through or sought exile from is expressed in an antagonistic attitude toward the postwar Jewish establishment, and an unwillingness to conform to the older generation's notion of a "committed Jew." In the view of some of these authors, a Jewish revival in Germany and Austria is an absurd concept.

Unlike their pre-Holocaust counterparts, most of these writers are best described as Jews writing in German, rather than Germans and Austrians who happen to be Jewish. Thus, these authors cannot, in any straightforward sense, be considered heirs to a continuous German-Jewish literary tradition. They can no longer assimilate into the German literary environment, "passing," as could their predecessors, for German authors. The uniqueness of new German and Austrian Jewish writing consists in creating a literature which is, above all, markedly Jewish.

Contemporary German literature tends to be abstract and impersonal; Jewish authors represent a different approach. They tell stories in which the author/narrator's personal voice is strongly felt. Their language is an instrument of storytelling, of soul-searching, not a cold medium for linguistic experiments. This is true of both the fiction and the nonfiction in this volume.

To tell a story is to try to remember and to understand a sequence of events which might otherwise vanish from memory. For postwar German and Austrian Jewish authors, the Holocaust is not an abstract notion, but a tangible issue affecting their lives and their writing. At the same time, it is a source of stifling and complex social taboos. These writers want to understand the crippling barriers between themselves and their parents, between Jews and Germans. They want to transcend and to break the taboos; to remember the past, but not to wallow in it.

Some German Jewish writers have been influenced by Jewish-American writing. This affinity expresses more than an ethnic connection; it also indicates a need to fit into a literary framework other than the German, a form of literary exile: writing in German without producing a recognizably German quality in their writing. A good example is the Rothian element in the fiction of Rafael Seligmann and Maxim Biller.

Several of the authors in this anthology have chosen physical exile, where they continue to write in German. Thus, **Barbara Honigmann, Peter Stephan Jungk,** and **Benjamin Korn** now live in France; **Henryk Broder** divides his time between Germany and Israel; and **Chaim Noll** lives in Rome. The concept of exile plays a central role in German Jewish writers' fiction and nonfiction, in various forms. In his essay, *"Heimat? No Thanks,"* **Henryk Broder** contemplates the history of Jews in Germany in relation to his own decision to live in Israel as a German citizen.

Chaim Noll's account of his refusal to conform to the East German regime is a story of an inner exile through books, which leads him to Judaism. Noll's parents were prominent Communist functionaries, and he was raised in an atmosphere in which the family's Jewish background was a taboo subject. Noll himself did not dissent from Marxist ideology until he began to discover his Jewish roots. His rebellion culminated in his refusal to be drafted into the East German Army. As a result, he was committed to a psychiatric hospital.

Both selections from **Barbara Honigmann's** fiction deal with exile, also from East Germany. The narrator in "Novel of a Child," an isolated, lonely single mother, speaks of her hunger for "foreign cities and foreign countries," and a longing for Jerusalem. Instead of this unattainable exile, she is drawn to the tiny East Berlin Jewish community, "the Jews of the Jews." In Honigmann's novel *A Love Out of Nothing*, the protagonist, who has emigrated from East Berlin to Paris, argues with a Jewish-American student about living in Germany: "He would always reproach me: how could Jews bring themselves to live in Germany after everything that happened to them there . . . He wanted to persuade me to come to New York with him . . . I said, No, no, once I'm at Ellis Island, I'll never get out again. Ellis Island is my home."

Maxim Biller's short story "Finkelstein's Fingers" contains an unusual exile motif. In a scene where a young Jewish writer from Germany becomes aware of the onset of Shabbat in an orthodox Jewish neighborhood in New York's Lower East Side, there is a sense of escape into a kind of atavistic Jewish utopia, a Jewish world unto itself, seemingly intact and untouched by the Holocaust.

As a journalist, Biller tries to describe without sentiment the pilgrimage of young Frankfurt Jews to Auschwitz and other "Holocaust sites" in Poland. Their encounter with Polish anti-Semitism is almost as powerful as their visits to concentration camps. In Germany, "the place of forgetting," raw, exposed anti-Semitism is a rare occurrence in these teenagers' lives. But in Poland they discover that it is as alive as if the Holocaust and the local aftermath had never happened, and as if that country's ancient, vibrant Jewish culture had not been dead for almost half a century. In spite of the fact that they hate their parents for raising them in Germany, the young members of the tour group to Poland welcome their return to Frankfurt as a blessing. In "See Auschwitz and Die," Biller's attitude to "the whole Holocaust shit" is neither cynical nor indifferent, despite his sacrilegious language and images. This author's bellicose ego tortures German and Jewish sensibilities alike.

Rafael Seligmann shares with Biller an impatience with both Jewish and Gentile taboos, and with the enormous accumulation of symbols and "forbidden" feelings on either side. These two authors have been accused of creating negative caricatures of both Jewish and non-Jewish characters, and of unnecessarily provoking sentiments which, some critics contend, are best left dormant.

Seligmann's novel *Rubinstein's Auction* has been compared to Philip Roth's *Portnoy's Complaint*. The principal points of comparison are the neurotic Jewish family dominated by a caricature of a Jewish mother, and the frequently masturbating adolescent son in desperate search of his first sexual experience. Seligmann's protagonist feels profoundly alienated from his parents because they made him leave *his* native Israel when he was ten, and decided to return to *their* native Germany, where he is very unhappy. This novel reflects the author's personal background. His parents fled Nazi Germany and made their home in Palestine, returning to Germany in the 1950s. Seligmann is thus the only one of the current generation of young German Jewish writers for whom Germany is, on the one hand, the home of his immediate ancestors and, on the other hand, doubly forbidden territory, due to his parents' returning there from Israel after fleeing the Holocaust. Unlike the American diaspora, which symbolizes freedom, the German diaspora carries the stigma of a forbidden home. Seligmann's protagonist resolves his inner conflict by finally arriving at the conclusion that, having grown up in Germany, he is no longer an ex-Israeli, but a German Jew. This author writes with brutal self-mockery and

frequent attempts at humor that often dissolve in anger and
self-pity.

Robert Schindel was born in 1944 in Bad Hall, Austria. His
parents were communist resistance fighters who had come back
to Austria from France under false names (Robert Schindel was
in fact born as Robert Soel), and were denounced and deported
to Auschwitz four months after his birth. His father was killed
at Dachau; his mother survived and managed to find her son
after the war. In Schindel's poem "Memories of Prometheus," the
author alludes to his family history in painfully concrete terms,
and defines his identity as a survivor.

In language usually reserved for poetry, Schindel's novel
Gebürtig ("Native") attempts to cover as much post-Holocaust
ground as possible: the children of the Final Solution's perpetrators or onlookers or even innocent bystanders meeting with,
living with, sleeping with, not getting along with (in various
degrees), or loving the children of the victims and the survivors.
It is a novel about the impossibility of breaking down the glass
wall between young Austrian and German Jews and non-Jews,
because of a past that remains unforgotten and unforgiven. Yet
it is also a novel about the need to live and to enjoy life, in spite
of the past and because of it.

Robert Menasse is a younger Austrian Jewish author. His
novel *Happy Times, Brittle World* tells the story of Judith Katz and
Leo Singer, both children of Viennese Jews who fled Austria in
1938 and ended up in Saõ Paulo, Brazil. Their first meeting takes
place in the 50s, in their parents' native Vienna, where they are
now students. Leo's parents have come back to live in Vienna
after the war, whereas Judith's refuse to return and she is studying in Vienna against their wishes. The excerpt in this collection
shows how Judith and Leo are affected by a pro-Nazi demonstration. Their argument reveals their differing attitudes in
general. He is full of self-hatred and impotence; she is a
committed intellectual with a tendency toward self-destruction.
Both are victims of the war, although physically they were
unharmed by it. They are second-generation survivors who have

become permanent emotional invalids. Austria, unlike Germany, did not officially acknowledge its role in the Holocaust until very recently. Instead, it hid behind the ludicrous pose of a "fellow-victim," when in fact it had been a very willing partner of Hitler's Germany. Austrian Jews are not as explicitly ("antagonistically") Jewish as German Jews. This is reflected in the subdued presentation of Jewish topics in Menasse's writing.

At first glance, **Esther Dischereit** appears to deviate from the storytelling pattern that characterizes the work of German Jewish writers. The narrative of her novel *Joemi's Table* is fragmented and seemingly disconnected. However, it is not abstract play with words and structure, but rather a coherent whole broken up into many pieces, like a shattered mirror. She tells the story of a Jewish woman born after the war who, after a lifetime of denying her Jewishness, faces the necessity of accepting her identity. The protagonist also comes to grips with the story of her mother's persecution under the Nazis, and her own sense of political justice, expressed in a lack of sympathy with Israel. The two histories, her mother's and her own, are intertwined in the text. This is an angry book, in which the protagonist offers herself to her German surroundings as "living history."

Matthias Hermann, a young East German Jewish poet, also presents a view of Germany in which history, *Jewish* history, cannot be separated from the present German landscape. One of his poems, "The Shower Rooms in Prison," speaks of "hereditary memory," which must necessarily draw a line between young Germans and Jews today.

This division is also the subject of **Thomas Feibel's** essay "Gefilte Fish and Pepsi: A Childhood in Enemy Territory." Feibel is the youngest contributor to this anthology. He describes his own sense of liberation when, as a teenager, he decided to rebel against his burdensome Jewishness—not by abandoning it, but rather by ceasing to make a big deal out of it. For Feibel, being a Jew should not occupy too much of an active young person's time, especially in Germany, where one can easily become paranoid and live one's life in unnecessary fear. Although he is able to get his parents and the official Jewish community "off his back," it is Germans who do not let him forget that he is Jewish. As a journalist, he is always asked to write on Jewish topics, as if he had nothing to say about anything else. So, for his first journalistic assignments he is sent back to his Jewish community.

Henryk Broder provides a more political account of German-Jewish relations. Although he was active in the German student movement in the sixties, he has made clear his disenchantment with the German Left's position on Israel and with its anti-Semitism disguised as "anti-Zionism." In "Our Kampf," Broder documents the German peace movement's behavior during the Gulf War. He achieves a chilling effect by quoting statements made by various German politicians and other public personalities during the war, and then drawing his own frightening conclusions. The past figures in these Germans' thinking only to the extent that it can be connected with their current political needs and views. But this would be the most benign interpretation. To put it more bluntly, as Broder himself did in one of his books: "The Germans will never forgive the Jews for Auschwitz." In two senses: as a reminder of their guilt and as evidence of their failure.

Benjamin Korn is a theater director and essayist. One of his essays, "Shock and Aftershock," deals with the Fassbinder Affair; in 1985, a number of Jews occupied the stage of a Frankfurt theater in protest against the planned presentation of a play by Rainer Werner Fassbinder that they considered anti-Semitic. Korn found himself witnessing the scene and being forced to reflect on the implications of each side's reasoning. His situation was unexpectedly complicated by the fact that his mother was one of the protesters. As a theater director and believer in artistic freedom, he could not identify with the demonstrators. But as a Jew, he could not fail to sympathize with the under-dog's—in this case his own—cause. Korn's essay provides an excellent example of the dilemmas and split loyalties Jews encounter in post-Holocaust Germany. As bitter as he sounds in this piece, the tone there is conciliatory compared to that of his essay "Witching Hour," a pointed comment on the questionable nature of the new, re-unified Germany.

Katja Behrens is also very sensitive to the "unreality" of a "wholesome new Germany." In her short story "Perfectly Normal," she describes the narrator's need to get beneath the surface of the pervasive sense of German "normalcy," the trademark of the postwar decades. She discovers that it is not only fragile, but to her, as a Jew, nonexistent. In the story "Crows of God," her protagonist goes to Israel, where she can stop dealing with the exhausting German-Jewish issue. But here she discovers a different problem, this time related to being a woman. She is obscenely propositioned by an elderly ultra-orthodox man in the streets of Tel Aviv. This encounter is juxtaposed with the memory of a Christian male religious figure, also clad in black, who had played a role in her wartime survival. As a woman, she feels equally threatened by both.

Leo Sucharewicz's story "The Girl and the Children" also deals with an attempt to find a haven in Israel. The narrator of this story is torn between his student life in Munich and his need to serve in the Israeli army. The "girl" of the title is the narrator's non-Jewish German girlfriend, who has no sympathy at all with her boyfriend's sense of duty toward an army in general and toward the Israeli army in particular. The "children" are the children of the Warsaw Ghetto, to whose memory the narrator owes his commitment to Israel as the secular symbol of post-Holocaust Jewish survival.

In **Peter Stephan Jungk's** novel *Shabbat: A Rite of Passage in Jerusalem*, Israel is a source not of secular, but rather of religious identity. Jungk's hero is a rootless, assimilated Austrian Jew in search of a spiritual home. He hopes to find one by discovering his Jewish God in a yeshiva in Jerusalem. But it is a difficult process, hard for the young man and presumably just as hard for God. The student asks God questions to which no Jew since the Holocaust can hope to receive a satisfactory answer. He also tries to reconcile his sense of a cultural home in a German-speaking country with a strong religious identity as a Jew, and fails: "There, where I grew up, everyone says 'Grüss Gott' when they greet each other. I share the woods, cities, tavern tables, I share the language of the inhabitants of that country and am obliged to forget, forget each day anew, what took place there, forty years ago. I must speak with You in their language, the only one whose subtleties I really know. I beg you, forgive me."

* * *

Imagine an old house burned down with the original inhabitants still inside, and then a gleaming new structure erected in its place. You might move into the new building and never feel a thing. But if you happen to be related to those destroyed in order to make place for the home you now call your own, chances are you will think about it a lot. This is the situation of young Jews in Germany and Austria. Although they are by no means a homogeneous group, the writers among them all try to cope with their ambiguous status as perennial outsiders in a country and language that are still hostile territory.

BENJAMIN KORN

Shock and Aftershock

THREE YEARS AGO I went to Frankfurt to direct a production of Molière's *Don Juan*. There I involuntarily became a witness to the Fassbinder Affair. The events that took place tangentially to my own work and kept the public in suspense for weeks on end have not lost their hold on my memory.

Just as an individual often needs years to grasp a decisive event in his life—and even then does not come to terms with it because the wound refuses to close—so a people often needs decades before a shock it has suffered can enter its consciousness. Since the end of the war, Germany has been half asleep. In school we went from the dinosaurs to the Weimar Republic three times, and then stopped when we got to fascism. The Second World War was the big bang out of which the Federal Republic emerged like a young butterfly from an ugly caterpillar. Let bygones be bygones, demanded newspapers, politicians, and our teachers, who had instructions from the principal to focus all their attention on the idea of a united Europe. Even we young people were happy to refrain from asking our fathers pointed questions.

From time to time, fragments of the big bang floated around our ears. On the heels of the Nuremberg Trials we witnessed the rehabilitation of the German armaments industry, smear campaigns against former members of the resistance, the elevation of old Nazis to the highest positions in the republic. In May 1985, at the military cemetery in Bitburg, Reagan and Kohl rehabilitated the reputation of the Wehrmacht and made a clean distinction between soldiers who had murdered, pillaged, dropped bombs, and shot people in the stomach in the name of the Geneva Convention, and members of the Waffen-SS who had done the same without the blessing of the Geneva Convention. Now Europe's dead fell neatly into two categories: legitimate and illegitimate. On his trip to Israel the German chancellor denied that his generation bore any responsibility for German history; now historians are busy revising that history. Racism is creeping out of eggs once laid in the mud, and from the eyes of a butterfly the old caterpillar stares back at us.

And the Jews? What brought them to Germany when the war was over? The desire to emigrate, to golden America or to Zion, to begin a new life? Certainly. But why did so many stay so long? Because it took longer to get visas for overseas than they had expected? And when the visas came? What kept them here, in such close proximity to a people they hated and among criminals they could pick out on the street by the way they handled their German shepherds?

Reconstruction was in full swing, and as a rule those who stayed found themselves better off than those who emigrated. There was more than just food, shelter, coal for heating. Dollars and D-marks earned on the black market, or through smuggling, or in deals with American soldiers, reparations payments from the government were transformed effortlessly into a bar, a stocking factory, a building lot. There was no alternative for those who had survived and did not belong to that small contingent of German Jews who returned actually intending to stay. The world had destroyed their world and catapulted them into a new one in which everything they had learned, worked for, done, and thought counted for nothing; the only thing that did count was what the war had taught them: how to survive. And there were ample opportunities for surviving, legal and illegal, in this country under American occupation whose economy seemed to have an infinite capacity for growth.

They had come planning to emigrate. They stayed because of the money. In their own minds they were just passing through. One day they would emigrate, or their children would. They initiated no contact with German society that went beyond business dealings. They did not speak of their wounds, or of nightmares in which the dead would not stop screaming. Matters of the soul had no place in business decisions. Those bridges politicians love to speak of on ceremonial occasions were built over their pain; the pain does not lessen. That is what we learned from the events that took place in Frankfurt in the fall of 1985.

Fassbinder's *Garbage, the City, and Death* was the talk of the town. One could not avoid discussions of whether it should or could be allowed to open. One would run into an acquaintance on the street, call up a friend, wish someone happy birthday— invariably the subject of the play would come up. One would open the morning paper and immediately find oneself reading a commentary on the issue, whether with an international or a domestic perspective, whether expressing concern or examining questions of principle.

Opinions were articulated by bishops and Jewish community leaders, high Israeli officials and local politicians of all parties, directors of theaters, historians, journalists. All either opposed the production in the name of the victims or favored it in the name of freedom of expression. Hilmar Hoffmann, head of the city's Office of Cultural Affairs, was simultaneously opposed in the name of the former and in favor in the name of the latter. Peter Zadek, a well-known Jewish director, wrote that the play was anti-Semitic but had to be produced nonetheless. The *New York Times* demanded that the play be canceled, the Greens demanded that it be performed, a Jewish organization in Berlin sued the theater for inciting to violence and pressed for an injunction. The theater's director and the Jewish community's cultural spokesman engaged in an exchange of newspaper articles in which both sides laid out their positions, repeated them, and batted them around until the whole thing took on the character of an athletic contest and became the stuff of talk shows.

The city seemed intoxicated, and the countdown to the premiere raised the excitement to fever pitch. The international press added to the coverage, one American network appeared on the scene and broadcast live reports overseas, Israel's Knesset chimed in, and the confusion of voices reached Babylonian proportions. Like oxen bashing their heads together, the parties to the controversy had trouble thinking clearly. They exchanged not arguments but volleys of gunshots, and both sides were using the same ammunition: freedom.

Frankfurt became the site of an absurd civil war between two civil liberties that had originally been closely allied; the Jews' right to protect themselves from anti-Semitic attacks was being balanced against freedom of expression in the arts. Two sets of minority rights entered the lists as if they were mortal enemies— rights for whose acceptance generations of German and Jewish freedom-fighters had struggled, from the time of Gotthold Ephraim Lessing and his friend Moses Mendelssohn.

Weren't the hands that in 1933 tossed the works of the German Enlightenment into the flames the same hands that would set fire to the synagogues five years later? And didn't the same spirit motivate those hands? Had the leaders of the Jewish community forgotten this when they invested Mayor Wallmann with the powers of a feudal prince, and asked him to defend his tax-paying Jewish minority by subjecting Fassbinder's play to political censorship and simply banning it? [. . .]

Freedom is as indivisible as the air we breathe. That is one lesson to be learned from the Fassbinder Affair. There is a second, related one: suppression has no power to educate. Did the Jews of Frankfurt really think that forbidding an idea would make it disappear from the face of the earth? Physics teaches us that in the universe no energy is ever lost, and history teaches us that obsessions thrive best under cover of prohibition. All forbidden movements have rallied their forces in the dark. Prohibitions poison our thinking. The play belongs in the light of the stage, and if it were dangerous, it would belong in the light all the more.

There were, it seems to me, reasons other than philosophical for sweeping the play under the rug. The almost unlimited right of the victims to be spared pain was a compelling argument, but was it being used as a pretext for stifling undesirable discussion of real estate speculation? And Friedmann, the cultural spokesman for the Jewish community, who repeatedly invoked that right—wasn't he engaging in some highly visible PR for himself and his political career? Those who were truly affected kept silent and allowed themselves to be represented by those to whom speaking came readily.

Ah yes, there were careers to be won and careers to be lost everywhere you looked, in City Hall, in the Jewish community center, in the theater. People do not want to fall through the social net they have worked so long and hard to spin. That desire is overwhelming; it crosses all religious and class lines. So in spite of everything that separated them, all the parties had something in common: in addition to sweating over ideas and fears, they were sweating over careers; this sweat flowed profusely and mingled with the other kinds of sweat, overflowing the banks of various brows.

And who had sweated more at the outset than the man who would later hold all the threads in his hand: Wallmann? I can still see him, weeks before the premiere, sitting in the first row at St. Paul's for the ceremony at which Teddy Kollek, mayor of Jerusalem, was to receive the city's peace prize. Wallmann was sweating something dreadful. His face looked transparent, as though the sweat were running down the inside of his skin. It was rumored that Kollek was planning to interpolate into his prepared speech a remark reprimanding the mayor of Frankfurt, to disrupt the harmony of this prize ceremony, so laden with symbolism for Germans and Jews, and to demand that the play be banned.

When it turned out that it wasn't Kollek but Stuttgart's mayor Rommel who wove a (gentle) reproof into his speech, Frankfurt's mayor nodded, as the close-up showed unmistakably, nodded overzealously, like a schoolboy who has just gotten off lightly. It was a nasty, revealing piece of byplay. Cowering inside this mayor was a typical German subordinate, and in this subordinate was an abject fear, the entire energy of which was invested in his career. Sitting in front of the television set that Sunday morning, I perceived that this man would not let a mere play trip him up on his way to the top.

And what about art? Who came to art's defense? After the war, the authors of Germany's Basic Law granted the arts a place of honor among the civil liberties, for the arts, too, had been gagged, burned, thrown into concentration camps, hounded from the German universities and theaters, and driven out of people's minds, the better to regiment them completely. Art has special rights because it has such weak legs. It is obligated only to the truth, not to any lobby in the Bundestag, to any caucus at union conventions, to any member of the Chamber of Commerce and Industry. Art, as Schiller tells us, is a daughter of freedom. Hands off!

Theater Director Rühle made a big mistake when, instead of insisting on this point, he tried to focus the discussion on the play's artistic merits. Instead of the contents of the play— prostitution around the Frankfurt railway station, homosexuality, Jewish bar owners, anti-Semitism, pimping, sexual violence— suddenly the issue became Fassbinder's artistry. That was a clever way to get everyone off the hook and avoid provocation. Experts on artistic questions sprang up like toadstools, criticizing the play's language or the woodenness of its structure.

Rühle, for his part, pronounced the play a brilliant urban ballad portraying the coldness of modern life. Yet a few months earlier, writing as a theater critic for the *Frankfurter Allgemeine Zeitung*, Rühle had called the play artistically uninteresting. Why this about-face? The result of a second reading? Or is a journalist's reading different from a director's? Was it more a physical than a philosophical process, a sort of shift in focus that altered his thinking?

In reality it did not matter whether the play was good or bad. The play's quality had no bearing on the right to stage it. This right exists independently of any aesthetic considerations; otherwise one would have to ban dozens of plays every year. At issue was an anti-social play that aired Frankfurt's dirty linen, and the high-minded discussions helped to distract people from the play's subject matter. All this also came at a bad time. The controversy had wormed its way in like a maggot between the peace prize ceremony and the opening of the new Jewish community center, between reconciliation focused on the past and the promise of a new, shared future. It was like a festive meal spoiled by odors from the latrine. [. . .]

No, people in the Jewish community said, the play was anti-Semitic not because one of its characters was a Jewish speculator but because this character was called simply "the Jew." What would people have said if he had been called Rosenthal, Bronstein, or Goldmann? In point of fact, is there any such thing as a Jewish name that would not be anti-Semitic? Fassbinder calls him "the Jew A." A. as in Aron? Why not B.? For heaven's sake, be careful—there are several B.s in Frankfurt; people might start making connections.

No, the theater replied, the Jew is the only character who awakens positive feelings; one just has to read the play carefully.

Everywhere a cap of invisibility was dropped over the play and its barbs.

The premiere approached, and discussions about the play itself gave way to discussions of strategy. What should be done if the theater were taken over by demonstrators? The actors were feeling the tension. It was rumored that one of the leading actors had asked to be assigned a different part. Another had been

attacked by his parents-in-law, who lived abroad, for partici-
pating in an anti- Semitic event. The box office had orders to
sell only one ticket at a time, so that the opponents of the
production could not purchase a block of seats. Hate mail was
coming in. In the hall where the offices were located, I repeatedly ran into an older Jew who seemed to know me by name
and who kept trying to change the theater director's mind. Bomb
threats proliferated. The police adopted comprehensive tactical
measures to protect the theater. Reporters for tabloids in
Hamburg and Berlin sat around in the theater café with
enormous ears and indifferent eyes, trying to snag bits of
conversation from the other tables that they could turn into red-
hot reports on the prevailing mood, and thereby earn their keep.

The two major Frankfurt dailies, which I read on the train
every morning on the way in for rehearsals, had taken opposite
sides. Caught up in the heat of the argument, they defended
their positions chiefly by attacking each other. In an article that
gave evidence of intimate acquaintance, a former colleague of
Rühle's at the *Frankfurter Allgemeine* characterized the theater
director as a "schoolmaster who has shaken off his inhibitions,"
while a well-known commentator from the *Frankfurter Rundschau*
fired a broadside against "Jewish investment capital," as if the
capital did not come from German banks and as if capital
bothered to ask, as Gretchen asked Faust about his religion,
whether an entrepreneur wore a turban, a yarmulke, or a
borsalino.. [. . .]

On the day of the premiere of *Garbage, the City, and Death*, I was
conducting a rehearsal of Molière's *Don Juan*, suppressing any
doubts I might have had as to the significance of what I was
engaged in. The play had been performed only three times in
Molière's lifetime and then not again for two hundred and fifty
years. The clergy had exerted all their influence to get Louis XIV
to prohibit this bitter comedy that made the Church the butt of
its humor. "A discreet nod from the immediate vicinity of the

King" had resulted in the withdrawal of the play, we read in the documents. Officially no censorship was practiced.

My evening rehearsal did not take place. I had canceled it so as to let those actors who had tickets attend the premiere. I myself had made no attempt to get a ticket. By late afternoon, however, curiosity drove me to the square in front of the theater. It was already dark, and at the theater entrance members of the Jewish community had gathered to demonstrate against the production. "Nip it in the bud," I read on a banner. What bud? Was something just starting? Was hatred of Jews beginning only here and now?

A procession of demonstrators made up of members of the ruling parties in the Frankfurt city council joined the protestors. Christian Democrats, Social Democrats, Free Democrats were standing shoulder to shoulder with Jews. An amazing community was forming here in the struggle against a past in which both sides had been involved. Was the idea to come to terms with that past or to cover it up? Among the people from City Hall wasn't there one here and there in whose pocket a check for a nursery school—handed him in return for help in securing a building permit—had been metamorphosed into a Mercedes or the foundation for his new house? Wasn't there one who had been blackmailed with photos showing him in the company of a prostitute? Here politics and money, careers and special interests went hand in hand. Their cap of invisibility was morality, their motivation a desire to draw the veil over past deals. The more egotistic a person's motives, the more noble the general welfare in whose name he speaks. There was only one problem: compared with the unspeakable things said against Jews at hundreds of German bars every evening, what the anti-Semite in Fassbinder's play says is small potatoes. The play does not give rise to anti-Semitism; it asserts that anti-Semitism exists, and it is precisely this that people were closing their eyes to.

Yes, it was a remarkable community of people gathered there to bury the play. Normally they eat at different tables and not infrequently wish each other to hell and gone, but this time they were helping each other hold an enormous shovel, with which they planned to bury this play once and for all. A play chock full of sexual filth, political deals, bribes and intrigue—in short, all sorts of human things. They wanted to bury it and trample on the last will and testament of the artist, who had wanted his play to be performed in Frankfurt.

I went to a side entrance, where I had to show identification in order to be let in. The offices seemed abandoned, but I heard voices coming from a corner room. Here, sitting in front of a monitor, were members of the theater—actors, dramaturgs, secretaries. They offered me a glass of wine. Demonstrators had occupied the stage—one could see this on the screen—and they were holding a banner that stretched across the stage. It was impossible to make out individual details; the video camera was filming the entire scene from a fixed position.

Dany Cohn-Bendit intervened in the discussion. His voice was unmistakable. Then I heard another voice I knew. The word "traitor" rose above the din. I peered at the screen. On the right was a moving form that seemed familiar, but it wasn't much more than a white speck. My need to be in the auditorium was so overwhelming that I had someone show me down there, past gates, barriers, and guards. I positioned myself in the belt of darkness behind the last seats. Leaning against the wall I looked toward the stage. That speck of white was my mother.

I hadn't seen her in years. I had a great deal of trouble following what was happening. I felt a weakness in my spine that radiated through my entire body and paralyzed my concentration. I hadn't been prepared for this encounter between myself, the people in the theater, and my mother. The two worlds that had shaped my life, Judaism and German culture, were in danger of colliding. I had learned to keep them apart— on the one hand the world of my friendships at school, my adventures in love, the student revolt, and on the other side life in the Jewish community, the undying memory of genocide, the celebrations and rituals, the family relationships which, as long as one affirmed them, provided protection and warmth.

And here and now, under extreme tension, they were meeting in hostility on my stamping ground, the stage, challenging me to choose between them or effect a reconciliation. I could not do it. All I had learned was to avoid the issue. I had avoided the Fassbinder Affair, rationalizing my silence by telling myself I did not want to add my spit to the spoiled soup of the discussion. I had always dodged the issue, taking refuge in art, in the socialist ideal, where the ridiculous fractures of life and its torments cease before one has actually solved them.

Now I was pinned. The moment to step forward and face the music had come. All the necessary conditions were present, and not only the condition of having no escape, which forces one to stand and deliver—no, I was also acquainted with the problem at hand down to the smallest detail and from all sides, was a child both of this city and of the Jewish community, was the son of a landlord, had experience with squatters, was very familiar with the history of the district around the railway station, the local political parties, was employed in the theater, knew what the theater and its actors were going through—yet I felt utterly paralyzed. What was wrong? Why was I gripped by such existential anxiety that beads of sweat formed on my upper lip? Was it fear of fouling my own nest (which in reality is the more deep-seated fear of cleaning out one's nest, because a nest is by definition dirty)? Was it fear of a family confrontation in the auditorium?

No, it was a petty fear, an ignoble fear—if such thing as a noble fear exists. I subsequently came up with the excuse that the events of that moment had overtaxed my understanding, but the fact was that more courage than I possessed was called for to think them through and to act, to leap onto the stage and to shout the truths I knew into the faces of all those present.

Unlike the heroes I take such pleasure in seeing on the stage, I found my own comfort more important than honor. I did not want to spoil things with either the theater or the community, either with Bubis or with Rühle, who put breakfast on my table, with my old political comrades or with my mother, or with the

critics. I did not want to poke a hole in the social net I had
worked so long to weave, and tumble into what seemed a
bottomless pit. It never occurred to me that I was behaving no
differently than all the others, whom I showered with scorn,
mockery, and sarcasm.

I, too, was fulfilling my contract with society, continuing to
work on the production of my own play while the Fassbinder
play was being aborted; actually I should have dropped the play
instead of salving my conscience by putting more and more
delicate touches on Don Juan's monologue against hypocrites,
which doesn't get a rise out of anyone these days. Yes, it was
easy to send out on stage, in my stead, a hero who says what
he thinks with brutal frankness and doesn't give a damn about
society's reaction. Molière himself had had to pay the price. The
least I could have done was to leave the stage bare, to break off
the production in protest against the wound inflicted on our
theater by political censorship. That would have been the only
honorable protest; of course it would not have healed the
wound. But what about our salaries? What about the reviews?
What about my family?

I accommodated my thinking to my banal cowardice and
provided myself with reasons to keep things running. It was
opportunism pure and simple; nothing compelled me to behave
this way. I was in no real danger, just worried about my career.
It was shameful, and I am still ashamed when I think back on
that period.

Frankfurt's Kammerspiele is a small theater. There is hardly any
distance between the audience and the stage. For those standing
up there, the auditorium became the stage, with the result that
two audiences were facing each other. They could see the whites
of each other's eyes. The determination of those who had occupied the theater had something extreme about it. They stood
there as if for their last stand, as if their struggle were directed
against more than "subsidized anti-Semitism"—the slogan on

their banner—against the shadow of history altogether, which had recently crept over the graves in Bitburg and against which they had not defended themselves.

The Fassbinder play was the fuse to a powerful powderkeg, and the members of the audience were functioning as representatives of those who wanted to ignite it: children of Germany. On the stage a symbolic occupation was taking place, and down below sat a symbolic audience. No one wanted things to be this way, at least not in the audience; those on the stage were there of their own free will, united behind their banner. It held them together—nothing else could. Leftists stood next to the religious, poor next to rich, girls who would be going to a discotheque afterward next to former concentration-camp survivors. Down in the audience, people who supported the production were arguing with people who opposed it. Way in the back sat a few right-wing extremists watching the spectacle with malice. Other members of the audience sat there as if paralyzed, and others just wanted to see the play and nothing else.

Yet the actual line of demarcation ran not between socialists and right-wing extremists, between humanists and racists, between the stubborn ones and the reasonable ones on the stage and in the auditorium, but between the stage and the auditorium. People were swallowed up by their identity as Jews or Germans. Hadn't the former comrade up there on the stage and the one sitting in the audience both been involved in violent encounters with NPD thugs? What now linked the former so strongly to the conservative property-owner beside him? Does tribal thinking always win out in the end? Do people when they feel threatened invariably fuse into archaic blocs? Do they lose their individual capacity for reason?

My mother up there on the stage was dividing all those present into friend and foe, Jew and goy, good Jew and Jewish traitor. This did not fail to have an effect on the audience, for she made it seem as though she were speaking in the name of the dead; but she was speaking in the name of hatred. The hatred the Nazis had showered on her people lived on in her and was perpetuated as a curse on later generations, but also as a curse within me.

The dead are not reconciled through hatred. Hatred produces more dead. I knew that, but I did not have the strength to shout that message to those on the stage. I did not want to be counted among the traitors, so I decided to keep silent. The children of the chosen people were standing and the children of the master race were sitting; or rather, the children of the chosen people were sitting on the high horse of suffering, and the children of the master race were standing at the pillory.

This was not an edifying moment; it was a moment of blindness. If people had just opened their eyes, they could have seen. Here the symbolic encounter between the peoples was finally taking place, that encounter of which the theater and all the arts dream. Instead of actors, real human beings were facing each other, called upon to solve a human problem, to put an end to war, hatred, vengeance, and to do it not in the realm of illusion, through art, but in reality. It was all so simple. The distance between the first row and the stage in the studio theater is so slight that one can easily shake hands. Dialogue was within reach; no metaphorical bridge was necessary. But I'm dreaming. Contact was made; and precisely because this was possible, the factions froze and withdrew into the snail shells of their souls.

From time to time Herr Rühle stepped onto the narrow line between the auditorium and the stage and politely asked whether the play his ensemble had spent so long rehearsing could finally be performed. He was greeted with laughter from the stage and applause from the audience. People were at a loss. Dany Cohn-Bendit called for the play to be performed behind the demonstrators; that way everyone's demands would be met—the audience's, the demonstrators', and the actors'. The actors were on the stage, too, but it was hard to see them. They were sitting behind the demonstrators, nervous at first, ready to jump up, shake off their creeping resignation, and start the play.

They never got the chance; on this particular evening they had to be satisfied with a minor role, and this role had a short script: one member of the ensemble got up and read in the dry manner of a press spokesman a statement to the effect that they didn't consider the play hostile to Jews; they had rehearsed for a long time and wanted to perform the play.

They did not stand their ground, as the actors had done 170 years earlier in Mainz when they kept going all the way through to the end of Schiller's revolutionary *Robbers*, aimed at a tyrannical aristocracy—despite reactionaries' bombs that brought down the front wall of the theater. They did not stand their ground like their colleagues in Paris in the 1950s, who forged ahead to the end of Genet's anti-colonialist and truly obscene play *Les Paravents*, in spite of Algerian War veterans who were provoking fights in the audience.

It would not have taken a heroic deed, but not a single actor forced his way into the midst of the demonstrators to protest being described as a state-subsidized anti-Semite. They sat there glued to their chairs, fulfilling their contractual obligation and not defending themselves.

But they had to get the play out in the open now or never; it was in their bodies, had become flesh of their flesh during the many months of rehearsals. They should have had the right to interrupt the aseptic dialogue between the opposing parties, engage in a genuine argument, take up the struggle against having their play aborted! Was their love for the play less than their fear of a scandal?

Those who had occupied the theater were not afraid of a scandal; they wanted one, and that was why they came out on top in the confrontation, not in the days preceding or following, but on this particular evening. Socially motivated fear of scandal decided the outcome of the confrontation, and this fear gripped not only those present and sitting in the eye of the storm, but also city, state, and national political figures. A couple of weeks later, Theater Director Rühle announced that the production had been canceled. This announcement followed close on the heels of his conversation with the mayor, slated to join the Bonn government soon and worried about jeopardizing his solid relationship with the state of Israel. It was hard for anyone to believe that he had reached this decision freely, that political pressure or censorship did not enter in. In obedience to a national tradition, deeply rooted in Protestantism, external pressure had been converted into inner freedom. Responsibility came to rest at one man's door, and the scandal fell in on itself.

Seldom had I witnessed such a peaceful occupation. Bubis, chairman of the Jewish community council, stood motionless for hours at a spot near center stage and conversed politely with Dany Cohn-Bendit, who was trying to mediate between the two sides. No one went for anyone else's throat, no one got pushed or shoved, no one insulted anyone. They were all stroking the beast of prey sleeping inside them. The talk was of freedom of artistic expression, of trespassing, of the right to demonstrate; but everything that was said seemed to be suffering from a sort of paralysis. Every argument sounded as if a third party were in the room. The dead. Brothers and sisters, parents, relatives, and friends murdered by the Nazis stood among us, stood there precisely because no one mentioned them. The children of the dead were standing before the children of the murderers, and the victims and their slaughterers were staring at each other through the eyes of their children. All those present sensed this, all knew it and recognized the connection. They passed this unresolved conflict on to the next generation. This act took place without words and was sealed with silence, like an ancient ritual—although other matters were discussed.

Guilt weighed heavily on everyone. Guilt is hatred frozen solid. Woe betide us if it ever starts to steam.

Could any people be more uprooted than the Germans? The Germans have no center and no sense of moderation; they have lost the ground under their feet and cannot recover it with the gravitational pull of money. Abroad one gets a look at them under a magnifying glass. A German tourist enters a restaurant in Holland with his family and does not dare to say "Guten Tag," because he would not want to be identified with the Germans who invaded Holland; even so, he feels guilty. This man is the civilized façade of the same man who goes to his club with fellow Germans and sings soldiers' songs, cracks jokes about the cowardice of Italian soldiers, and will not let the waitress clear the table because at the end of the evening they have to count how many beer bottles they've lined up in military formation.

The Germans are a schizophrenic people. The hatred they feel for their own identity comes from the lost war, forced democratization, and the incomprehensible crimes of the Second World War. They hate their guilt feelings and, without realizing it, those who occasion them. Both the unconquerable desire "to be someone again" that expresses itself in this people's legendary capacity for work, and this resurfacing xenophobia spring from the same source, as does the tendency to agree too quickly with adversaries and thus not allow criticism to be aired. (Wasn't something similar happening with the German reporters who tried to balance the pain of Jewish demonstrators against freedom of artistic expression? In the scales of guilt, freedom doesn't stand a chance.)

Nothing in this country's consciousness has done as much harm as the notion of collective guilt. The fascists' crimes were unloaded on the entire people, and the executioners, the fellow-travelers, the merely indifferent, and the resistance fighters were all tarred with the same brush. The differences between them were obliterated, and the Nazis won the struggle for people's consciousness. All were guilty but none responsible; it was like original sin: where there is so much guilt, there is also much forgiveness. If Herr Krupp's chauffeur is as guilty as Herr Krupp, both may feel free to continue going about their business—or neither. Thus the Germans blocked themselves from calling their criminals by name, from distinguishing between them and the fellow-travelers, the indifferent, and the resistance fighters, and building their future on the right people.

Not guilt but shame would have been appropriate. Guilt is a religious emotion and obscures one's understanding. But a person who feels shame about something contemplates that thing and tries to get to the bottom of it, even if that means pursuing his fathers' crimes until he feels in himself the ability to repeat them. Then he can purge them and live without guilt. The child who promises to be better only because of a guilty conscience is already paving the way for the next misdeed. This child was raised in Germany.

And what sort of Jewish child was raised in postwar Germany? For one's spiritual equanimity it is pleasanter, or so it seemed to me, to be a child of the victims than to be a child of the murderers. But the fear does not go away; for if the dead whom people kept mentioning in my childhood are always present, the murderers cannot be far away; they are running around in the streets. What does this woman on the streetcar want of me when she asks me where I'm going with my Hebrew Bible? I have just been to see my rabbi, but I lie and say the Bible belongs to a friend. I could never forget the story of the Jews whose skin was made into lampshades, the dreadful word Auschwitz never left my mind, and I saw before me the gold teeth that were pried out of the mouths of the dead, and pictures from the *Yellow Star* that showed heaps of corpses and people starved to skeletons staring out at me from the page.

Every young Jew had to build for himself the famous bridge that is so often mentioned on the holy days; but usually it was just a footbridge across which social or sexual contact took place.

The time has come to lift the blockade. The Jews must help the Germans. The Jews have an easier time of it; their vision is not distorted by guilt (unless by the guilt of living in Germany, a guilt imposed on them by their brothers in other lands). All they have to do is get down off the comfortable hobbyhorse of suffering, where they have been able to ride immune from reproach. They must stop responding to any criticism by charging anti-Semitism, must stop exploiting the Germans' guilt. They have been toying with the Germans' guilty conscience, a dangerous game.

What justifies us in looking down on our fellow human beings, whether circumcised or not? Did we choose the color of our skin, our religion, the part of the world into which chance has cast us? What credit can we take for those things? When I was five, I knew nothing about them, and neither did my friend Norbert Schmidt, the son of our building superintendent, and we would have exchanged religions and origins without hesitation if it had been a question of preserving our friendshp.

The border between bestiality and humaneness is not located between peoples or between individuals. It is located in each of us, and the more powerful side is peopled by hostility, arrogance, selfishness, and bigotry. In this respect—as the history of the children of Israel from the conquest of Zion to the present day teaches us—the Jews are just like other human beings, no better, no worse, no different.

But we, who came into the world imperfect, like to focus on the imperfections of others. Just so, on that evening in Frankfurt, the two audiences stared at each other, and they are still staring at the whites of each others' eyes.

Above the theater that evening there were stars in the sky, but we never looked up at them.

KATJA BEHRENS

Perfectly Normal

I'VE TRAVELED ALL OVER THE WORLD and still haven't been able to shake it, this feeling of having to go into hiding. Nothing anyone says helps: I have nothing to conceal, haven't had anything for a long time, even have things to show off.

We had things to show off when I was a child, too. It was just that we couldn't let people know *what we were*. Something very bad. What was bad about it I didn't know, only that we weren't like the others in the village where we survived. That we didn't belong I sensed even before I learned to speak, in a charming dialect with a sing-song intonation and a rolled *R*.

I forgot that dialect after we returned to the country where we were supposed to have been gassed. But the sense of not belonging stayed with me.

Something about us wasn't right, just as before. In spite of praying, *lay me down to sleep . . . soul to take . . . Jesus' sake*. In spite of badminton and girlfriends, Heidi and Toxi, *there's no place like home*, in spite of cowboy-and-Indian stories and dancing lessons, bouffant petticoats and Harry Belafonte. Like all the others. But the others didn't agonize over people I don't even remember, people whose names I've forgotten, along with their faces, everything. Except for the fact that there were millions of them, whether it was six or not. I flailed around, but my vehemence didn't help. They refused to be convinced.

It took a long time for me to realize that talking did no good. They were human beings, too, I thought. Had to have feelings. Had to share our feelings. Feel outrage. But they didn't. It wasn't six million, they said, and I said, So what, even if it was only four—and they said, like accountants, But it makes a difference—as if only the numbers counted.

It's part of my heritage, like my freckles, my stubbornness, and my nose. I know that now. But at the time I thought I could somehow rescind Mother's staying behind and groveling, taking off her glasses outside the door to some government office with the Führer's picture above the desk—*they make you look more Jewish*. I thought I could belatedly emigrate, on behalf of those who had stayed, so to speak, on their behalf and retroactively, for it wasn't essential anymore, at least not essential to one's survival; one got *picked up* only at dance class now, and Mother received so-called restitution, even if she continued to go around with her eyes on the ground, no question of holding her head high. Head bowed to the end, lower and lower, whether out of shame at her nose or shame at having survived only she knew.

Belatedly emigrate and no longer be among people who rationalized, who kept silent, who blamed the victims, who knew nothing, who forgot; no longer be there where people said things like *It's a gas* and *go up in smoke* and *This way to the gas*. And not only *people*, but also the decent, the concerned, the well-meaning, friends. Even your own brain picks up these phrases, and it's only your mouth that balks at actually pronouncing them. Phrases heard so often, from early childhood on, ever since I can think, already drained of meaning. Drained of meaning, but normal.

What do you expect, that's perfectly normal, my girlfriend said. But was horrified at the photos in a magazine of heaps of corpses. It was the fifties. Children might see these, my girlfriend said. As if these naked, murdered people were something obscene that children's delicate souls had to be shielded from.

I sensed that my friend's mother was speaking through her mouth, and she was a perfectly normal woman.

It's time to let bygones be bygones, her husband agreed.

That was perfectly normal at the time; most people thought that way.

We were the ones who weren't normal, in our normal town, on our normal street, inhabited by normal people.

For instance, there was an inconspicuous, ordinary, and respected man, of whom it was said in our household that he had *skeletons in his closet*. At the time it wasn't clear to me what *skeletons in his closet* might be.

The man lived with his family in a handsome old house on the hill.

Under a false name, my mother said. Everybody knows that.

His daughter's birthday parties were something very special. Once I was invited, too. The man danced with me. It was the first time a man danced with me. I think he was a tailor. His suit was made of some fine material. That's what I noticed. Nothing else. A normal man. The only special thing about him was that he was the master in this handsome house. It never occurred to me to be afraid of him. And he, too, probably thought nothing of holding in his arms a girl he might have smashed against a wall as an infant. Or tossed alive into a pit on top of her dead mother. That was over and done with, it had been a job, a dirty job, but it had to be done.

A nice man. He taught me a dance step, tango or foxtrot. I didn't catch on, stepped on his feet, was ashamed. I was always ashamed about something, back in the fifties, when everyone was normal except me. Today I realize that that's normal, too: it's always those who are kicked who are ashamed afterward, not those who do the kicking.

At some point in the first months after we moved to the street with all the normal people, a woman we didn't know rang the bell. She wanted to come up. No special reason. Just to see someone who'd been in a concentration camp. Normal curiosity. A rumor was going around the neighborhood. It would have been normal for us to have been in a concentration camp. Mother denied it, as if it were something shameful. Should have realized long since that there was no chance of being a normal person.

Even so, she raved all the time about a nose job. An operation that would confer the joys of normality. If it was too late for her, then at least for me.

When she finally got her *restitution pension*, she wanted to pay for a cute little snub nose for me. I rejected the snub nose and went away, to Noseland. I stayed there for two years and came back. Nothing had changed.

They're educated. They're progressive. They're terribly nice. Together we kept silent vigils for peace and marched at Easter.

And then, suddenly, you hear a sentence—

—they certainly like wheeling and dealing. You can't deny it. It's in the blood.

Or silence. Speak a word that recalls persecution, expulsion, or extermination, and silence settles over the group, an embarrassed silence among people I felt close to just a moment ago, a silence that tells me I put my foot in my mouth. In the silence, the gulf between us becomes apparent.

It happens again and again. During a nice dinner in town or a balmy summer evening over wine and olives.

Crickets chirping and a conversation about music. The man was my age. A German church organist, cultivated. Had had a bit to drink.

To get anywhere in the music world, he said, you have to be Jewish or gay.

I saw the little blue veins in his forehead pulsing and thought, I must have heard wrong.

No, really, they're everywhere again, they've cornered all the key positions. What? All gassed? Not at all. They earmark all the good positions for each other, I'm telling you.

I saw the blue veins under his alabaster skin.

Since going away hadn't helped, I tried staring the past in the eye.

Let's let sleeping dogs lie, my former teacher said when I went to see him, or, to be more precise, looked him up. He was

still teaching at the same school. Had gone gray. Otherwise
unchanged. The hair combed back smoothly. The too-small
turned-up nose. The sardonic eyebrows.

When I phoned him, I was amazed that his voice sounded as
if he were a human being, just a human being, a perfectly
normal one. No trace in that voice of the things I remembered.

The stairwell smelled of cleanser. I saw him through the door,
open just a crack, saw his outstretched hand, and for a moment
it was like old times.

Then I noticed that something had changed.

There was no finger pointing scornfully at me. Only a
question: had I found my way all right? And no dark allusions
to my nose.

His invisible wife had set the table for coffee. He sat across
from me in woolen vest and slippers.

The coffee service on his table was a pattern I hadn't seen in
any other household. Except mine. For years I'd been drinking
my morning coffee from these cups, eating my bread from these
plates. I couldn't believe I had anything in common with this
bastard.

There was a piano in the room. The cover was down. No
sheet music was lying around. Nothing was lying around. No
books, no newspapers, no knitting, nothing that would have
given evidence of life. Everything was neat and clean. The silent
piano polished to within an inch of its life.

I asked where he was born.

In Silesia, he said.

Had he been in the army, I asked.

The vest and slippers contrasted strangely with the military
precision with which he rattled off the number of his batallion
in the *Volkssturm*, as though he'd forgotten that I was sitting
there, his former pupil, a surviving parasite on the *Volk* that he'd
done his best to stamp out, who had now looked him up, seek-
ing liberation from the past. It was a long number, but it came
shooting out, as if from the barrel of a gun, almost half a century
after he had last stood at attention.

Let's let sleeping dogs lie, he said, quoting his own old teacher. We have to look to the future now. I asked whether he still told his pupils that Hitler built the autobahn.

He threatened to terminate the conversation.

We sat there in silence. I stared out the window. On the balcony hung laundry. My former teacher was jiggling his foot.

I didn't let him off. But the damage was done.

. . . must ask you to leave, unfortunately.

I handed him the pencil he had lent me. After we'd drunk our coffee, I'd rooted around in my pocketbook but found nothing to write with. I had taken everything out of my pocketbook and still found no pencil. With my wallet, lipstick, and compact on my lap I'd felt strangely naked.

He helped me into my coat and wished me a safe trip.

On the way back, I felt as though I'd traveled a great distance. I got to my apartment and was surprised I had a place I could call home. I looked at my furniture, and it was like something one had forgotten one owned.

No sense of liberation. He was stronger than I was. For him the past was laid to rest. He looked as though he slept well. They all sleep well. They have nothing to fear. That, too, seems normal.

And when I find a new friend, the question is always lurking at the back of my mind: Would you offer me space in your attic? Share your ration card with me?

CHAIM NOLL

A Country, A Child,
But Not the Country's Child

MY MOTHER WAS THE MOST BEAUTIFUL woman in the
world. She had hair as black as night, chestnut-brown eyes, soft,
delicate skin, looked entirely different from all other mothers,
sang wonderfully, and her speech was a spirited, lively-leaping
melody. In the afternoon she would wheel my carriage through
the streets of Berlin, streets strangely gray, smoke-darkened from
the fires of the last war, streets with gaping holes in the houses
that lined them. We passed ruins and freestanding firewalls that
jutted up toward the sky. Here and there, ten years after
Germany's debacle, you could still see bullet holes in the stucco
of the façades. When I asked about them, I received an
astonishing answer: even after it was clear the war was lost,
German soldiers had fought doggedly to the last.

So the streets were not merely streets but symbols, and the
city a symbolic city. Here a great army had met its end, an
empire had collapsed with a thundering crash, with plumes of
dust and fire billowing into the sky. I had powerful mental
images: pockets of resistance in the flayed houses, shots being
fired from skylights, suicide squads made up of little boys in
uniforms much too big for them, and courts martial hastily
improvised by the SS. An old man who lived upstairs from us
had been deaf ever since being caught outside when a bomb
exploded in the middle of the street. That made him an interesting figure to me; I pictured him hunched over and dashing

across the street, then hiding in a cellar. All old men had hidden in cellars. That thought occurred to me when they shouted at us like drill sergeants, when they leaned out the window and shook their fists, threatening us because we made too much noise playing.

The country to which our part of Berlin belonged called itself the GDR. That name stood for three claims: Germany, democracy, and republic, none of which would bear close examination by itself—a blurred trinity, a noncommittal abbreviation consisting of three initials. One saw them everywhere, in block letters: on bridges, on roofs, in store windows among baby carriages and cabbages. Usually associated with promises of a brilliant future.

My childhood was sheltered. I was not deprived. On the contrary, my father would cross into West Berlin, where one could get anything, and buy me Alete baby food, and toys, and bananas. The adults made a great fuss over us because we were the first generation after the inferno, and our uninhibited twittering provided a life-affirming contrast to the wailing sirens of those nights when bombs rained from the sky. Our colorful little swarm offered the first touch of color against the blackened firewalls. Yet there were militant demands: "Down with the old ways!" "Progress!" and "A new beginning!" Most disastrous of all was the promise they fed us.

It hung in the air. Reduced to a simple formula, it went like this: now everything will get better, from now on everything will be handled properly. The promise was all-inclusive, applied to the whole world and to the entire human race, which—as I later read in Marx—was supposed to evolve inexorably "from the bottom to the top." When lofty aspirations were expressed for Germany, it was meant to be symbolic for all peoples, and anyone reluctant to believe in them 'would be helped along. The whole country basked in this vision, for Germany had sunk so low that things could only get better. The Germans in the west focused on what seemed most immediate and reveled in their "economic miracle," while those in the east placed their hopes in a rosy future, when the masses would be triumphantly on the march. Each side wanted to prove to the other that the German variant of its chosen principle represented the *ne plus ultra*. Their rivalry permeated the city of Berlin, where people were fever- ishly building, painting, and renovating, and cocky slogans appeared on the walls of buildings. Underneath the paint, the old walls were crumbling.

Sparked by a fierce commitment to betterment, a German-German competition sprang up that seemed to restore a sense of pride to this country that had fallen so low and had such a craving for recognition. I grew up in the east, where the break with the past was supposed to be final. The word "tradition" was equated with a "reactionary" mentality, and anything reactionary was unforgivable. A *tabula rasa* mood had seized hold of my parents' generation, and where a white elephant like the Berlin Stadtschloss stood in the way, it was dynamited with- out further ado.

My father was enjoying a successful career in this country, so we moved. Our huge new apartment was across the street from a park. We had a neighbor, a Professor Stein, who was eighty-four. Allusions were made to his having been "persecuted." Apparently he drew a special pension, which explained why he could afford his large apartment and the woman with a gray bun who kept house for him. Professor Stein was a dignified gentleman with a mustache, a walking stick, and a hat that the grown-ups called a borsalino. He differed from other old men in that he never shouted, threatened, or scolded.

In the apartments of old ladies whom we visited when my father had manuscripts for them to type, we saw photos of young men, usually blond with light-colored eyes, in uniform. They smiled above their tightly buttoned collars, and their chests displayed an eagle with outstretched wings. "Who was that?" I would ask on the way home, and would learn that the young man was the woman's son or husband, "killed in the war." I thought all these young men looked alike; there were some vari- ations in the color of their hair or eyes, in the size of their noses, or the firmness or softness of their chins, but they all had the same haircut and the same odd smile on their faces. They looked so much alike, and so different from me.

Many people with whom I dealt—the women next door, salesgirls in shops, the fat policeman on the corner—seemed to screech, to bark, to growl, but not to speak. The speech with which I was familiar from home was music; the voice rose and fell, made little hops and trills, did not always stay at the same pitch. These unknown grown-ups also seemed to have no sense of humor; it took them a long time to grasp things, they reacted ponderously and unpredictably, their faces seemed dull, and their phony smile—when they chose this mask over a perpetually grumpy one—would unexpectedly give way to a sardonic grin. Years later I found these lines in a poem by Wieland Herzfelde:

He who laughs, grins,
He who doesn't laugh is suspect.

As a small boy I seemed uncanny to the salesgirls, maids, and women at the post office. They would ask, and a saccharin friendliness would spread over their faces, "Didn't you wash your eyes this morning?" This question puzzled me, until my mother explained that they were referring to the darkness of my eyes. Such eyes were uncommon in this country, even frightening, for they reminded them of something. No one said anything more specific, but the menace in the question did not escape me. I looked different from the way people looked in this country. The children with whom I played in the devastated streets were not the ones who made me aware of it; it was the grown-ups, who had been alive "in the old days."

"In the old days" was a gloomy garden, a labyrinth, a chamber of horrors. It conjured up the war, hiding in the cellar, or, in Professor Stein's case, "being persecuted." I was living in a country where every memory of "the old days" was loaded, among people who were quick to take offense. They turned hostile, swore, or sank into embittered silence. "In the old days" was when the smiling young men with the silver eagle on their chests had lived and then "fallen," when sirens had wailed and bombs had reduced the cities to rubble. "In the old days" my mother, then a child, had been hidden away in a monastery, and, as I heard my Berlin grandmother say, we could bless our lucky stars for that.

My other grandmother lived in another city and came to visit us now and then. I never felt close to her, because she always seemed so sad. It was very easy to make her angry; she reacted, as my parents said, neurotically. Whether she was reading, drinking cognac, or making a telephone call, the expression on her face remained sad. She had been "persecuted" too, had been in prison and then in a concentration camp for years, and pronounced the word "survive" with an emphasis that made a deep impression on me. She had been arrested before the general wave of deportations because—as my father put it—"she wouldn't stop grumbling," not even "when she had to wear the yellow star." She really did love to grumble, waxed indignant at the slightest provocation, flared up, and then suddenly, at the height of her inexplicable rage, broke out in a serene smile. My Berlin grandmother also liked to laugh at herself and her "malheurs," sometimes to the point of tears. Both of them loved me because in that respect I took after them.

When they were together, they played solitaire and talked in great detail about "the old days," mostly in French and behind closed doors. Both had "witnessed incredible happenings," had "come to know human nature," both were loud, had deep voices, and dominated any room they entered. They were the opposite of self-effacing, although they tried to appear restrained, or "diplomatic," as my Berlin grandmother called it. One shouldn't provoke "those people" unnecessarily; by that they meant the Germans. It was better to tiptoe around them, like sleeping beasts. On this score I did not take after them, and for that, too, they loved me. It was their secret joy to see me so brash and loud in a country where, if things had turned out the way the Germans had figured it, I would not have even existed.

What a strange feeling, to grow up being aware that your

existence is not generally welcome; something in the atmosphere, something extremely powerful opposes it. The majority of people around you, people you have learned to call your "fellow countrymen," once did everything in their power to make sure that someone like you would no longer be found in their part of the world. Your birth, your parents' coming together, your first signs of life, even your childish prattling—all constitutes an affront. Supposedly, this is your home, or at least no one would dare to contest that openly—you are not a black child, not a little Chinese—yet people stare at you as if your very existence were a silent reproach. My mother likes to describe how she "smuggled" me through my childhood; what was considered cute or forgivable in other children would in my case elicit an unexpectedly solemn response, undue sternness, a persistent wish to teach me, at three, five, or ten, a lesson, to change me once and for all.

Yet as a child I knew almost nothing of my forebears' peculiar history. A "Jewish problem" was not a topic of conversation in my family; indeed, the subject was shrouded in impenetrable silence. Today I can partly understand this attitude, even if I cannot condone it. Fear at times becomes so overwhelming that it banishes all reason, and the victim often succumbs to the delusion that apparent harmony with his persecutors renders him safe.

The ability to lie to ourselves is highly developed in German Jews. In order to be accepted and "loved" by the German public, even merely to obtain a professorship, Heine, Börne, and thousands of Jewish intellectuals had to convert and forswear their origins. If one reads Heine's autosuggestive reflections on the "moral superiority" of Protestant Christianity, one senses how wretched these Jews must have felt. But the longed-for harmony with their persecutors outweighed all their memories, all their knowledge of thousands of years spent as outsiders. Their "entry ticket," as Heine called his conversion, the unavoidable concession to society, produced widespread desire for assimilation.

In Germany it was called "Germanification." It ranged from enthusiasm for the First World War, to "Jewish self-hatred" and anti-Semitism directed against Jews from the east, all the way to a willingness to tolerate even Hitler. I hate to remind people of this, but in 1933 the Reich Association of Jewish Frontline Soldiers issued a declaration of loyalty to the just-elected Reich chancellor Adolf Hitler. The signatories, who had fought in the World War, most of them as volunteers, and had been decorated with the Iron Cross, etc., said they were placing themselves at the disposal of the "national awakening." We know how the Germans rewarded this attempt at submission a few years later. Seldom in history have Jews, longing to be assimilated, made such a poor investment; never has their self-denial ended more tragically.

The explanation for the desperate devotion of many Jews to Germany lies in their fundamentally ambivalent psychological state, almost impossible to reconstruct today, a combination of high-flying hopes and deep-seated fears. The Germans, for their part, have never really acknowledged what their country owes to the strangers in their midst, especially to the Jews; they have never liked foreign influence and have always feared it; traditionally they cannot be counted among the nations that have welcomed Jews. Ample proof exists that it is not a German trait to tolerate the irritant of people who think and feel differently, to allow lively discussion, even to listen to and want to understand what an outsider is saying.

The Jews' ancient fear of this narrow-minded host nation was calmed for a short time in the 19th century, for the Germans themselves seemed to calm down after the establishment of the Reich in 1871. For the next few decades it looked as though Jews were tolerated, and as though their assimilation and their subsequent efforts to be more German than the Germans made sense and might even prove liberating. Bismarck was no anti-Semite, certainly not after the Jewish banker Gerson Bleichröder financed Bismarck's war against France and thereby made a major contribution to the German victory. In addition, the House of Hohenzollern, which owed its rule of the Reich to this victory, had long since emerged as one of the most tolerant German dynasties as far as the "Jewish question" was concerned. Since the days of Moses Mendelssohn, Berlin had been the center of the German-Jewish intellect, and since Frederick II Jewish immigrants had been welcomed as citizens, receiving equal rights under the law from later kings. Rahel Varnhagen's salon was visited without hesitation by ministers, dignitaries, and the Prussian prince Louis Ferdinand.

Toward the end of the last century, the German-speaking realm seemed less hostile to Jews than ever before, and given their terrible experiences in previous centuries, this "less" must have caused Jews to feel great hope—unjustified hope, as we now recognize. The fin de siècle, the twilight of the Kaiser era in Berlin and Vienna, the republican era that followed in the twenties—never had this region known an atmosphere less hostile to Jews. Many Jews in Berlin, Vienna, and Prague became part of German literature and scholarship as if they were completely at home in German. Knowing that people tolerated or ignored their Jewish origins filled them with a pro-German enthusiasm that would be incomprehensible if we did not know about their grim experiences in earlier times and their foolish hope of outrunning their ancient history.

The illusion did not collapse until 1933, when the majority of Germans decided to embrace Hitler, with his program of national cleansing and *Gleichschaltung* (a euphemism for eliminating opposition), and thereby a degree of anti-Semitism far exceeding that of the Middle Ages. Yet the "golden decades" before and after 1900 must have seemed so hopeful that to this day many a German Jew cannot get over the shock of the relapse and still cannot grasp the German people's fall from apparent civilization into soulless barbarism.

As far as I can determine, in my forebears from this period the desire for assimilation outweighed any other impulse. A great-grandfather is supposed to have emigrated in plenty of time to Palestine, but as little was said about him as possible.

The striving of those who remained behind could be summed up in the formula, "I want to be a German." My parents substituted a socialist content for this formula's nationalist one, but fundamentally the attitude remained the same, just a newer form of conformity. So much for the milieu that produced me and that I have now left behind.

I am not the first Jew to assume a rejected legacy of Jewishness, not the first to want to return to where his ancient roots lie, and I will not be the last. It is senseless to try to resist these memories that will one day prove more powerful than any craving to fit in. As far back as I can remember, I have got along better with Jews than with non-Jews, laughed at their jokes and tragicomic stories more readily than at those of the Germans—if, indeed, I could ever laugh at German jokes—and have felt more deeply stirred and better understood by Jews. Even a Jew I do not like is never incomprehensible to me, even antipathy and enmity are profoundly familiar. All of this would seem to have little to do with Germany, and was already ancient history in Babylon.

History—that is the word I use to classify my return to a Jewish sense of self. Being a Jew can mean various things; to some it means primarily strict observance of the mitzvoth, to others it has to do with one's maternal descent. To me it meant accepting our history, its symbolic uniqueness, captured over the centuries in books, its concentrated, magnificent humanity. "In the Old Testament," Heine wrote, "I read today through the entire first book of Moses. The holy world of bygone times filed through my spirit like long caravans." As a poet he saw the ancient images under the aspect of the word: the word "emerges in the terrible nakedness that frightens and stirs us," we find there "naked truth without the cloak of art." And two weeks later in the same travel journal, still under the spell of that text: "Fear and hope alternate in my spirit, and I find myself feeling very uncertain."

Fear of even pronouncing the word "Jew" has beset me since I was a small child. I was born in Germany because my parents were determined to stay here and conform all over again. They jettisoned the previous history of their dispersed people in favor of the illusion of a new beginning, completely in tune with this century, which likes to succumb to the delusion that history can be canceled out as never before. In vain, of course, for history catches up and punishes such arrogant notions, as it has every time.

And whom would history punish more severely than Jews who worshiped false gods? "Thus the Lord separated them from the tribes of Israel, as smoke is separated from fire and blown away," the Spanish rabbi Joel ibn Schuaib called five hundred years ago after the apostate Marranos; "let them be undone by that from which they hoped to escape. For you there is neither refuge nor salvation, neither on earth nor in heaven." His curse took on a horrifying contemporaneity for the assimilated and converted Jews of the twentieth century, especially for the German Jews. The communists among them experienced the same thing, somewhat later but to no less a degree.

"I am a Jew"—to write this sentence meant to break with everything I had been raised to believe. I had been raised to play along, to live unobtrusively in the midst of an unloved, alien, basically anti-Jewish nation. My parents were made to feel every day that they were not liked. They attempted to protect themselves by entering into an arrangement with the state, an arrangement directed against its citizens. They mistrusted the latter, without telling me why. My mother used to entertain us by imitating the way our neighbors complained, acted envious, pretended to be friendly; as a child I would laugh heartily, not suspecting how little reason there was to laugh. I grew up feeling we were safe in the GDR, since my parents were treated obsequiously wherever we went, and apparently belonged to the respected, important people, to the winners.

In their attempt lies much of the tragedy of those Jews who threw in their lot with communism. To belong to the communist movement, then to the caste of functionaries, seemed to provide security, like being a German nationalist a generation earlier. To be implicated was more acceptable than the old role of victim. Since Yurizky, Trotsky, and the Jewish people's commissars, since Yagoda and his interrogators, since Jews have been implicated in communism to the point of criminality, since Jews have betrayed other Jews and denied their identity, many have followed this path just to be part of things, to come out on top. Yet in their being there was always something fragmented, something irremediable; something in the role they were playing seemed irreconcilable with their ancient genotype. I do not know why the sight of them turned me against communism more than anything else. I felt they were selling themselves cheap, humbling themselves before people who, God knows, did not deserve it.

All one needs is suddenly to pause in midstream and ask oneself: who am I? Where do I come from? As if coming out of a deep faint, I admitted to myself one day what I had long been feeling: I could never be a "proper German." Not a German patriot and not a German socialist—I had watched my family fail in these attempts to conform. Not a "German Jew" either, for I did not believe there could be such a thing anymore. The historian Michael Wolffsohn goes so far as to call himself a "German-Jewish patriot," as the good Jews of the Central Association of German Citizens of the Jewish Faith once did. Since Auschwitz, such an identity is an absurd if well-meant construct, born of the effort to achieve reconciliation. It rests on that same self-denial that to my mind has been the undoing of German Jews. As for reconciliation: I feel it should not be up to us to work so hard to achieve it.

In the longer run, the German nation will not be forgiven for Auschwitz, or for the calculated attack on humanity this word has come to symbolize. How Germany comes to terms with this is its own problem. When a people makes such a spectacle of itself, its name becomes emblematic of something revolting; for centuries that was the case with the Huns, Tatars, and Mongols. The Germans will not succeed in making people halfway forget Auschwitz unless they consistently behave like civilized people.

So far, the East Germans at least seem to be recidivists: the penitentiaries of Brandenburg, Bautzen, and Hoheneck, the women's prison, were still going strong forty years after the end of the war.

On August 13, 1961, my Berlin grandmother was sitting with us by the radio. Sunlight was shining in the window, and her eyes were half closed with strenuous concentration as the announcer declared, "The border-crossing points Friedrichstrasse, Oberbaumbrücke, and Sonnenallee have been closed. . . " A critical decision had to be made that morning: should one try to find a spot to slip through into West Berlin, or stay for good? She decided to stay, for the sake of my brother and me, brash offspring of timorous parents. She was weary and would have liked to spend the rest of her days unnoticed, being spared further frights, and she would probably have given in to this weakness had there been no offspring or that transcendent goal invoked by books: survival.

At first we could observe the half-city on our side becoming more boring, orderly, and dreary with every day that passed. At night I would hear clattering and loud noises out on the street, and my father would say, "It's our tanks." I was taken along when he reviewed "our border troops," young men who sat on iron vehicles and resembled the fallen sons in the pictures: a similar uniform, a similar look in their eyes, loyal, ready to follow and obey. My grandmother, angered by my parents' loyalty to the state, predicted war, Old Testament-style disaster: "I've seen more than you have." As if suddenly awakened, she announced passionately, "One must be fair. They're human beings over there, too."

No sooner had she left the house than I heard my father saying, "They're bourgeois, and always will be." He claimed to be more clever, modern, progressive, free of the blemish of not fitting in. As a communist he wanted clear demarcations: the city divided, the swamp drained, an end to the confusing back and forth. He had long since been gripped by the worst, most corrosive fear of all: the fear of being an outsider, of possibly being "persecuted." The world, so I learned from him, was evolving in the direction of progress; magnificent things were going to happen, a general reconciliation of contradictions and liberation from everything subsumed under the phrase "the old days." We had only to struggle consistently for "socialism," if need be by giving our lives, like many heroes whose names I learned early on. I also learned early on about an arcadian land called the Soviet Union. Dark forces in the west were trying to block what could not be blocked: the advance of the tanks, the determination of "our border troops," "our cause," of which we—my father, his comrades, and I—would one day make a gift to the entire world.

My grandmothers secretly tried to pull me over to their side: "Your father doesn't say what he really thinks." They had no chance of success; my parents were closer to me, what they had to offer more interesting. The older I got—eleven, fifteen, seventeen—the more grandiose that picture seemed, impervious to any oldsters' objections. History's turmoil stopped in its tracks in a scientifically predetermined fashion, the wretched of the earth were liberated, and the universal panacea was found that would cure the quirks of human nature. My parents' loyal, optimistic attitude was favored in a country that has always persecuted the bad, "subversive" Jew but has occasionally tolerated the good Jew. "Ach, what's this about being a Jew? There really is no such thing anymore." Splendid Zero Hour, an escape at last from a hopeless, confused, tragic history, the old dream of assimilation realized, and in harmony with the progressive forces in the world, no less.

I owe it to my father's successful career in the communist German state, to his complicity, that I was able to grow up there unimpeded. Imagine what the teachers, day-care workers, and supervisors of my childhood would have done with me otherwise. They were coarse and prone to bullying, most of them from Saxony, transplanted to Berlin as part of Ulbricht's resettlement policy. The husband of my elementary-school teacher, who came from Geithahn near Leipzig, was an officer with the

Stasi. That teacher yelled at us in a voice so loud it followed me into my dreams. But she fawned over the children of functionaries, took out her hostility on those whose fathers were low-ranking employees or workers, hurled her heavy bunch of keys across the room at a little slowpoke. In the classrooms and corridors of my school, one heard shouting like on a parade ground. It offered little comfort that the voices yelling commands were women's voices, and certainly not to the child who was ordered to stand in the corner, to sit in the hall, or to pass his notebook to the front.

The teachers clearly embodied power. The mothers and fathers were intimidated when they were summoned to the school for a "conference," which could happen at any time. With only a few exceptions, among them my father. When he got out of his big Soviet limousine, wearing his fur-lined coat, a decoration on his lapel, always in a hurry, the faces of my wardens, usually so lordly, became accommodating; their grating voices tried to adopt a chatty, modulated tone. "Your son," they would say, "is such a joy to have in class."

I really was a good student. "Since you stick out like a sore thumb anyway," my parents told me, "make up for it by doing well in school; that's the only thing that provides any assurances." They taught me to view my inborn nature, my appearance, my character as a risk factor that could be compensated for only by emphatic conformity. I became a Young Pioneer and a Thälmann Pioneer, sang in the school chorus, "Today my dad's on reconstruction shift," even though I had no mental image of what that might mean, wore blue neckerchiefs that my mother ironed, because whether a neckerchief was ironed or not revealed one's parents' political commitment. I learned poems by Stefan Hermlin and Evgeny Dolmatovsky by heart, drew doves of peace, red stars, Lenin's head, marched through the gray streets of Berlin feeling I belonged and was doing everything right. I joined the Free German Youth, wore a blue shirt, and my right sleeve was adorned with stripes, indications of rank, never too low, never too high. I assumed various functions, learned to bow to the will of the majority on the steering committee, and when addressing the actual majority, sitting silent in the auditorium below, found words as eloquent as if I had been expressing my own decision.

The world was full of turbulent motion, while the picture we were given of it was static. In the meantime other wars had taken place, yet because they did not touch me directly, I adopted the official opinion of them, condemned the "American aggressor" and learned to praise the "peace-loving Soviet power." Everything was developing according to plan: people were rising up and discovering—how could it be otherwise—socialism, a worldwide liberation movement. I was doing the same on a small scale. But one day a war came along that made me lose my faith in my teachers, Israel's Six Day War.

Something had always disturbed me about classes in school, afternoons with the Pioneers, our "Polit-Information" sessions: the poverty of the language used, a stupidity in the choice of words, a lack of sensual, musical qualities, its hammering, one-sided, chanting tediousness. The language customarily used in such settings clearly fell short of the possibilities I had discovered for myself. My language had found a direction of its own, and what gave me delight occurred only in books, never in "social life." I had given up looking for it in this life, just parroted what they demanded in order to be left in peace. In secret I had entered a second world and opened up a second existence, that of literature, where I could roam freely, without boundaries.

Surrounded by shelves extending from floor to ceiling, I lay on the rug and read, while outside a November afternoon in Berlin sank behind tiresome roofs. I read of rich people rising and falling, of princes despairing, of pastry-vendors becoming nobles and senators becoming beggars. I came to recognize injustice and baseness in the edifying stories I was fed every day, and cleverness and goodness only in rare individuals, who usually met a bad end. I began to suspect that what counted for wisdom in school was a mockery of the truth, an impermissible, revolting ruse. The people I read about seemed neither consistently "good" nor "bad," and they were not on the proclaimed path "from the bottom to the top;" they seemed to be simply human beings in all their puzzling awkwardness, fallibility, unwieldiness, with rare flashes of beauty, and I no longer believed that their fundamental nature would ever change.

The less their nature was described as "logically explicable," the more convincing it seemed to me. As I read, I lost the certainty my Marxist teachers had tried to instill in me, their certainty that human beings and the construct of society, which they were always making fresh attempts at building, could be "transformed." When I was sixteen, my love was focused on the psychological portraits offered by writers at the turn of the century: they showed the human being as an imponderable, inexplicable even to itself. I read of young Tonio Kröger—also not a "proper German," like me—who tried to explain to his school friend how he had been stirred by Schiller's *Don Carlos*, and was not understood. My school friends did not understand me either when I tried to tell them, as if our salvation were at stake, about Hamlet's ennui, Werther's last letter, or Akaky Akakyevich Bashmachkin's terrible search for the overcoat, when I tried to catch them in the web of my world after I had spent long afternoons hunched over the rustling pages of a book. They did listen when I said I had adventures to recount, but these were adventures of the intellectual sort that refreshingly called into question our political and scientific dogmas. They laughed and slapped me on the back, but they were not prepared to consider the world of books more significant than getting ahead and the concomitant need to conform.

So I was probably crazy in much the same way as my heroes when I drew more life from the printed page than from "reality." My solitude was made bearable by the knowledge that I was in the best of company, if one that allegedly no longer existed. At the time I particularly liked letters, because in them the author's "I" found direct expression, that subjective, forbidden "I" that the guardians of my childhood were trying to drive out of me.

One day I was reading Heine's letters when I came upon something for which everyday experience had already prepared me. Heine referred to a people with whom I felt a deep, mysterious bond, a people of the book, who had survived the most incredible torments thanks only to its extraordinary devotion to the written word. "The Jews," I read, "known to this day as the 'people of the book,' a name that is deeply fitting . . . One book is their fatherland, their sovereign, the source of their happiness and their sorrow. They live within the walled precincts of this book; here they have their inalienable civil rights, here they cannot be expelled, despised, here they are strong and admirable. Immersed in this book, they noted few of the changes occurring round about them in the real world. Peoples rose to prominence and vanished, states flourished and were extinguished, revolutions stormed across the face of the earth. . ."

It was not "this book" that transformed me into a rebel; I did not discover the Old Testament until later. But this much I understood, in spite of all my indoctrination: that the Jews, who allegedly no longer existed, preferred books to any other company. In time of war and during outbreaks of turmoil they sat there, the last of the faithful, bent over their folios; they hauled books with them whenever they had to flee, and went to the gas in Auschwitz reciting psalms from memory. They would come up with a literary *bon mot* even when all around them the world was sinking into rubble, and they continued to fuss over words in times of speechlessness.

Back to the Six Day War. I heard what I had heard so often before: Israel was the "aggressor," the "warmonger," the "running dog of U.S. monopoly capitalism," had even before that been a fomenter of international intrigue, a "string-puller." I remember one statement clearly: "Tel Aviv is spinning the threads." Zionism was a form of racism, a notion confirmed not long afterward by a U.N. resolution that subjected Israel's "disregard for humanity" to worldwide condemnation. World peace in danger, the "peoples' legitimate aspirations to freedom" destroyed, the "balance of power" shifted in favor of our enemies. I was fourteen, and kept my mouth shut. The charges being made seemed perfectly logical and meaningful within the framework of what I had been taught: a picture of the world as consisting only of "comrades" and "adversaries," and no one in between.

But this time I could not go along. The state of Israel, I told myself, this gruesome spawn of "reactionary forces," apparently has Jewish residents. Jews like your favorite writers. Emigrants from Europe, people who fled Hitler, people who share those secret convictions that mean so much to you. Wasn't one of them the poet Else Lasker-Schüler, to whom you feel as close as to your grandmothers, who gazed into the world with the same dark eyes as you? Didn't you get a whiff of home from her "Hebrew Ballads," from reading her biography, which could easily be yours?

No matter if "reason" argued against Israel, no matter if it was eminently logical, or scientific, as our doctrine would have it, to claim that the "world policeman," the U.S., or "world capitalism," or, as Ulbricht said at the time, "the World Bank" was behind the war and Israel was merely their "bird dog" waging a "proxy war"—I could not condemn that country. I was in the grip of more than childish obstinacy. It was an old certainty, much older than all the ephemeral truths with which they bombarded us, and against which I now unexpectedly and uncannily found myself armored. For the first time I came to realize that there was a knowledge older than all the "reason" with which I was surrounded.

It's a funny thing about Marxism: if you cease to believe in its infallibility in one small detail, the entire ideology loses its power over you. My deviation on the subject of Israel was nothing more nor less than the tiny flaw that would cause the entire monolith to shatter for me; the rest was only a question of time.

According to my teachers' and my parents' theories, there

could be no more Jews in my country because socialism had gratifyingly solved the confusion of the different religions and had at last provided that people of homeless wanderers with a home, in "progress." That meant I could not be a Jew. For the first time I admitted to myself how awful such a prospect was. No more Jews, no more people of the book? No more living symbol for the existence of the oldest truth, the truth of the written word? Where could I find refuge, where could I flee from the book-hating, language-abusing environment in which I spent my days?

For the time being, without really believing in the Jews' disappearance, I continued on my path as I had been taught, left the Free German Youth to join the party, tried without success to smuggle in a better form of socialism, dared to raise half-hearted objections, got myself punished and accepted the punishment. I traveled to Russia and drank brandy until I was able to discover hopeful features in that crumbling empire. I assured my friends that in spite of all my criticisms I believed firmly in socialism. The question of whether one could improve it, whether the teachings of Marx and Lenin did not contain a kernel of usable truth, preoccupied me. Rereading and reexamining their ambitious theories absorbed all my energy, and in this way several years passed.

Self-deception can assume stubborn forms, especially when it has been inherited from one's parents. Halfhearted participation in something in which one no longer believes can be more comfortable than putting an end to it, which may be wrenching—because where does one go next? One's inner back and forth can last a long time, but eventually the day arrives when they demand a commitment, when one has to take the oath.

I was prepared to pay lip service if absolutely necessary, but I felt incapable of "service with arms" in the East German army. The uniform this army wore was too reminiscent of that earlier one, and I will never understand why the GDR government was so stupid as to show its hand this way. The color was a little different, the cut the same, and when certain German faces showed above the collar, the impression was complete. Above just such collars those smiling young men had gazed out into the world, foolishly confident of victory, those young men whose pictures with black crepe pinned to them hung in the apartments of elderly ladies. I was familiar with the rest of the uniform from other photos: firing squads executing Jews. From friends I heard that things in the new army were much like in the old one, with physical violence and "self-training," with meaningless harassment and daily humiliation.

"When a noble purpose is at stake, even a hero's death is beautiful." These words could be found in a brochure entitled "Marxist-Leninist Aesthetics and the Training of Soldiers," written by a Russian major-general called Milovidov. "The sight of a rocket prepared for launching awakens aesthetic feelings in the soldier and stimulates the growth of his moral powers." That struck me as absolutely outrageous: I was supposed to find this revolting business "beautiful." Such texts were accompanied by more pictures of smiling young men, gazing out of the turrets of tanks, marching across rough terrain, or strolling with their girls. I simply could not imagine my own face above this uniform. For that reason I decided not to put it on.

My comrades, who had taken it for granted that I would, did not understand my refusal. When I stuck to it, with threadbare pretexts but implacably, when I went on a hunger strike to make myself unfit through illness, their lack of understanding turned into anger, naked and menacing. My not wanting to cooperate constituted resistance to their state, which I was supposed to love more than anything in the world. To avoid a public scandal, the authorities finally decided I must be mentally disturbed. This verdict saved me from going to jail.

I found it somehow appropriate: in this state everything was upside-down, and if they labeled me insane, I had reason to hope I was sane. Besides, the psychiatric facilities to which they committed me had a major advantage over prisons: the inmates were allowed to read. Without books I would not have made it through those months unscathed. I resolved to use the time to figure out just what was going on and, if I survived the whole thing, to write about it. The step from reading to writing becomes easier when one has such experiences as material.

I left the GDR soon after that, but inwardly I had emigrated long before, in the same way Jews have done for centuries: with the help of books.

BARBARA HONIGMANN

from

A Love Out of Nothing

ON THE MAP OF PARIS, which was the first picture I tacked up on the wall of my basement apartment, I looked right away for the streets where my parents had lived before the war. I even circled them in red pencil, although I was not at all sure whether I should go to see them—what could I expect to find there? After all, I did not want to follow forever in my parents' footsteps, even though I also knew that I would not get away from them, and that my emigration was perhaps only the dream of a real separation, the wish for a rootless life. More than anything else, perhaps, I was running away from my parents, and in spite of that I was still tagging along behind them.

When they lived in Paris, my parents did not know each other yet. My father was married to another woman, and my mother to another man. She had come from Vienna as a refugee, and my father was a correspondent for the *Vossische Zeitung* before he too became a refugee.

My mother told me she was wealthy in those days, had an apartment on the Quai d'Orsay with a view of the Seine, an apartment with huge rooms, ballrooms, and a vast bow window, and she knew the entire Paris art world, *tout Paris*, and all the expatriates from every imaginable country. She threw grand parties and danced the night away in a rose-colored silk gown with a deep décolleté and a hat with a plume. And in the cellar of our Berlin apartment house I actually came upon an old cardboard box containing a plume and a rose-colored silk evening bag that must have matched the dress. My girlfriends and I used to play grand lady with it; I could hardly believe that these props had once had a role in my mother's life.

At some point I walked along the Quai d'Orsay and stopped in front of her house; I picked a house at random because I had no idea which one it had really been. Of course there was absolutely nothing to see there; it is as if a wave had washed over her presence, and everything had simply vanished.

When Hitler followed my mother to Paris, she moved to London. There she married my father, who in the meantime had become a reporter for Reuters; the *Vossische Zeitung* no longer existed. He had left his first wife, and my mother her first husband. Hitler did not follow them to London, but every night he dropped a hailstorm of bombs on the city, so they were always having to look for a new apartment, the old one having been bombed. At night they slept in the windowless bathroom, because if one came through alive, shards from splintering windows presented the greatest danger. By day my father worked at Reuters, putting together war reports for the English newspapers, while my mother worked in a munitions plant, assembling English submarines for the war against Germany. They wanted to fight back. And Hitler was defeated. He lost, and my parents won. They left England and went back to where it had all begun, to the place Hitler had chased them out of, to Berlin.

My father arrived first, with a couple of suitcases, after a long, arduous journey through all of Europe; the war might be over but it was hardly peacetime yet. During the trip he had decided not to work for Reuters and the British anymore but rather to go over to the Russians in East Berlin. He had become a communist.

My mother returned almost a year later, as though she had hesitated. From London she had first traveled to Bulgaria to check on her family and friends and to show them that she was still alive. Only then did she rendezvous with my father in Berlin. She arrived wearing blood-red nail polish, as he told it.

Because they were Jews, the emigration and the bombs falling on London were not the worst of it. My parents could count themselves lucky, but for the rest of their lives they would have to live with the images and the tales of those who had not been lucky, and that must have been a heavy burden, so heavy that they always behaved as though they had had nothing to do with it at all, as though they had no connection with anyone who had perished in a ghetto or been gassed in Auschwitz. My father much preferred to talk about his ancestors who lived along the Bergstrasse in Hesse, physicians and bankers at the court of the grand dukes of Hesse-Darmstadt. After all, my parents had come to Berlin to build a new Germany, where everything was supposed to be entirely different from the old one; therefore it was better not to mention the Jews anymore. But somehow not everything turned out right, and the day came when they even had to explain why they had chosen a western country for their exile rather than the Soviet Union. My mother thought she understood why she was feeling worse and worse. She had been on the move too long, from country to country; now she wanted to go home. But for my father it had been a homecoming— Germany was where he came from—even if not to Hesse-Darmstadt but to East Berlin, to the Russians, the Communists. But perhaps it was this betrayal which, when he considered his origins, made his new home seem like a foreign country. At all possible moments and occasions I heard him say, Actually I don't know where I come from; nor do I know where I belong now. And once he added, Perhaps it's all just been a continuation of Martha. When I asked him, Who's Martha? What about Martha? Tell me, what happened to her? he said, It's something that goes way back to my childhood, but I suppose it never ended. All my ideas, my careers, my women, even all the places I've lived in my life—just a continuation of Martha.

We were carrying full shopping bags along the road from Upper Weimar to Belvedere Castle. My father went down to the little government-run store in the village almost every day to buy whatever they needed: bread, milk, butter, eggs, beer. The clerks in the store always addressed him as Herr Professor, although he had explained countless times that he was not a professor and never had been. We put down our bags and rested at the intersection at which one can choose between two routes, one that goes by way of the broad Belvedere Allee, where one walks in the shade of the old trees that line the avenue, or one that goes by way of the meadows along the Ilm River and the fields, the back way, a path that gets fairly steep at the end and is actually not very good for climbing with full shopping bags, but gives one an unobstructed view of the whole area, all the way across to Buchenwald.

When I was a little boy, my father said, I once wanted to write and put on a play. I was completely obsessed with the notion, and announced it to my parents; it was to be called *Martha*, and they were supposed to invite the whole family for a certain day, when the premiere was to take place. My father, the professor, was proud of me and invited the whole family and his colleagues from the sanatorium to our grand apartment in the large villa in Wiesbaden. I set about preparing for the big evening, making costumes, transforming the parlor into a set, writing the program, inventing the characters, even sending out additional invitations and announcements to selected people for the premiere of *Martha*. But when the moment arrived and the uncles and aunts and colleagues from the sanatorium were assembled in the theater-parlor waiting for *Martha* to begin, when the great moment for which I had prepared so long finally arrived—at that point it suddenly became clear to me that in all the excitement I had forgotten one thing: to write the play. *Martha* had been merely my dream of a play, a dream of a grand evening that would be mine alone, my success and my glory. But the play did not exist at all; I had completely forgotten to write it. I appeared onstage nonetheless and said:
This is frightful.
This is terrible.
This is absolutely awful.

And that's all there was to *Martha*.

*

Sometimes it seemed almost impossible for me to bring some kind of order to my life's work, which had fallen out of the shipping container totally jumbled. I was already exhausted by the impressions of the new world. I almost didn't have the stamina to keep sallying forth, and would much rather have simply stayed in, lying on my bed to catch my breath. It often seemed to me that I had had enough of major changes and would do better to stop this constant motion; I was already out of breath.

And why had I dropped everything and left it behind like a fugitive?

There had been this notion that one must keep striking out for a new country, a new home, even if it was just another province. All over Berlin people talked of nothing else but that one cannot remain in the same spot forever, that it would be childish, like never leaving home. They talked about this everywhere, in the cafeteria of the Berlin Theater or in my apartment, where we sat around the big table in the kitchen. Actually, during that period we hardly ever ventured out of our apartments; there was no reason to do so, for everything was so familiar we were sick of it. Indoors we sorrowed after and fantasized about everything that was "outside," and could hardly picture the reality of another life and other countries and cities: whether it was similar or entirely different there, and how people behaved. We played loud music at night, Bob Dylan or a Bach cantata, until the neighbors came and asked had we gone out of our minds and didn't we have to go to work the next morning.

I had a small place in the north end, a room where the washing machine stood next to the desk and where I never did manage to get a telephone installed. In front of the building was the bus stop for No. 57, which I had taken to the university for years, and for more years after that to the Berlin Theater. It was the same theater where as a child I had stood in the wings with my father, watching his third wife, the actress. In the meantime I had become a dramaturg, and had to draft the program notes, run to libraries to look up background material for productions, or write up comments on the rehearsals, which I showed to the dramaturgs who had been working there for decades; I was their assistant. At some point they threw me out of the theater; that is, a contract that had been provisional for years was not extended, a contract against which I should have long since registered a grievance before a labor court, but since things had somehow gone all right up to that time, I had been too lazy to put up any resistance to the injustice. And I had gradually grown tired of working at the same theater all the time, always taking the same route, always catching the bus in front of my building and going to the Berlin Theater. I had quarreled with my friends, or maybe we were just tired of each other, the result of friendships that had gone on too long; maybe we had just had enough of always hanging out together. The familiar had become familiar to the point of boredom, leaving me with nothing but a sense of weariness and weakness, and a profound existential lassitude that alarmed me.

Once, after the first performance of Goethe's *Egmont*, I, like all the others, received a bouquet of roses from the general manager. We stayed up until early morning celebrating, and then I walked home at dawn. It was June, the beginning of summer, and not at all chilly. I had not closed the window in my room; both casements stood wide open, and in the nearby trolley yard the first trolleys were just crawling out of their barns. Beyond lay the stockyards, from which a biting, nauseating stench of animals' death wafted over, day and night. Next to the Leninallee municipal railway station, banners on Werner Seelenbinder Hall were announcing some sort of party rally. Beyond that, factories and smokestacks stretched to the horizon, punctuated by a small, pale-blue church tower. The sun was just rising above all this scenery as I came in the door from the cast party. It tinged the dark gray of the waning night with the red and yellow gray of morning, and I stood there with the bouquet in my hand and gazed out at this landscape, which was like a restless and menacing ocean—the streetcars and the barns, the squeaking pigs trapped in their enclosures, the smokestacks, and the morning sun splashed over all of it. In my room I already had many bouquets. I had dried every bouquet I had ever been given and displayed them on my shelves and dressers. A dusty primeval forest, a cemetery of flowers had grown up, gradually overgrowing and overrunning the landscape of my room. But this morning, after the first performance of *Egmont*, at the sight of the wide-open window, I did not want to dry and preserve any more flowers. I tossed the bouquet of roses in a high arc out the window. It landed somewhere in the trolley yard, and then I cut down the primeval forest and leveled the cemetery of flowers on my dressers and shelves, throwing all the other dried bouquets after the roses.

Sometimes at the Berlin Theater, when we were sitting in the cafeteria, one of the actors would recite these lines from Rilke's "Departure of the Prodigal Son":
and go away: where? To parts uncertain
off to a warm and unrelated land
that's there behind all action like a curtain,
a backdrop of wall—or garden—on demand;
and go away: why? From instinct or frustration,
from lack of patience or from expectation,
from failure to be understood or understand.

Then we would argue about Rilke, whom some of us worshiped like a god and others rejected completely, and about the uncertain foreign land, the failure to comprehend and be comprehended, and it was half serious and half just casually tossed out, and usually ended with someone exclaiming, Oh, just forget it, will you! But then if someone in this circle really set out to seek a new province, a new land, the others would become very indignant, and he would be condemned by those he had left behind as if he had betrayed them.

The first they discussed this way was Alfried. He was a director, and among the first to leave the theater and the country. They accused him of thoughtlessness and asserted that he must not know the price he would have to pay. All those who left later were accused in the same terms, and I listened and knew that some day my turn would come.

At home in my room I sat among the dessicated flowers, stared out the window at the trolley yard, at the stockyards, and could hardly believe that Alfried had simply torn himself away from everything. I began to write him long letters, yard-long accounts of my life and my love for him, which took shape as I wrote. The letters piled up on my desk because I had no idea where he was now and where I could send them. So they stayed there, and in the end I threw the stacks of yard-long letters into the garbage chute, where everything one throws in falls so far down that one cannot find it again or retrieve it.

Alfried used to wait for me sometimes after the play was over, and we would go out for something to eat or walk through the Friedrichshain, first up Mont Klamott, the hill made of rubble, and then around the little lake, or on Sundays we would take an excursion to another city. And we always wrote each other letters, or rather little notes that we pushed under each other's doors, not when no one was there, as other people do, but rather precisely when the recipient was home, because that way we could hide from each other. We never said, I love you, and never, I love you, too. We just made gestures, and they could always be understood in a number of ways. But above all: not a word. An enigmatic pantomime.

When Alfried visited me, it was always late at night. The front door would be locked already, and he had to stand below in the courtyard and call out my name loudly, because there was no bell. Then I would run down, unlock the door, and let him in. He stayed only a couple of hours and left before dawn, so that by day no one ever saw the man who had shouted so loudly in the night, and often I was no longer sure myself whether I had seen him. The next day we would be colleagues again at the Berlin Theater.

Alfried told me he did not wish to receive me in his apartment, but he never gave a reason. He said nothing, and I did not ask; we kept silent about it, as about everything else. But I could not understand it, and one day, to get even, I decided to break into his apartment, just to see what he had to hide. He had said something about a concealed key, I remembered, and one time, when he was away for a few days, I set out, planning to retrieve the key from its hiding place and open the door, and I took other keys with me to help with the break-in. Once inside his apartment I wanted to rummage around, burrowing through and pulling out everything, and leave a note saying I WAS HERE, to put an end to the imposed silence. Or even better, once I had pulled everything out and thrown it on the floor, I could sit down in the midst of the chaos and wait until he came home and found me. I wanted to see what he would say.

I did not find the hidden key. I tapped and scratched and knocked on every inch of the walls and the window sill and the window frame by the door, all in vain. But one of the keys I had brought along, when I chose it at random and inserted it into the lock, opened the door quite easily: it sprang open before me and suddenly I was standing in Alfried's apartment. I walked through his rooms, saw where he worked, where he slept, his kitchen with a little balcony outside the window, and noticed that he had not washed the dishes before he left. I saw everything, but I could not bring myself to touch anything, and I did not want to look anymore—among his things I felt like a burglar. I did not feel closer to him but rather more remote than before. I did not stay, did not pull anything out, and did not leave behind a note saying I WAS HERE, but left everything untouched and locked the door behind me with my key so that everything would remain as it had been.

From the beginning I hated Alfried's name. I could not bring myself to say it, because it sounded so Teutonic and I did not want to love a Teuton, for I could not, would not, and was not allowed to excuse the Teutons for what they had done to the Jews. Because the Teutons had been murderers, I could not speak Alfried's name, and said "sweetheart" and "love" instead.

For I did love him, almost against my will, and this love often seemed to me like a connection or even a bond from which we could not escape.

Sometimes I wished or feared that we would have a child. But I saw the child in nightmares, loosely put together out of individual parts that did not stay together, and it would fall apart and shatter and not stand upright. I never told Alfried about these dreams, because I knew he did not want to hear about them. He avoided any discussion of our origins, our resemblances or differences. He had no desire to see the reality of my life, which I had not chosen, but which weighed so heavily and whose inner truth was at once apparent and hidden, even to me. Perhaps he had problematic origins, too, but we kept silent about everything, as if it were not there; a mere allusion was too much, and every question an imposition. Perhaps it was the fear of a misunderstanding or our inability to recognize each other's reality, and there was even something like a rivalry between us. It was always a question of a winner and a loser, and we were fighting not for victory but rather for defeat. Each of us felt like the loser and charged the other with being the winner. The less we talked about things, the more clearly this struggle emerged. All the while we never really looked at each other properly, just furtively and bashfully from the side or from a distance, never directly in the face. It was like the fear of seeing each other in the light of day after a terrible night, a blood wedding.

After he left, Alfried sent me postcards from every conceivable city in Europe, never a letter, and none of the cards carried a return address. In the cafeteria of the Berlin Theater, people said what they had heard about productions he had put on in other cities, this or that play here or there, in Hamburg, in Frankfurt, in Munich, and occasionally someone would bring in a newspaper review, which we passed around.

And I sat in my apartment in the middle of the flower cemetery and no longer felt right in my skin and thought that leaving could be a kind of metamorphosis, in which one simply slipped off the old skin. I wanted to emigrate, preferably to Paris, to learn a new language and start something entirely new, perhaps also travel on, to America, for instance, where no one I knew had ever been. I would really be the first to get there. No one would know me and no one would ask me questions, and if someone did, I could answer whatever I liked, something invented from an entirely different life; I could make a fresh start.

I wanted to tear myself away from the nest of familiar people, landscapes, political conditions, and language, and from the sense of security I found in it all, knowing I might very well never find it again.

For a few months I continued to carry all this around inside me, but then I went and submitted the necessary application, in a building I had no trouble finding, because it was the same one where over the years I had repeatedly put in my request for a telephone, to no avail, and had picked up the forms authorizing wood and coal deliveries for the stove that stood next to my washing machine and my desk.

Before long I found the white card in my mailbox that gives the signal for leaving the country and initiates the bureaucratic procedures at the end of which one is informed that one can leave now, just as one wished, and that one has only a little time left; before this period is up, one must be gone. They delivered the shipping container to my room, and whatever I wanted to take with me vanished into its depths. It did not hold that much, and I weighed every piece for its utility and its place in my life. I chose primarily things I did not want to part with: photos, pictures, books, letters, a couple of manuscripts of plays, my easel, household items, a few tools, and clothing for the various seasons.

Then I had to say good-bye to my friends—in parting I had made up with them, and also with my colleagues at the Berlin Theater. It felt like a breaking and wrenching when I said that this story was supposed to end now, and I did not know what would come next. I cried a lot those last few days, first thing in the morning, because I had gone to bed the night before crying.

But one morning I left the apartment, locked the door, and did not put the key in my bag as usual, but rather took it to the housing authority and turned it in. Then I no longer had an apartment to come back to; it was locked behind me once and for all, and I was on the outside. In order to hold fast the exact moment of my departure, I looked at the clock. It was nine in the morning, as it was every day, my neighbor was going grocery shopping, as she did every day, and she told me she had heard that the first tomatoes were finally available at the store, six marks fifty a kilo, outrageous.

During my first weeks in Paris, I was often afraid of going under. A lot of people gave me good advice—friends of friends, whose addresses had been written in my notebook, or old friends who had left long before me and ended up here. But for the most part they were already well adjusted to the new environment and so caught up in their lives that I had trouble recognizing them. They said they wanted to help me; I should call again and come again, another time, later, and they gave me addresses and named new names, and after we had discussed everything, we often sat together a while longer or went somewhere else, had something to drink, and told each other about the adventures we had experienced since emigrating. We asked each other interminably, in a sort of litany, Do you know so-and-so, do you know so-and-so, do you know so-and-so?

Looking for work, I made the rounds of the names and addresses they had given me, a list that kept getting longer because they were always adding more addresses and names of theaters, publishers, bookstores, little magazines, and theatrical agencies. But actually I did not want that kind of work anymore, because I knew that I would be made an assistant again, which was what I had been for far too long at the Berlin Theater, and I thought I should do something else with my life.

So one day I stopped trying the publishers, theaters, bookstores, little magazines, and theatrical agencies and struck out on an entirely different path. I went to the Ecole des Beaux Arts, applied for a scholarship, and immediately registered for courses in painting, nature study, and life drawing. Instead of letting the waves of new life roll over me and wear me out or even drown me, I wanted to ride them to a new location.

I had brought my easel from Berlin. It was just a light, portable easel, designed to be carried around and set up outdoors, but mine had always stood in my room and had often tipped over when I painted, usually at night—self-portraits, as if to reassure myself that I was still there; sketches of Alfried, to be closer to him, because he always concealed himself; the view from my window of the trolley yards, the stockyards, and the little gray church tower on the horizon; and portraits of poets whose books I loved, as homage and a response to them. Painting was a means of holding on to things whose presence was unstable and unreliable, like the easel itself, which came from my friend Blanca, who had inherited it from her father, a Spanish painter in exile. When Franco finally died, her father went head over heels back to Spain and left the easel behind. Blanca gave it to me before she herself left for England. The exile was over, but aside from the legends her parents had told her, she had never come to know Spain, and she was afraid they would mistake her for a German there, as she had been mistaken for a Spaniard in Germany for so many years. Now that she finally had a choice, she preferred a third country, a neutral one, to live in.

Now I sometimes take the easel and fold it up; it looks like a little suitcase. I wrap my paints and brushes in a cloth and tie them to the top, and go out to paint a view of the city. Most of the time I do not succeed, because I cannot select, cannot limit myself. Then I go back to my basement and paint the objects on the table, things left over from breakfast; or scenes from photos I pull out of my boxes, or the view from my window, which to me, because I can see only halfway across the street, offers a neatly defined sliver, and so I am not thrown into dire confusion by the vastness of the city.

The first person I saw here often and regularly was Mark, who in Paris called himself Jean-Marc. He was an American from New York, but his parents were Jews, originally from Riga. They phoned him every week, and he did not have the courage to tell them they were calling too often. He had almost finished his studies in architecture, but he still came to the nature-study class at the Ecole des Beaux Arts, where we sat next to each other. We took the Métro home together or walked all the way, even though it was far, and looked for spots and views to draw. Jean-Marc knew the city much better and was more observant, perhaps because he studied architecture and looked at houses as if they were people.

He lived not far from me, in a garret; I climbed flights of stairs to visit him, or he came down to me in my basement. On Sundays he worked in a laundromat near the Place de l'Italie, and I would keep him company now and then. I would pick up fruit or something to drink from the épicerie around the corner, which is always open, even on Sundays and late at night. In the short time since I have been here, it has already changed owners three times. First they were Turks, then Arabs, and now they are very dark blacks, and the whole family is always crowded into the store.

Jean-Marc did not have much to do at the laundromat, so we could read and talk; sometimes I would bring sketch pads and pencils or pen and ink, and we would do drawings of each other. We spoke French—that was a compromise, so that neither of us would have the advantage of speaking his native language. Mostly we talked about our family stories, about our parents, where they came from and how they had fled from the Nazis. Their emigration routes and experiences in foreign countries were the myths of our childhoods, indeed of our whole lives, like the travels of Odysseus: legends told over and over again. Now we repeated them to each other, almost sang them in chorus, like different strophes of one and the same song.

Jean-Marc spoke of New York, and I told him of Bulgaria, Weimar, and my life in Berlin. Jean-Marc corrected me: I should

say East Berlin. But I explained to him that for us there was only
one Berlin. There were no halves, only the city in which we
lived, and then there was West Berlin—but that was not the
other part that belonged to our part; it existed in another dimen-
sion. He could not understand that. And there was something
else he could not understand and for which he would always
reproach me: how Jews could bring themselves to live in
German after everything that had happened to them there. He
himself would never set foot in that country. And when I said
one time that I would love to show him Berlin and Weimar, the
Belvedere and the Gingko Biloba, he said no, that would not
interest him at all. In school he had done everything he could
to avoid learning German, choosing Latin and Greek instead
because no other languages were offered. I objected that German
was my native language, and that what he was talking about
was tantamount to a boycott. Yes, he said, a boycott—that's what
I have in mind, like the one imposed on Spain. Spain expelled
all the Jews, who never came back, and that put an end to the
Golden Age in Spain. We argued about whether that was right
or not. We did not argue, as I remembered doing in Berlin,
about the place where one wanted to live or could live, but
about whether it was permissible to live in one place or another.
It was not easy for me to explain the reasons that had brought
my parents to Berlin, so just as I had quarreled with Alfried, I
now quarreled with Jean-Marc, and we reproached each other
for things over which we had no control. But where Alfried had
withdrawn into himself, Jean-Marc tried to pull me completely
over to his side, and it was very tempting simply to let myself
be drawn into his world. He wanted to persuade me to come to
New York with him; he said he knew I wanted to, and although
that was true, I could not take such a step. He said that if I
wanted to immigrate he would marry me, and then everything
would be easy and I would get through Ellis Island very quickly.
But I said, No, no, once I'm at Ellis Island I'll never get out
again. Ellis Island is my home. Oh, said Jean-Marc, they stopped
using Ellis Island ages ago.

HENRYK M. BRODER

Heimat? No, Thanks!

When I delve into a topic that is new to me, my first step is usually to look up the central concept in the dictionary: "*Heimat:* a territorial unit experienced subjectively by individuals or collectively by groups, tribes, peoples, or nations in terms of a feeling of a particularly close bond" is what I find in Mayer's. This dictionary also lists a number of variants and combinations of *Heimat,* for example *Heimatkunst* [folk art]; *Heimatmuseum* [museum of regional history]; *Heimatschein* [certificate of domicile]—a peculiarity of Swiss communal law; *heimatlose Ausländer* [homeless foreigners]—apparently doubly cursed, first as foreigners and then as people without a *Heimat*; *Heimatschutztruppe* [home defense militia]—a subdivision of the territorial army of the Bundeswehr intended to protect our *Heimat* if things get serious, which makes one wonder what job the rest of the army has if war *per se* is nowadays construed as a defensive operation.

Even the most tentative approach to the concept of *Heimat* leads one more into the wide realm of ambiguity than to the desired clarity. The word and its background seem highly suspect. There is something stifling, provincial, stale about it; it is redolent of farmhouse kitchens, homemade brandy, and cow barns. Willy-nilly I associate it with peasant costumes, half-timbered houses, and shooting matches; apparently my concept of *Heimat* is rural. I might be mistaken, objectively speaking, but this is not a random association. I am reproducing images and impressions that have been conveyed to me as embodying *Heimat.*

It's no accident that *Heimatkunst* and *Heimatdichtung* [rural literature] are not the offspring of cities and metropolises, that the very words have a robust, all-natural sound to them, like "home slaughtering" and "volunteer fire department." And if a *Heimatdichter* from Berlin or Munich is mentioned, the stress is not on the urban origins of the writer in question; no, the accidental circumstance that he lives in a city becomes secondary to the dialect in which he writes or the district where he lives, in short, to something one can easily get a handle on. To that extent, the concept of an urban *Heimat* artist is a contradiction in terms and at the same time an attempt to impose something homey on an environment associated with decadence and alienation, the wish to be able to discover a bit of rural idyll even in the middle of the asphalt jungle.

The sense of *Heimat*, as differently as it may come across, is conveyed through the way people define themselves out of and through the surroundings in which they appear. They're not there by chance, or if they are, then they want to belong there, want to be accepted. Nor have they moved there for better living conditions; on the contrary, they've remained true to their *Heimat*, often taken burdens and hardships upon themselves so as not to betray their *Heimat*. One can compare the sense of *Heimat* with those Russian nesting dolls; it can be separated into smaller and smaller units. A German may feel lost in France, a Rhinelander in Hamburg may feel as though he's in a foreign country, and a person from Cologne who grew up on the left bank of the Rhine may refer to the parts of the city on the right bank as if they lay on the other side of the moon.

I know hardly anyone who lives where he was born. There may be such people, but in my milieu it's more the exception than the rule. From this perspective I consort with nothing but people who lack a *Heimat* or have been expelled from their *Heimat*, who at most can claim a *Heimat* they've chosen, a second-choice *Heimat.*

I was born after the war, in 1946, in Katowice. Both of my
parents had been in concentration camps and numbered among
the fewer than 10 percent of all Polish Jews who survived the
so-called Holocaust, an unbelievable stroke of luck, especially
when one considers that my older sister also escaped, hidden
under mattresses in the house of a petty-bourgeois Polish family.
Twelve years after the war, in 1957, my family moved by way
of Vienna to the Federal Republic of Germany. My sister, who
was a Zionist at the time, was the only one of us who went to
Israel. For me, leaving Poland was a move, nothing more. At the
age of eleven I'd developed neither a sense of *Heimat* nor other
emotional ties. The only thing that caused problems for me and
made me sad to go was that I had to leave my dog, an old
dachshund, behind; he was given away. For my parents it was
a little different. My father came originally from Galicia, my
mother from Cracow. Both of them had been shaped by the
surroundings in which they'd grown up, he by the shtetl and
she by the culture of the Austro-Hungarian colonies. But with
the war, my father's shtetl had disappeared, and Cracow had
long since ceased to be a suburb of Vienna.

Nonetheless my parents did not find it all that easy to leave
Poland. The persistent Polish anti-Semitism helped them reach a
decision; they moved to Germany primarily for linguistic
reasons. Both of them had grown up with the German language
and did not want to live in a country where they could not make
themselves understood. In Israel, with Polish, Russian, German,
and Yiddish, there would have been no language problem either,
but that was a country somewhere in Asia with a terrible
climate, and in any case, so many Jews in one place wasn't a
good idea . . .

The first years in the Federal Republic were relatively free of
problems. I can't say we had found a new, a second *Heimat* of
our choice—it was and remained a provisional solution of
unspecified duration—but I don't think our situation was so
much different from that of a family that had come to the
Rhineland from East Prussia, for example. At times I felt as

though I were on another planet. When Carnival broke out in Cologne, an event that occurred as regularly as Easter and therefore just as inevitably, I felt like Captain Cook visiting some strange, primitive tribe. There I was among all those natives, who became jolly on command, rocked back and forth to the music for hours like autistic children, and laughed at jokes I didn't even understand. At Carnival, especially during the so-called Wild Days, which one has to take literally in Cologne, it became clear to me: this isn't my home, there are worlds between these primitives and me.

On the other hand: whenever I got back to Cologne from a trip, and the towers of the Cathedral appeared on the horizon, whenever I crossed the Rhine after several hours on the Autobahn and saw the Old City lying before me like a postcard, kitschy and beautiful from a distance, I did have the feeling of coming home. Some nerve was touched, a sentiment stirred in me. One could live with this ambivalent attitude—being happy to return to a place where I didn't feel comfortable—especially since Cologne has a major geographic advantage: it's close to Holland. And thus an excursion to Maastricht could satisfy two needs: the need to run away and the need to return. Without my being conscious of it, the whole thing was a Jewish joke, transformed into reality, whose punchline went: "You're better off keeping moving." As often as I could arrange it, I kept moving. It wasn't just a longing for distant places that motivated me, but an enjoyment of changing places, of movement for its own sake. One might say this is a typically Jewish characteristic. If there is something like a mass soul, a collective character, a behavioral pattern that marks a particular group, then Jews have a nomadic trait as part of their set of common characteristics. The exodus from Egypt, the forty-day wandering in the desert, occupy a central role in the Jewish psyche. For three thousand years that event has been celebrated annually at Pesach, as if it had occurred only recently. Moving away, moving, emigrating, giving up a place of residence, looking for another—these are normal occurrences for Jews that have been repeated over and

over again in the course of history. Ahasuerus, the Wandering
Jew, is still roaming around. But the idea of a person who has
been expelled and damned to eternal unrest and life without a
Heimat is a non-Jewish idea. It originated in the New Testament
and can be found since the beginning of the seventeenth century
in numerous writings and legends, stylized into a sinister figure
of horror.

It's pointless to debate whether character determines one's
life circumstances or the other way around. In any case, Jews
have always had a fairly flexible relationship to stationary existence, even in areas where they've been settled for a long time.
The possibility that a pogrom might erupt at any moment led
them to develop certain habits that took the looming danger into
account. It was best to have everything portable. A little pouch
of gold and diamonds could be taken along more easily than a
house or a piece of land. Material things that weren't useful
were not important. A bed, a chest, a table had to be not beautiful but practical. Learning was important, food was important,
family cohesion was important. The lack of aesthetic refinement,
whose consequences one can observe today in every second
Israeli home, and the emphasis on abilities a person can put to
work anywhere, such as abstract thinking and skill with one's
hands, were both cause and effect of that mobility that is
considered typically Jewish and that, in the form of a negative
stereotype, constitutes the image of the rootless Jew, Ahasuerus.
For Jews, *Heimat* has never been a territorial concept.

It was the poet Heinrich Heine who spoke of a "portable
fatherland." Some of its components were religious heritage,
tradition, a way of life. Whatever Jews needed for feeling at
home they always had with them, if necessary in the bags they
kept packed in case they had to flee. Whether in Lemberg or on
Long Island, the candles were always lit on Friday evening to
mark the beginning of the Sabbath, at Pesach matzoh was eaten
everywhere, and on Yom Kippur the fast was observed. The
thought that *Heimat* might include a piece of land of their own

did not even occur to Jews until the second half of the last century, much later than with other peoples.

"Let people give us sovereignty over a piece of the earth's surface sufficient to the legitimate needs of our people, and we shall take care of the rest," Theodor Herzl wrote in 1896 in "The Jewish State: An Attempt at a Modern Solution of the Jewish Question." Nowhere was rejection of his ideas as resounding as in the Jewish milieu, which resisted with all its might being transformed from a cultural nation into a territorial one. The Jews took several approaches. An orthodox minority behaved as though the Enlightenment and emancipation had never taken place; they made a point of continuing their lives as if in the ghetto, even after the ghetto walls had come down. A secular minority saw in the Jewish question neither a social nor a religious question but a national one, which had to be solved with political means, "in the council of the civilized peoples," as Herzl formulated it; this was to be one of the functions of the Zionist movement. The majority of Jews in Germany attempted to establish a symbiosis of Jewish and German culture; these were the "German citizens of the Jewish faith," who wanted to differ from their Christian fellow citizens only in religious practice. Thus at the beginning of this century Jews had three different concepts of *Heimat* to choose among: a spiritual one, in the sense of a portable fatherland; a national one, in the sense of Zionism; and a "symbiotic" one, in the sense of assimilation.

We know which course history chose. All attempts at assimilation proved futile; the desperate struggle to be recognized as good Germans was merely the prelude to the greatest catastrophe in Jewish history.

"Jews have lived on German soil for more than a thousand years. Common fates and participation in German intellectual life have created an intimate bond between them and those of another faith. German is our language, German our intellectual formation, German our culture. Germany is our fatherland, and German Jews are indissolubly tied to it . . ." These words stand at the beginning of a pamphlet issued early in this century by

an anti-Zionist committee to which a few dozen prominent
Jews belonged— doctors, manufacturers, government officials,
judges, lawyers, bankers, businessmen. "The Zionist movement
mistakes the communal feeling of those united by origin and
belief for national feeling; for the German Jew there is no Jewish
national feeling—he is a member of the German cultural
community and therefore his national feeling is German, like his
language. By contrast, the Zionist movement's goals lie outside
the German fatherland and thereby undermine the political,
economic, and social position of the Jews," the pamphlet goes
on, and its signatories assert that they want to reveal "to our
people the danger posed to us and our children by the pursuit
of Zionism." The pamphlet concludes with the words, "Anyone
familiar with the nature of nationality and national feeling
knows that the German Jew belongs to the German people. Anti-
Semitic injustice has not been able to rob us of our love for the
fatherland. We do not want Zionist agitation to jeopardize our
struggle for our rights. German Jews are struggling for equal
rights because they are not foreign elements but German
citizens—by language, culture, education, and sense of *Heimat*."

To these German Jews it was perfectly clear where they
belonged, where their *Heimat* was. It was clear to them that the
Zionist "Jewish nationalist movement posed a serious danger to
the German Jews," and that "overcoming Zionism" was an
"existential question for German Jews." At the beginning of this
century the German Jews, who had committed themselves so
emphatically to the German language, culture, and education,
and to the German sense of *Heimat*, could not imagine that this
very commitment contained a threat to their existence.

Another document of German-Jewish love for the *Heimat* is
even more shattering and astonishing to the present-day reader.
On March 30, 1933, just before the Nazi boycott of Jewish shops
in Germany, the official newspaper of the Central Association of
German Citizens of the Jewish Faith carried the front-page head-
line: "We 565,000 German Jews Solemnly Protest."

What were the German Jews solemnly protesting on March

30, 1933? The emerging measures the Nazis were adopting against the Jewish population? Anti-Semitic speeches and threats by party functionaries? Neither nor. They were protesting the charge that they were encouraging anti-German propaganda abroad.

"Unrestrained atrocity propaganda against Germany is raging in the world," began the solemn protest in the Central Association's paper, and it continued: "We German Jews are as deeply affected as any other German by every word spoken and written against our fatherland, by every call for a boycott. Not under compulsion, not out of fear, but because certain circles abroad are besmirching the honor of the German name, are harming the land of our fathers and the land of our children, we have risen without delay to protest. At home and abroad we have denounced the lies being reported about Germany and the new government. . . "

Although the German Jews came to the defense of German honor, they were held responsible for the anti-German propaganda.

"People charge that the campaign of hatred and lies emanates from the German Jews. They say it would be appropriate for the Jews to rebuke the liars but that the German Jews do not want to do this. Before all of Germany we 565,000 German Jews solemnly register our protest against these unspeakable charges. The German Jews have not instigated anyone in Germany or the world, directly or indirectly, to these shameful libels or to any action against Germany. The German Jews have, to the extent of their ability, done their utmost to render impossible any insult to their *Heimat*, any offense to the government, any harm to the German economy."

The solemn protest concludes with resigned pathos: "Before God and man we stand justified. With dignity and courage we shall endure the pitiless measures of Germans against Germans on the soil of our *Heimat*. . ."

To repeat, that was March 30, 1933. At that time, German Jews worried less about their own future than about the threat to the reputation of their *Heimat*, to whose defense they came and for whose honor they spoke up. Even the more clever and prescient among them were filled with a love of *Heimat* that in retrospect seems like an exercise in masochism.

The philosopher Theodor Lessing had already left the German Reich at the beginning of March 1933, after being attacked for years by super-patriotic students and the nationalist press. He sought refuge in Czechoslovakia. There he wrote for the *Prager Tageblatt* and delivered a series of talks and lectures that was brought out around the middle of 1933 by a German-language publishing house in Prague. Even in exile, indeed especially in exile, Lessing insisted on being a German, although he denied having anything in common with the Germans who had the say in Germany at that time:

> If the language spoken today in Germany is German, then I have never been a German. And if the spirit of today's leaders is the German spirit, then it is as little suitable for me as for Goethe or Kant to be a German. "Land that we love, you should beg our forgiveness or never have our ashes," Coriolanus said before he left his homeland. So, too, we German Jews leave our *Heimat*. No armies behind us? No! That is not how it is. Behind us the army of our forefathers, Abraham, Jacob, Moses. But behind us also all German guardian spirits. Leaving Germany with us are all those who have a home in our hearts, and would perhaps have a home nowhere on earth if not in us: Goethe's worldly-wise, lucent humanity, Schubert's comforting song, Dürer's loyal childlikeness, Hölderlin's hymnic blessedness . . .

The guardian spirits that Lessing thought were following him must have stayed home. On August 31, 1933 he was murdered by two paid Nazi assassins, who did not have Goethe's humanity or Hölderlin's blessedness in mind, but the price that had been placed on Lessing's head by the Nazis—80,000 Reichsmarks. Lessing became the first victim of the Nazis' lynch justice after their seizure of power. His books had already been burned in May 1933 in the great purge.

Yet one cannot assume that the German Jews experienced their first identity crisis with the outbreak of the Third Reich. Or that they hadn't begun to think about their relationship to their German *Heimat* until 1933, under the sign of the swastika. What today is glorified by many as the time of German-Jewish symbiosis was a very one-sided love affair. "To be sure, the Jews tried to have a dialogue with the Germans," writes Gerschom Scholem, "from all possible points of view and positions, demanding, pleading, imploring, obsequiously and indignantly, in all tonalities from touching dignity to godless indignity . . ." — but: "They were speaking to themselves, in fact one was shouting louder than the next." The only ones who took the Jews seriously as partners in conversation, Scholem remarks cynically but aptly, were the anti-Semites, "who did answer the Jews, but not helpfully." German-Jewish literature provides numerous examples of this conversation Jews carried on with themselves, which the Germans at best listened in on. One of the most gripping examples can be found in Jakob Wassermann's essay, "My Way as a German and Jew":

> Recognition of the hopelessness of any effort turns bitterness in one's breast into a fatal convulsion.

> It is futile to beseech the people of poets and thinkers in the name of its poets and thinkers. Every prejudice one thinks has been laid to rest brings thousands of new ones to light, as carrion yields maggots.

> It is futile to offer one's right cheek when the left has been struck. It does not make them at all thoughtful, it does not touch them, it does not disarm them: they strike the right cheek, too.

> It is futile to counter raving cries with words of reason. They say, What, he dares to answer back? Gag him!

> It is futile to try to provide a good example. They say: We know nothing, we have seen nothing, we have heard nothing.

> It is futile to seek shelter. They say: The coward, he is hiding, his guilty conscience is driving him.

> It is futile to go among them and offer them one's hand. They say: What is he up to with his Jewish pushiness?

> It is futile to be loyal to them, whether as a fellow combatant or
> as a fellow citizen. They say: He is a Proteus, he can seem
> anything.
>
> It is futile to help them throw off the fetters of slavery. They say:
> He must have made a tidy profit doing that.
>
> It is futile to detoxify the toxin. They will brew a fresh batch.
>
> It is futile to live for them and to die for them. They say: He is
> a Jew.

Wassermann's "My Way as a German and a Jew" appeared
in 1921, at a time when most Jews were firmly convinced they
would be accepted as German citizens of the Jewish faith. Since
1848 Jews had participated more and more in German political
developments, and many had achieved positions of high and
even the highest rank: Eduard von Simson, raised to the nobility
by the kaiser, president of the National Assembly in 1848, then
of the North German Reichstag of 1867, of the German Reichstag,
and also the first president of the Supreme Court in Leipzig.
Many, in their devotion to their German *Heimat*, became tragic
figures.

The Jew Alfred Ballin, an adviser to Kaiser Wilhelm II and a
proponent of the kaiser's policy of building up the German fleet,
committed suicide in 1918, filled with despair at Germany's
defeat in World War I. The Jew Walther Rathenau, who had
organized the supply of raw materials for Germany during the
war, and after the war represented the Weimar Republic as
foreign minister, was murdered in 1922 by a German nationalist.
And it was a Jew, the consitutional expert Hugo Preuss, who
drafted the outline for the Weimar constitution. Yet a German
writer as successful as Wassermann could sum up his experiences with the people of poets and thinkers in the resigned
statement: "It is futile to live for them and to die for them. They
say: He is a Jew."

In the middle of Germany, Wassermann was a native without
a *Heimat*. He spoke German, wrote in German, thought in
German, and yet a barrier existed betwen him and the rest of
the German people. This may be something experienced particu-

larly often and intensely by Jews, but it is not an exclusively Jewish experience. When, for instance, there is talk of "homeless" intellectuals or leftists, that is, those without a *Heimat*, this is not a reference to people who have no permanent residence, who sleep under bridges and roam the land like vagabonds. These are people who do not belong; of course, who belongs is decided by those who have the say in their *Heimat*. Aside from all attempts to define *Heimat* territorially, to make it a characteristic that determines who are fellow countrymen, *Heimat* designates an ideological arena, a spiritual state, a kind of mental congruity, in short, a community of the like-minded. What follows is that wherever there is a *Heimat*, there must be people without a *Heimat*. Not refugees, who maintain their dialect and their folklore, but those who are not admitted to the community of the like-minded or have been driven out of it.

Heimat is always restrictive. It fences people in, and therefore also fences people out. *Heimat* requires not only clear but also clearly visible conditions. Therefore *Heimat* is almost automatically identified with country, village, and town, with morality and decency, with a network of relationships in which everyone knows everyone else, where no one steps out of line or out of his role, where the most powerful group coherence exists. The city, by contrast, stands for decadence and confusion, for anonymity and individuality, and especially for plurality. Marginal figures and outsiders who wouldn't stand a chance in the country can live in the city and survive. The more urban a metropolis, the more pluralistic it is, but that also means that it poses a stronger threat to souls in need of harmony and addicted to *Heimat*.

In a blurb for Fassbinder's "garbage" play, the playwright Heiner Müller writes as follows: "Fassbinder's *Garbage, the City, and Death* depicts in large, glaring images the devastation of a city, through the example of a victim's revenge. The city is known as Frankfurt. The instrument of revenge is real-estate speculation, with all its ramifications. The distortion of human relationships by treating them as commodities demonstrates the

Biblical wisdom that the first fratricide, Cain, was the first builder of cities . . ."

This is as pretentious as it is confused, and even as a Biblical allusion it's only partially correct. But it sounds like a prophecy: He who murders his brother is also capable of building a city. In these few sentences an entire panorama of blood-and-soil mythology is presented in contemporary dress; history is unfurled from behind, so-to-speak: building cities perverts human relationships, speculation is an instrument of revenge, and revenge, one knows, has something to do with Jews and the Old Testament. Thus one piece of Biblical wisdom is linked to another.

The connections are clear. In classic anti-Semitic propaganda, too, the city was always portrayed as a Jewish monstrosity, while the village represented Aryan innocence. Here the morass, there the productive field.

In 1981 a publishing house in Hamburg issued a book by a writer who was no longer young. This man presented himself to his readers sometimes as a "writing cultural worker," sometimes as a "nationalist Communist." The book was entitled *Germany— An Attempted Homecoming*, and the title page carried a sketch of a peasant parlor in lovely, warm pastels. The author, we learn from the blurb, had an "extraordinarily happy childhood under Hitler," later lived in Frankfurt, Berlin, and Hamburg. The sketch on the title page must refer to his childhood, if to anything. But what is the title supposed to mean?

The author is no returnee from prisoner-of-war camp, emigration, or banishment. He never went to sea or lived abroad. In the physical sense he cannot return home. Something else must be meant: a return to the bosom of the larger whole—let us call it the *Volksgemeinschaft*—a collective from which the author excluded himself for a time on the basis of his political orientation. And this return, called a homecoming, takes place through a symbolic door, above which hangs a sign saying "love of *Heimat*." The blurb informs us that this is a book "that risks the tension between love of *Heimat* and the horror that *Heimat* once generated and still generates."

So love of *Heimat* is a sort of house of horrors. One shivers a little, but wouldn't miss the experience for anything. This belated homecomer does not want to commit himself unreservedly to love of *Heimat*. He questions his ambivalence, and then at the end of the exercise he says, Well, why not? Thus love of *Heimat* serves as the formula on the basis of which the members of a *Volk* community can come together, a lowest common denominator for collective identity. Since love of *Heimat*, as the author just quoted assures us, is a "spiritual state," it becomes a question of sharing this condition with as many members of the national family as possible. For in contrast to national awareness or even nationalism, love of *Heimat* is not discredited, but is seen instead as a harmless emotion. One loves one's *Heimat* as one loves one's family, one's language, one's garden, one's pets. But even those who argue this way occasionally admit that something more is at issue with love of *Heimat*. "As a German I am sufficiently lacking in a *Heimat*," writes a young left-wing author, who regrets not his outward but his inner lack of a *Heimat*, "to see it as my task to put down roots, to try to establish links with German history, even if it be the worst of all possible histories, and at the same time"—watch out! here it comes!—"with the silent majority of Germans, to whom we will otherwise not get close in a hundred years . . ." Translated, this means that the rediscovery of *Heimat* as a spiritual state creates the link between leftists without a *Heimat* and the silent majority; this rediscovery constitutes a simultaneous homecoming and bridging, after all other attempts at rapprochement, such as calls for socialism, for disarmament, or for involvement with the Sandinistas, have proved unsuccessful. One might also say: when appealing to class consciousness or international solidarity fails, love of *Heimat* comes into play as *ultima ratio*.

Where there's a *Heimat*, there must also be people without a *Heimat*—people who are refused permission to belong or who renounce belonging: not belonging to the language, the culture, or the same tax bracket, but to that diffuse mixture of pretentiousness, sentimentality, and aggressiveness that also goes into love of *Heimat*. The author who wanted to try to approach the silent majority with the help of this very instrument describes in the same connection what "is annoying about Henryk Broder and Lea Fleischmann": that they "turn the historical tables and now exclude us, as people with whom there is simply nothing to be done."

This is a revelation of praiseworthy unambiguousness. The historical sword is pointing in the right direction when the Jews are marginalized by the Germans, as is fitting, but it's seen as a piece of particular chutzpah when the situation is the other way around, when it's the Jews who separate themselves from the Germans. That shouldn't be allowed—*quod licet Jovi non licet bovi*. A young German leftist would rather cozy up to the silent majority, which doesn't want to know anything about him, than allow a couple of Jews to turn the historical tables and for a change do what they've always had to take from others.

The longer I focus on the concept of *Heimat*, the more obscure it becomes to me. I really don't mind when a person loves the pounding surf of the North Sea or the fragrance of the forest after a storm. That isn't the problem. But those who suddenly and unexpectedly discover their love for their *Heimat* remind me of shareholders in a company who give themselves preferred shares and then justify their action by insisting on their irrepressible love for the stock market—at a time when these shares happen to be going up. Love of *Heimat* is first and foremost a means for creating and preserving the *Volk* community, for bridging contrasts and containing conflicts. That precisely those who until recently were busy analyzing social relations have now switched to the field of love of *Heimat* must be considered one of the curiosities of this transitional period, and *ex post facto* downgrades their exercises in classless society and proletarian internationalism to the status of intermezzos in their revolutionary cabaret.

I don't know when it began or who started it, but at some

point in the "we're somebody again" movement, the question of nationalism was posed in the so-called progressive camp. People said one couldn't leave concepts like *Nation, Heimat, Volk* to the rightists; the leftists, too, or the part of society that considers itself leftist, had to fill these formulas with content. (At this time the debates over whether an alternative *Bild-Zeitung* could be published were already forgotten.) True, the Nazis had abused this terminology and used it for their own purposes, but that didn't mean one could remove *Heimat* or *Volk* from the political dictionary! What sounded quite plausible at first soon led to a new form of repression and rationalization. Where the rightists babbled that the figure of six million was a lie—they wanted to get out from under the historical shadow of the mountains of corpses at Auschwitz—the leftists were attempting to unload the burden of history by displacing the guilt.

"Overcoming our German past consists in solidarity with the Palestinians!" A young German leftist reduced to this brief formula his attempt to, as he put it, "sneak away from German history." Either strategy served the purposes of a reconciliation with oneself, restoring a "spiritual state" in which it was possible not only to speak the words *Heimat, Volk,* and *Nation* without shame or embarrassment, but also to rehabilitate the associated period in history. And as always when the question of nationality is raised in Germany, the Jews came up. Even as shadows of their former selves, they stand in the way of the "Germans' becoming good again," as Eike Geisel calls it. German self-discovery always used the Jews as a catalyst, and it still does.

The blessing of having been born late, to which Chancellor Kohl likes to allude, corresponds at the other end of the political spectrum to the one-sided declaration made by the Frankfurt Schauspielhaus in conjunction with the Fassbinder play that "reconciliation should and must come about," whereupon the Jews who refused to step forward and be reconciled were reproached for having rejected the outstretched hand. Deputy Fellner demanded that the Jews show more understanding for the sensitivity of the Germans and not always make demands.

And a member of the audience called out to the Jews who had occupied the stage, "Don't always bring up your Auschwitz!" A mayor from a town on the Rhine made the cheap crack that to balance the city budget they should kill a few rich Jews. On a considerably higher intellectual plane, a well-known liberal theater critic said much the same thing when he called for unmasking the role played by Jewish capital. When a group within the leftist party Alternative List demanded demonstrations against the visit of Shimon Peres, the Israeli prime minister, on the grounds that this was important "for the establishment of German identity," they were taking up an old tradition.

Jews have always helped Germans develop a sense of unity and solidarity. Even the Alternatives' identity still depends on this vehicle. The common practice among German nationalists of counting Auschwitz, if it is even acknowledged, among the "war crimes of the Allies" is supplemented in leftist circles by the observation that the Israelis will do to the Palestinians what the Nazis did to the Jews, and the use of the expression "final solution to the Palestinian question." Thus the victims of yesterday are made into the perpetrators of today, and the perpetrators of yesterday become the moralizing referees of today. This is what Jürgen Habermas has called "the decontamination of the past."

And that belated literary homecomer I mentioned recently wrote in a review of my book *The Eternal Anti-Semite* that one shouldn't hold my lack of sound scholarship too much against me, for one should ask oneself how the German "revenge-foul" would have looked, assuming Jews had murdered six million Germans." One reads this sentence, stops short, reads it again, and sees that one was not mistaken. The Germans killed a few million Jews, and forty years later a Jew writes a book about German anti-Semitism. This is seen not only as revenge, arising from the well-known Old Testament spirit of vengeance; it is a *revenge-foul*, an unfair, nasty blow below the belt, against all the rules of sportsmanship. Six million dead against one book.

This fellow member of the *Volk*, from the leftist-nationalist side of the *Heimat* stage, considers it pure happenstance that it was the Germans who killed the Jews; he thinks it could easily have been the other way around. What if the Jews had killed six million innocent Germans, he asks; how would we, the Germans, have behaved afterward?

I'm happy to respond to that. If we're going to play this old game of comparing apples and oranges, let's at least think it all the way through to the end. If history hadn't gone the way it did, but the other way around, if the Jews had subjected the Germans to a holocaust, then even forty years after the attempted final solution there would be neither political nor human relations between Germans and Jews. No Jew would be allowed to step onto German soil, and no German would allow a Jew to say that there should and must be a reconciliation. The Germans would not consider any Jew's late birth an extenuating circumstance, and they would not allow any Jew to give them advice as to how they, the Germans, should behave toward their minorities. There would be no debates over collective guilt, collective shame, collective responsibility; every Jew would be held responsible for what happened, and no Vatican council would exonerate the Jews after two thousand years. No Jewish theater would dare to schedule a play that dealt with an exploitative German someone had forgotten to gas; and such an undertaking would certainly not be able to be justified with a declaration that closed season was over. No one would say it was time to draw a line under the past; and if a Jew suggested that one merely had to kill a few rich Germans, it would cost him not only his job but his head as well. The Jewish state, if there were one at all, would not be a respected member of the international community, and no Jewish politician would have the courage to tell the Germans that they shouldn't carry on so and should be considerate of the Jews' sensitivities and not always be reminding them of the past. And no one would think that paying money would put the whole business to rest once and for all . . . This would be more or less the state of affairs if history had turned out the other way.

Heimat, to return to our starting point, is not a geographical entity, not a place one can find on the map; *Heimat* is a spiritual state. Reacquiring *Heimat* is, therefore, a return to an inner condition in which the homecomer is at one with his surroundings, is reconciled. A person who characterizes himself as without a *Heimat* suffers the opposite: he lives in dissension with himself and his surroundings. It's understandable that such a condition cannot be tolerated in the long run, or must result in serious damage.

The Jewish concept of *Heimat* did not envisage a harmonious relationship to one's surroundings, for those were almost always and everywhere hostile to Jews. So what mattered was to preserve and perpetuate one's tradition. There was no need to restore a spiritual state that had been thrown out of equilibrium, for in spite of persecution and suppression, or perhaps precisely because of it, the Jews' inner balance hadn't suffered any damage, aside from those who abandoned their Jewishness or assimilated; these were people who wanted to escape not only from the religion, but also from the shared fate of the Jews; among them one can observe that phenomenon for which Theodor Lessing coined the expression "Jewish self-hatred." Not until they received recognition as citizens with equal rights did Jews feel obligated to manifest their devotion and loyalty to their external *Heimat*; they transformed themselves from Jews into Germans of the Jewish faith.

"The noblest German blood is that which was spilled for Germany by German soldiers. To these belong as well the 12,000 casualties of German Jewdom, which thereby in turn passed its solemn and admirable blood test in the German sense . . . " is what it says in the preface to a volume commemorating the Jewish soldiers who died in the First World War. The book was issued by the Reich Association of Jewish Front Soldiers in 1932. The definitive proof of being a German was the privilege of dying for Germany. By doing that, 12,000 German Jews had passed the blood test in the German sense.

That misunderstanding is now history, although there are a few Jews in the German army again, and the chairman of the

Central Council of Jews in Germany, a reserve officer in the Bundeswehr, explains: "I see it as my task to present the correct picture of Germany, its citizens and parties, whenever the tendency to paint the 'bad German' on the wall arises. . . " This reminds one of the position taken by the Central Association of German Citizens of the Jewish Faith in March 1933, which also defended Germany's reputation against those who would have slandered it. The chairman of the Central Council was rewarded for all his loyalty by being urged by a Bundestag deputy to consider whether his own behavior might not be stirring up anti-Semitism in Germany.

But these are marginalia, small points noted in passing. The actual Jewish problem with *Heimat* answers to the name of Israel. After a gap of 1,900 years, the Jews have had, for almost forty years, a piece of land where they are sovereign. This is a historical accomplishment whose value cannot be overestimated. But at the same time it is a fact that causes the Jews problems and places new burdens on their spiritual state.

About a quarter of the Jewish people live in the Jewish state, our "historical *Heimat*," as we say. To have this homeland is sufficient to most: three-quarters of all Jews prefer to stay in the Diaspora and say the prayer "Next year in Jerusalem" every year at Pesach, although they could come this year if they really wanted to. One may ask whether the Jewish state maintains a large Diaspora community of potential citizens, or whether the Diaspora, for insurance reasons, maintains a state just in case worse comes to worst, which everyone hopes will never happen but knows one can't dismiss. The simple fact that Israel exists protects the Jews in the Diaspora from greater discrimination and persecution, but at the same time thrusts them into inner crises and external conflicts.

Many have a guilty conscience because they don't live in Israel, and they compensate with a "love of *Heimat*," i.e., long-distance Zionism, which often takes on embarrassing features. Others, in turn, compulsively distance themselves from Israel, so as not to come under the reputation-damaging suspicion of being Zionists. To this inner conflict is added the reproach by others that they have divided loyalties. They teeter between the country in which they live and the country with which they feel solidarity or from which they distance themselves, but with which they are in any case emotionally involved. But even when they make up their minds and settle things once and for all, that is, stay or go, the dissonance doesn't cease. When a German television station does a feature on the topic "Do the Jews have a future in Germany?" Jewish existence in Germany is treated as a problem, and the question is directed not just at temporary residents but also at those Jews who by staying have already supplied an answer. On the other hand, those who just a short while ago were shouting "Jews to Palestine!" don't like it either when the Jews follow their orders, because now it's a matter of combatting the imperialist-expansionist ideology of Zionism. And finally, our Arab relatives are right when they ask the question why someone born and raised in Brooklyn should suddenly turn up in Hebron and declare that this is his true homeland, and from now on he must live in the city of the patriarchs, for otherwise the two-thousand-year history of suffering will have been in vain.

To discuss the political and practical implications of Zionism as it is actually practiced would be a topic worthy of separate treatment. But one thing can be said: with the establishment of a Jewish state, a particular set of problems caught up with the Jews which left them only one choice: between wrong and mistaken. It would be wrong, unthinkable, to give up this state. It would be mistaken and not doable to dissolve the Diaspora, to settle all Jews in Israel. So we're stuck with the Jewish state here and the Diaspora there, and the split personality in the middle. We can reflect on the tension between a spiritual and a real *Heimat* and also on the question as to whether the latter doesn't exist at the expense of the former. There is no solution to the problem, but problems aren't there to be solved; they're there to be worked out.

For six years now I've been living in Israel with a German passport. To many, who like to have things neat and tidy, this may seem inconsistent, but it's far less inconsistent than living in Germany with a membership card for a Zionist organization in one's pocket and one's suitcases under the bed. I admit I'm making it easy for myself. I've withdrawn physically and spatially from the alternatives of becoming an alibi-Jew or a Jewish Michael Kohlhaas in Germany. Germany is very stressful for a Jew; it can be tolerated, and liked, much better from a distance. In Israel, as a Jew but non-Israeli, I have a privileged status. I live in the country without having to wrestle with the difficulties its citizens have. So I pick the pleasant things from both sides. Perhaps that's what makes my German leftist friends without a *Heimat* so furious with me: they, too, would like to get out, if only they knew where to go. Walter Boehlich recently described me as a Figaro who is sometimes here, sometimes there; one never knows just where he is. Apparently I've violated the commandment of belonging somewhere which Walter Boehlich firmly espouses from his living room in Frankfurt. He garnishes his super-clever analysis of my gypsy-like way of life with a few anti-Semitic digs, reproaching me, among other things, with "meddling" in the affairs of the Federal Republic. He's right: if the Jew escapes from the anti-Semite's blows, he shouldn't make a stink from the other side of the fence.

If you ask me whether *I* have a *Heimat*, and where it is, I reply in classic Jewish style: evasively. I think I have a *Heimat*, but I can't localize it. It's the odor of gefilte fish and potato pancakes, the taste of borscht and pickled herring, the melody of the Hatikva and the sound of the Internationale, but only when it's sung in Yiddish by old members of the Bund in Tel Aviv on the first of May. It's the Marx Brothers' night in Casablanca, and Ernst Lubitsch's to be or not to be. It's Karl Kraus's *Torch* and the autobiography of Theodor Lessing. It's a spot on the Aussenalster in Hamburg, a little stairway in the old harbor of Jaffa, and the Leidseplein in Amsterdam. Isn't that enough?

The big problem with *Heimat*, it seems to me, is that a person is expected to choose one. It would be better simply not to have one. Or best of all: to have a whole lot of them.

ESTHER DISCHEREIT

from

Joemi's Table
A Jewish Story

HERE I AM, sitting on this stupid swivel chair. After twenty years of being a non-Jew I want to be a Jew again. I've spent ten years thinking it over. What does the man behind the desk have to say? "Tax evasion," he says, and smiles. I have to do penance for four years and pay the back taxes. I tell him: Mother dead, Papa a goy—fourteen years old, shipped off to the country, no letter, no nothing from the community—and I come back after twenty years, want to be a Jew again, and the Jew tells me, "Approximately 800 marks—or should I let you do the calculation yourself?"

Must one be a Jew? I've asked myself that long enough. The congenital mark of Cain, forgotten under the waters of socialism, is shining through on my skin.

History's dead caught up with me, and drew me in. I didn't want to be drawn in, was determined to be a perfectly normal leftist— oppressed in the standard repertory of classes, class struggle, of rulers and ruled.

My attempt proved a complete failure. I'm on the street recruiting, class struggle, and someone asks me my nationality. Neither proud nor self-confident, certainly not indifferent . . . should I say German? German is what one probably should say. BUT then . . . BUT what? But Jewish. There it is, bold and heavy, the word that was pinned to my lapel, that hung on a string around my neck. The string is cutting into my neck. My comrade on the rug we've spread on the sidewalk, piled high with propaganda brochures, leaflets, and our canister for contributions—he doesn't know. And why should he? Rome wasn't built by history's chronic losers.

I'll forget this question about being German, I decide. In the evening the news comes on. In some connection a clip of Nuremberg flashes across the screen, and again I'm upset, like this morning. Why does the news upset me so? There's enough terrible news as it is—isn't there? Of course I know that . . . and am all the more upset. Stupid question, is that allowed? Distribute feelings of injustice properly. Has reason gone mad?

What a feeling—when I don't even like them, the rich, evil, building-larded Jews, and also those who take other people's water for themselves and joyfully plant saplings on the houses of other peoples, as though it had to be that way and were decreed by Providence. I, too, danced around the tree, far away in a German city. We had bought it—thinking aloud in song of thrusting the spade into foreign soil. A distant land, which would always be a place of refuge, always? Perhaps that's why we didn't go there? No, we never went there, never. To go there was like undertaking a pilgrimage to Rome, or the Haj to Mecca. We didn't make a pilgrimage. We might have seen the children of the Haj. We might have seen the ruins of their destroyed houses. We might have seen parents without their children. Or we might not have seen all that—and the Dead Sea, it holds you up. It holds you up so wonderfully that no one can drown. Even so, it's dead, and perhaps no one can live who cannot drown. [. . .]

* * *

What do you want, Jew, soap or heat? The Jew says, I want heat. So the chimneys smoke, and soap is extra. — The blond, short-cropped hair leans way back with laughter. He's been in this job for six years, was trained here, has stayed here. Three evenings a week he goes to practice. Soccer. He's already getting fat, drinks too much beer.

He wants to talk, especially about last night. And how things just flowed. And the whole thing again from the beginning. He breaks off uneasily when the boss's son comes in. "Here's your, um— appointment at 3:00 P.M." The door closes. That business last night went until the early hours of the morning. Quite something, you should see how red my eyes are, colleague. He picks up the paperwork; everything's in there. He can't read it, again. Breathes mint fumes on his superior's vest and then slowly turns away to his typesetting machine. One time he went away for a summer course. The boss couldn't believe it. Then he got back and had a lot to tell, as usual. Thought there would be soccer, but there was also stuff about society and so forth. The guy really impressed him, said some things about the Jews. Say, I don't think I've ever really seen one. What do they look like?

I stand there and listen to him. What do these Jews look like? In the past one had to show one's ear for passport photos and at the border. Hey, colleague, you want to see my ear? Finally I say it.

He's all excited. He'll have to tell his instructor. He actually met one; probably he's the only one in the course. The next time he tells a joke, he pulls himself up short. "Sorry." At lunch we have hamburgers. Are you even allowed to eat this?

Maybe next time I can go along for the summer course. Then they'd have me right there in the flesh and could actually touch history.

* * *

"Nowadays we're more enlightened about these things, you know . . . actually I don't know any . . . Jews, I mean. They were somehow, you know, at the time they were already in a

separate school, well, sometimes in the courtyard, yes . . . pale
. . . different-looking, I don't know how to put it. Simply no
opportunity to get to know them."

His wife told me over the telephone that he was going to
Israel—his second time already. It really appealed to him there,
she said—maybe not the right way to put it. Oh—this Promised
Land. In his day the Promised People were pale and tubercular.

He feels deeply moved by this people and its fate, especially
in Germany.

. . .

"Your identity, couldn't your identity—somehow interfere
with your performance of your duties . . ."—he didn't mean to
say that, "but you understand—a case where in connection with
your identity you might have—a conflict of interest . . ." Aha, a
genuine, pure, racially healthy Jewish conflict of interest—you
see, the man's making an effort—or isn't he? One could have
refused at the beginning, after all . . . Somehow this Judaism is
archaic—the Antichrist is abroad in the land, is not abroad in
the land. Of course, the Sermon on the Mount. Nevertheless,
Paul indubitably implies the possibility of working with Jews.
God, how grateful I am to St. Paul.

Eyes behind glasses smile noncommittally. He can't help that,
to be sure.

Now and then he glances up. The tasteful tabletop mirrors an
angel, probably an archangel. In the annunciation lives Jesus.

"Would you like another cup of coffee? You know, these long
meetings—actually too much coffee. Of course my wife has
already adjusted to low-calorie cooking—we're not used to this
anymore. Yes, earlier one was really grateful for every piece of
bread. You know, recently we were invited to dinner, my wife
and I, it was really a lavish meal, more than lavish. . ." Before
my inner eye appears salmon filet, coq au vin, vanilla ice cream
with raspberry sauce, cream truffles . . .

"I said to my wife—you know, it's grotesque, in a way—back
then everything in our town revolved around bread, dry bread.
My first memory of the railroad station back then. In September

1945. A military policeman: he pulls this piece of bread out of his pocket.

"Well—back to you. Thank you for going to the trouble. I've been able to get a pretty good idea. Please don't get me wrong." "Good-bye." "Good-bye."

A light drizzle is falling on the paths outside the large house. Educational facilities usually offer drizzle in the evening—or ping-pong. Did you know that he's really well preserved—I mean for his age.

"What I have to ask you, just between you and me: do you know anything specific about . . . that Jew who was just here— I mean, how should I put it, his conscience. . ."

What's this about a Jew's conscience?

"Please don't get me wrong, that's not what I meant to say. . ."

What didn't he mean to say?

"How do you think?"

I think Dreyfus and thank Emile Zola. The whole business took place so long ago, and yet it's caught up with me. What's special about this story? Really? My friends don't understand.

Haven't we all been kicked out somewhere and somehow. We're always being kicked out somewhere, my friends and I, since we pick up stones. But this time—this time I don't have a stone in my hand. The stone around my neck the others can't throw.

* * *

"I have a confession to make to you. You don't know me. I'm approaching you, how should I say, with embarrassment. You know, you look like Ruth Deretz. She was in my class back then. And somehow also a little—well, as attractive as you, a big girl, pretty, you understand. Then she . . . I was born in 1921. Was in the Hitler Youth—of my own free will. I'd volunteered. Then I was on a U-boat off the coasts of Africa and Spain. Please don't get me wrong, I regret it today. I had to watch shootings—some

of my fellow soldiers didn't want to participate anymore . . .
And I'll tell you straight out: Heddernheim, VDM, there was a
concentration camp annex there. Anyone who says today he
didn't know anything about it. That's not true at all—we knew.
Not the full dimensions, of course not. But still—we knew.
Recently we had a class reunion. I suggested all of us should go
to Auschwitz together. You should have seen how they came
down on me—I was shook up. No, to think they still haven't
learned anything. I can't begin to tell you.

"I know, you actually came just to apply for admission. Yes,
we'll get to that right away. Please excuse me. Could you repeat
your name again, I mean spell it. Your address, please, oh yes—
up here at the top, I already have it, of course. All right: we
don't have your age: 30 years. I really wouldn't have guessed to
look at you. All right, I'll read the whole thing back to you to
make sure we have it all right. Misspelled? I don't understand."

First rays of sun sparkle through the dusty office window
and catch a corner of my application. I, Ruth Deretz—I'm
hungry.

*   *   *

The landlord is a Sudeten German. Sudeten German—it's all
right to say that, isn't it? Of course it's all right to say that. The
landlord from the Sudetenland now has two buildings—acquired
thanks to the work of his hands and the equalization-of-burdens
program, as I hear later. In our family are none with the work
of their hands, because my mother's hands shake. They shake
quite without reason. They really could stop shaking now. But
they shake. For this shake she receives reparations. In return she
can say that she has no profession, no school diploma, no
parents, no brothers or sisters—just her life and this shake.

When she applies for a housing subsidy, they deduct this
shake from the extra allowance. Yet she went very early in the
morning, so as to have the shake still under control.

If the landlord knew he'd rented an apartment to us. It isn't known.

Above us lives an older man. We hear he's a minister, and his wife was very angry when the children played their flutes after school. Jews always want to be better than other people. Playing the violin, pianists, that doesn't happen by accident.

How to explain this flute? I didn't ask for anything for Christmas. What would one of those trees with candles be doing in the home of a Yid anyway?

When Hannah from the village comes into the city and is divorced from her husband, the goy, she dares to wear the Mogen David again, though only under her dress, of course. But still.

I see the candle-decked trees of the people we encounter on the street, of the other girls at school. Don't I at least have some decorated greenery at home, they ask; what am I supposed to tell them? That my mother doesn't love me? Christmas is a custom at least. Hannah has a second one, and that's Hanukkah—but in the community. So Hannah asks her daughter what she wants for Christmas. And now back to this business with the flute.

Hannah's daughter says: Nothing. And nothing the following year, and nothing for her birthday, only a beautiful flute of her own, a shining silver concert flute. Two years earlier she also said Nothing when asked, and Nothing again the following year. Hannah should make up with her divorced husband, her father. Hannah didn't answer. Now that's two years ago, and now her daughter asks for the flute. The heavy ebony flute was the first instrument she was allowed to learn, borrowed from the music school. She herself is the great exception, Hannah says, the only one who doesn't understand anything about music, has no ear and can't carry a tune. That's why Hannah's daughter wants the flute.

And since Hannah didn't marry her father again, Hannah's

daughter plays the flute. And plays, till her raised arms are ready to drop off.

Frau Rau pauses on the landing when our door opens. She and her husband, she says, did belong to the Confessing Church back then. I look at her. Bitterness has twisted her mouth. It's stretched down to her neck. Sensible shoes, a wool suit flecked with gray, like her hair. I didn't understand that, the business about the flute and the church.

The neighbors next door to us, I don't know anything about them. And because I don't know anything, I take in our laundry in the evening. I suspect them of being from the same region as our landlord. They will certainly turn out to be equally hard-working.

* * *

"We come from Wullachen in the Bohemian Forest. All the Germans were expelled, so to speak. We got word that by ten in the morning the next day we had to be in Gilowitz. With fifty kilos of baggage. No more. We were in a transit camp there, and then we were taken to Hohenfurt, Kaplitz, to the station, and there we were loaded into cattle cars."

My ears repeat: Hannah loaded into cattle cars.

"I was twelve years old at the time, I should add. At that age we still had a sense of adventure."

She was six years old.

"Until cold reality struck, and we had to stand in line for food in the camp."

. . .

"The only thing I haven't forgotten. It was a magnificent day in May. We had a big dog at home, and he ran after us."

Her sister ran after her . . . and stumbled and fell.

". . . when we had to get onto that truck."

. . .

"We had to leave everything behind. In Butzbach we were assigned to families. There were people there who took in refugees."

Where were there people who took in refugees? In England? In Germany? Where?

"We were given an unbelievably warm welcome . . . Then in 1956–57 the parish church gave us this piece of land. Then everyone helped out. Yes—and there was also an equalization-of-burdens program."

Reparations, right?

"Most of us were in agriculture at home, large-scale agriculture. We were remunerated accordingly."

Terrible pain, numbers tatooed into our arms, the sums were calculated accordingly.

"Somehow I've really come to feel at home here."

Have I come to feel at home here?

"We can tell the children all sorts of things about home. But they don't really feel connected."

She's told me nothing, almost nothing. Oh—if only I didn't feel connected!

"Somehow all that's in the past."

Somehow, that's true, it's in the past.

*   *   *

Asking what it all means . . . yes, a mixture of pimples and a too-short skirt. A good thing all that passes. When things have to be taken care of, purchased, removed, called up, brought up. Imagine this unsolved question as to what it all means, an adolescent girl with hair falling to her shoulders in dark braids.

When she passes the building site, a young construction worker whistles at her—he seems to be buried in the earth up to his hips. His eyes bore into her knees. St. Bernadette—is passing. If an angel blushes. She isn't fair-skinned. No blood rushes to her cheeks.

World or non-world—a god who has abandoned us. Why did this god-damned god allow this? Who broke the laws, that you should punish us this way? Is God an exterminating angel from the land of the Mizrayim? Do you even exist, since you abandoned us? If penance is to be done, then preferably the way the Catholics do it, no? To be allowed to be a victim, the fascination of renunciation. If eternal life is more beautiful, why not right away? . . . A bit of death, perhaps? Bernadette began to love this unknown death, which the fatherless child thought of as masculine. In any case, death is doubtless something typical of men. Otherwise men would die feminine deaths.

In any case, Bernadette caressed her unknown death. Among her relatives there were no deaths. Not any longer. That was all long before her birth. The dead don't die. For death she feels the pulse in her wrist, runs her hand over knife blades.

A brightly patterned apron. Later on, wearing aprons went out of style. That must have something to do with washing machines. She knots the strings of the apron together, winds them around the rail of a bunkbed—for the sake of drama I have to say: low-income housing. — The strings are not attached high enough. Her feet brush the ground. For a while her neck carries the marks of these strings. From the psychiatric point of view: an entirely normal suicide attempt.

Can't an empty heart find comfort in God the Father, the Son, and the Holy Spirit? By all means, says Pastor Becker, though not immediately. In four or five years, at the latest. But what's this business with the Holy Spirit? The spirit is closed to her, and in any case Jesus just wants her to be a human being. Nevertheless Pastor Becker wants her to swear, even if her soul won't go along with it. Do you know the picture of pious Helen in the book by Wilhelm Busch? The final scene, where her spirit flies away?

The wafer tastes like paper. She never tried it again. This is the second time she's failed to escape being a Jew.

ROBERT MENASSE

from

Happy Times, Brittle World

FOR A WEEK LEO SINGER managed to keep his resolution not to phone Judith immediately, but rather to wait and see if she called him. To tell the truth, he did try once, but Judith wasn't home. He found this one attempt extremely humiliating. Sweating profusely, he pressed the receiver to his ear, and cleared his throat several times as he listened to the monotonous beeping; he grew increasingly tense at the thought that she might actually pick up the phone. But after this he remained absolutely steadfast, not least of all because he got sick right after trying to call her. He was already feeling sick at his parents' the day after he met Judith—"the day after the accident," as he would have put it. His parents had invited him because of his birthday. To be sure, his birthday didn't come until April, but his father would be away on business then, and he wanted to see Leo before he left.

Leo was planning to ask his father for money to get his car fixed, perhaps as a birthday present, even though he was sure his parents already had a present for him. Since the family's return to Vienna, he had always received the same thing, with downright religious monotony; they never asked him what he wanted as a gift. For Christmas and his birthday he was given "something warm," a heavy vest or sweater, thermal underwear, sometimes a blue suit in some thick, wintry material; he went around in these suits even in summertime, since he didn't own any others. And he also unfailingly received a pair of gloves; by

now Leo had the largest private glove collection in Vienna. This
pattern of giving no doubt had something to do with his father's
having built up a wholesale clothing business in Vienna; whenever it was time to come up with a gift for Leo, his mother
would pick something out of his father's "stock," as she put it.
She wrapped it in used wrapping paper from a department
store. Every time she bought something, she had it gift wrapped
and added the paper to her supply of used wrapping paper,
which she kept in a hulking armoire that also held the boxes of
candy and the bottles of liquor that people brought on various
occasions. She left them in their original wrappings, and took
them as hostess gifts when she and her husband were invited
somewhere. The package for Leo would be on a highboy topped
by an ornate mirror, which she called "the Psyche." When he
arrived, she always said pointedly and coldly, as though she
were afraid to touch this junk and sully herself with the taste-
lessness she attributed to her son, "Your present is on the
Psyche, Leo!"

Leo hated his mother so much that he would gladly have
killed her, but only if it could have been the perfect crime; if he
had had to serve time on her account—on her account!—that
would have been yet another victory for her. On the way to his
parents' Leo began to quiver with hatred once again. For the
mere fact that, as far back as he could remember, his mother had
not once made a gesture of tenderness, spoken a kind word, or
even given a glance that could be interpreted as minimally
affectionate to his father, to this soft, in every sense roly-poly
man, who was as proper as he was weak, as hardworking as
hopelessly life-loving and in need of affection, who was like a
water balloon, almost bursting with a completely unfocused
expectation of happiness and an infinite, skewed optimism—for
this Leo could never forgive his mother. Though of course he
also despised his father—for this weakness, for his pathologi-
cally conformist nature. As Leo changed at the Ringstrasse from
the number 58 to the J line, he was thinking that he admired
Judith's parents, as he pictured them, admired their refusal to

return to Vienna—in Vienna we were persecuted, but here we can live and work in peace! Such an attitude made perfect sense to Leo; it seemed to him clear, strong, and consistent. His parents had also had to flee Vienna to save their skins, and then things had gone well for them in Brazil, and he had grown up in Brazil, and that should have been sufficient to allow the conclusion that Vienna was merely the name of their birthplace, nothing more. Why return? Why give the Zahradniks the chance to engrave this grim story line onto their tombstones: Born and Died in Vienna? But it was not only that Leo's parents had returned to Vienna despite having already established them-selves in Brazil; to make it worse, they had not returned in triumph, self-confidently, as victors; no, on the contrary, they had always been obsequious, anxiously concerned for some putative reputation, and his father had bowed and scraped before officials who had once served in the Nazi bureaucracy—all in hopes of receiving a ridiculous thing called restitution. And as if that were not sufficient, and that was bad enough as it was, in Vienna his father had begun to celebrate Christmas, because "everybody does it." Here he sent a modest contribution every month to the Jewish congregation, yet he also began to celebrate Christmas—"that's just what you do here, it has nothing to do with religion, it's a social, cultural, basically a business necessity." From clients and business associates he received Christmas gifts, for the most part those boxes of candy and bottles of liquor that Leo's mother stored in the ghastly armoire, and he felt obligated to give Christmas gifts in return and to throw a Christmas party at work. But at home? At home, in their apartment, where no one could check up on how con-formist, how assimilated, how submissive he was, a tree was put up, and Leo's flabby, oleaginous father was not ashamed to sing Christmas carols before presents were exchanged, which meant for Leo the pair of gloves wrapped in used wrapping paper from Gerngross's. At least his mother just stood there, stiff as a board, her cold gaze checking to make sure the ceremony took its proper course and everything was done the way she thought it should be. Meanwhile Leo's father worked himself into a frenzy, as if all the baptized Catholics in Vienna were watching him sing "Silent Night, Holy Night."

As the J car negotiated the turn from the Ring to the Landstrasser Hauptstrasse, it derailed, "for undetermined reasons," as the newspaper account said the next day, but Leo immediately felt guilty; without being fully aware of it, he was convinced that his pulsing hatred, his vibrating, uncontrolled rage at his parents had caused the accident. All the passengers had to get off, but while most of them stood around in clusters studying the accident and offering a running commentary, Leo stole away as fast as he could, like a perpetrator leaving the scene of a crime. Since the derailed J car was blocking the way for any other streetcars using the same tracks, Leo had to walk all the way to Rudolf-von-Alt-Platz, and he knew, as he felt the cold wind whipping his sweat-drenched skin, that he would not come away from this madness unscathed.

His father opened the door. His face gleamed as if freshly oiled. As always when he greeted his son, he seemed at first to want to give him a hug, but then he suddenly extended his arms stiffly as one does when trying to keep a person at arm's length, after which he let his left arm fall to his side, and with his right hand he gave Leo two quick punches on his upper arm, and said, "Hello there, my boy." As always Leo was taken in by appearances and instinctively opened his arms to hug his father. This time agitation and his guilty conscience made the gesture more vigorous and emotional than usual, but his father's movements imperceptibly went over to the defensive, his fear of personal contact being too great after all and having won out yet again. As always, Leo stood there in a foolish, contorted position, which was so embarrassing that his father promptly wheeled around, said, "Come on in, Leo," and hurried on ahead to the living room. There his mother was standing stiffly, one hand resting on the back of her chair at the table, already set for tea. He gave her a hasty peck on the cheek, which she offered him rigidly, and as he felt a rush of disgust and pity at his mother's facial hair, which had increased noticeably of late, she inquired, after looking him critically up and down, "Don't you ever comb your hair, Leo? That's not how one goes out in public!"

Leo said it was very windy out, and—"In that case one wears a hat!" his mother said. "Have a seat, Leo," his father said, constantly rubbing his hands as if incalculable pleasures awaited them. "Sit down! So tell us: what's new?"

A small platter held four thin slices of cake. Leo's mother served first his father, then Leo, then herself, and then poured tea in the same order.

One does not talk with one's mouth full. This offered a pretext for not launching into his account immediately, and Leo wolfed down his cake with a relief bordering on panic. Too late he noticed that his mother was staring at him disapprovingly because he had picked up the cake with his hand instead of using his fork. He heard the noise his parents' forks made on the plates, as if a bony finger kept poking him reproachfully in the breastbone. But it was too late; his plate was empty, and he gazed longingly at the last piece of cake, still lying on the platter in the middle of the table. "Help yourself, Leo," his father said, "there's plenty. There's more out in the kitchen, isn't there?" he asked his wife. "So help yourself, Leo."

Leo looked at his mother and said, No, thank you, he was full. The waves in her hair looked as though they had been made with a curling iron.

Leo noticed that he was tied in knots with tension. He pushed back his chair a little and crossed his legs, inadvertently bumping one of the table legs, which made the cups rattle in their saucers and the tea almost slop over the rims. He felt a wave of heat wash over him, followed immediately by a chill.

Why did Leo describe all this so circumstantially a week later, when, barely recovered from his cold, he met Judith at the Landtmann Café? Judith seemed distracted and edgy. They were sitting in a window niche, and Judith kept glancing out the window at the Ringstrasse or past Leo into the main part of the café, as if looking for the waiter so she could pay and leave immediately. Leo, too, was highly irritable. He had been home alone for a week with a fever, and to him the busy café was as stressful as a huge crowd. The general hum of voices seemed as deafening as political chants being practiced. He thought he understood why Judith was jumpy, since he felt the same way, but his own irritability was exacerbated by hers. Judith's impatient and distracted air gave him the feeling of having very little time to talk, yet every sentence he spoke set in motion so many associations and memories that he thought he had to include more and more detail and provide even more background to make himself clear. But the faster he spoke, in order to squeeze in at least the most important things, the faster he came up with one reason after another for spinning out indefinitely what he was saying.

"You have to realize how many things welled up in me when I bumped against that table leg," Leo said.

Leo bent far forward, as if to whisper something across the table into Judith's ear. Judith puffed nervously on her cigarette, and the smoke she exhaled formed a sort of delicate grillwork before Leo's face and billowed like a thin curtain, behind which Judith inclined her ear toward him—no, she was glancing out the window again; what did Leo want, to make confession and be absolved? Did he want to convert, out of despair over a father who celebrated Christmas?

Leo pressed his face between his palms and began to talk as agitatedly as if it had all happened yesterday: he described how once in São Paulo, when he was a small child, his parents had taken him along when they went to play bridge with another emigré couple from Austria. He had sat there for hours in a chair off to the side of the card table, and he had kept quiet, as was expected of him. He had had no thought of doing otherwise, that is, there was nothing he could do but sit there quietly and look at everything in the room. And he had already seen everything, had circled the room with his eyes so many times. And then suddenly, Leo said, his mother turned on him, after paying him not the slightest attention since their arrival, and said, "One does not wriggle one's legs." Then she picked up the cards that were just being dealt and continued playing.

"That just came to me," Leo said, "my mother's brutal disdain for anything out of control; to her, anything that is not constantly reined in as tightly as she is herself seems bestial, impulsive, simply despicable. She always made me feel I was the epitome of crude instinct; she was absolutely withering, and—and," he repeated, because Judith was looking out the window again, she was even leaning close to the glass—what was all that racket!—Leo raised his voice a little, but really just a little, for he still had a bit of a sore throat, and besides, he did not want to shout out these very intimate things, which he was revealing to Judith with feverish nervousness. "And," he croaked a little louder, "that wasn't all." His parents had taken him along very seldom; the regular exceptions had been the visits to Löwinger, who had always insisted on seeing Leo. As a rule he had been left at home under the care of the maid. Leo recalled this *empregada* as a girl with a coarse, ungainly body, a repulsively unhealthy skin color, like ashes, and an extremely submissive and timid demeanor toward his mother. For his mother had the habit of putting on a pair of white gloves when she came home and sweeping through the house, running her fingers over the furniture, the deferentially and nervously quivering *empregada* in tow. Woe unto the girl if the spotless tips of the gloves picked up a trace of dirt or dust. "Picture that," Leo said, massaging his temples, "but that wasn't the worst: Maria, this *empregada*, was so afraid of my mother that when my parents were away she always tied me, a little child, to a leg of the dining room table with a length of clothesline. She tied me to a table leg so that while she was cleaning and tidying I would have no chance to get anything dirty or messy behind her back, for which my mother would have punished her. Not until she heard my parents coming did she hastily untie me and then follow my mother on her inspection tour."

"That can't be true," Judith said.

"Oh yes, it's true all right," Leo said, "and that's what came back to me when I bumped against the table leg, and my mother looked at me so reproachfully again, she of all people. Instead of— oh, I don't know. When I think about it now, I can't understand why Maria didn't simply quit, and why I didn't tell my mother about the clothesline. I probably thought she knew all about it anyway, and wanted it that way, because that was exactly what she always wanted: for me to keep quiet."

The noise in the café was increasing. For a moment Leo had the impression that people at the other tables were commenting in horror on his stories about his mother; behind him someone exclaimed, "That's criminal!" Leo's body flushed with heat. He must have gotten out of bed too soon and was now having a relapse; the fever must be coming back.

"And did you get money to have your car fixed?" Judith asked.

Leo said he had told his parents about the accident, even though the atmosphere at home had been so messed up from the instant he got there, but on the other hand that had always been the case, so he had mentioned the accident, just briefly and in the most general terms, a collision of the sort anyone could have, and had said that with his birthday coming up, if he could ask for something specific he would like some financial help for a change so he could pay for the repairs, an out-of-the-ordinary expense that was not covered by the allowance he received monthly for his studies.

"Money for your birthday?" his mother had said. "One doesn't give money. Your present is on the Psyche, Leo."

"I should explain," Leo added, but he had no chance to continue, because at that moment a few people at tables in the middle of the room and in booths along the back wall of the café jumped up and surrounded the window tables to look out at the street. Suddenly the waiter was standing next to Leo, also staring out the window and saying something about the crazies who were out in force again. Leo turned from the waiter's black tuxedo to the window, where all he saw was a lot of chaotic

running, with people sweeping along the Ringstrasse. They
rushed past the café window like a pack of black shadows in
the dusk, while car horns blared and—were those shots? Some
kind of detonations at any rate, sharp reports that sounded
strangely unreal inside the café, with its babble of voices, as if
the explosions were packed in cotton batting.

"The anti-Borodajkewicz demonstration," Judith remarked.

"The anti-what?" Leo asked.

"Borodajkewicz. The old Nazi who teaches at the Institute of
International Trade. Come on, Leo, I'm sure you've heard about
him. The anti-fascists are demonstrating because he keeps giving
far-right, anti-Semitic lectures. The day before yesterday there
was a rally, and neo-Nazis attacked, and—"

"How am I supposed to have heard about it?" Leo asked.
"I've been sick."

"And another demonstration was announced for today, and
this is it," Judith explained. "And the Nazis are attacking again.
Come on, Leo, we have to get out there."

"They should stick to their studies," the waiter remarked.

"Come on, Leo, we're going," Judith said, and she paid for
her coffee without leaving a tip. Leo left a larger tip than usual,
out of embarrassment.

"Such an idiot," Judith said as she pulled on her coat.

"What are we supposed to do out there?" Leo asked. "I
mean. . ."

"Come on, Leo, you don't really want to sit there while outside the neo-Nazis are beating up the anti-fascists."

"I mean," Leo said, slowly buttoning his coat, "what good
does it do if we let ourselves get beaten up, too? Judith, listen—"

She was already on her way to the door of the café, and he
hurried after her—her taut, erect gait, her ascetically slim body,
no, she did not remind him of his mother, whom he saw in just
such terms. He felt numb and filled with anxiety, not so much
because of the danger that might be waiting outside, but because
of the danger that he might lose the love of this woman, which
he so greatly coveted, before he had even had a chance to win

it. Outside Leo took Judith's hand in alarm, a woolen mitten in a bulky fur-lined glove, an awkward sensation that lacked the distinct feeling of physical contact. The square between the café and the Burgtheater and the Ringstrasse was thronged with people, thousands of people, all in motion, running, pushing. The mitten slipped out of the furry grip of the glove. "Over there!" Judith shouted, and Leo was running after her when suddenly he saw directly in front of him three young men in leather jackets who were swinging heavy chains. Leo had just ducked and darted off to one side when firecrackers and what sounded like small mortar fire went off; he wanted to get away into the outside lane of the Ringstrasse, but from there a group was descending on him in closed formation, shouting, "Heil Auschwitz!" He pressed himself up against the wall of a building. The noise was deafening—"Free speech! Let him teach!" Where was Judith? Leo hurtled off in the direction Judith had taken earlier, but what was this? Knives! Knives were flying through the air, and flaming torches, whirling like will-o'-the-wisps in a high arc above the shoving crowd. "Ho, ho, Nazis gotta go!" All this seemed to follow a choreography that Leo didn't understand at all. He felt dull blows on his back and his side, and now he was flailing around, too. All he wanted was to get out of here.

Suddenly he found himself at the foot of the steps to the Burgtheater. He ran up and half hid behind a column. From this elevated spot he could look out over the entire scene of chaos. Eggs, oranges, and tomatoes were flying through the air. In the middle of a group of students carrying banners opposing Borodajkewicz, smoke suddenly began to rise, the banners collapsed, and the group scattered, heads down and arms covering faces. "Those assholes are throwing teargas bombs," shouted a student who suddenly appeared beside him, out of breath, "teargas bombs, those assholes." Leo saw an uninterrupted stream of people running away, but amazingly the square did not empty out, and the tumult kept reviving. People pushed their way forward again, tried to regroup. This was particularly

amazing, and Leo even caught himself admiring their persistence. Then he saw young people trying to hold at bay with flag-
poles others who were attacking with chains, hoses, and iron
rods, and he was overcome with fear again. "Ho, ho, Nazis gotta
go!" — "Jewish swine! Jewish swine!" And organizers with arm-
bands were shouting, "To the monument to the Republic! To the
monument to the Republic!" They were trying to reorganize the
demonstration and give it direction. Leo stood there bemused,
and from his elevated vantage point gazed at the scene below
as if through a reversed and fogged-up opera glass. The dissi-
pating smoke from the teargas grenades and torches hovered
before his eyes like a dirty, milky aura in the darkness etched
by the streetlamps, and his impressions, as sharp as they were,
seemed clouded. Now the organizers running by were shouting
agitatedly, "To the Parliament! To the Parliament!" Suddenly he
also saw police. They established a cordon between the anti-
fascist demonstrators and the neo-Nazis, but the demonstrators
again formed a procession, moving away to the accompaniment
of chants, while the neo-Nazis bawled counter-slogans. He heard
"Commie pigs!" The Ringstrasse in front of the Burgtheater
began to empty out. Strange, Leo thought, the anti-fascists have
on windbreakers, the neo-Nazis leather jackets.

Where was Judith? Apathetically he looked around for her in
the thinning crowd, but of course he did not find her. Two or
three times he wanted to call out "Judith!" when he made out a
girl among the demonstrators. Only then did it occur to him
how few women were taking part in this demonstration. They're
all sitting in cafés with their boyfriends, he thought, or lying in
bed with them. Judith. He just stood there for another quarter
of an hour, like a blind man at a busy intersection waiting for
someone to take his arm and guide him across. Then he noticed
how cold he was, shivering in spite of his heavy suit and warm
coat, and even his hands were freezing in the fur-lined gloves;
for his birthday he had received a new pair, and a woolen vest.
"One must keep warm; if one keeps warm, one can survive anything," his mother had said, as if she owed her own survival,

her successful escape from the Nazis, to her clothing. "You know," his father had said while his mother cleared the table and stepped into the kitchen for a minute, "you know, Mama means well, she wants you to be nice and warm, but of course you also have to get the car fixed, I can understand that," whereupon he had hastily pulled two banknotes out of his wallet and thrust them into Leo's pocket. "Thanks, Papa," Leo said, and of course at that very moment his mother came back into the room. "And how are your studies going?" his father said in an unnaturally loud voice. "Thanks, Papa, just fine."

Good. Was he working on his dissertation? He was standing at the entrance to the Burgtheater watching an open-air performance. As an extra, who wanted a role in the life of a female extra. He was so cold. He set out for his car, which he had parked between the Burgtheater and the Volksgarten. He walked slowly, in case Judith might be looking for him. Suddenly he stopped in his tracks and headed back to the café. Perhaps she was waiting for him at the café; after all, that was where they had originally planned to be. But she was not there. It was warmer inside the café, but that was all. So back to the car and home.

When he got to the car, which he had picked up at the garage only that morning, the hood was bashed in and the front bumper was bent down sideways. Probably demonstrators had climbed up on it and jumped around. Leo wept. That the demonstration had left one person dead he would find out only days later from the paper. With a loud cry Leo swung himself backward onto the hood of the car parked next to his. But he did no damage. Apparently it was not so easy to dent a car. His coccyx, on the other hand, would hurt for two days.

Leo looked really sick the next evening when Judith came to see him. She had phoned, and he had said that he was sick, a relapse, and could not leave the house. But he would like it if she came to see him. Not only was he visibly congested, he also had such a suffering expression on his face that Judith was strongly tempted to mother him—put him to bed, give him hot tea, make him sweat it out, and then watch over his sleep and his feverish dreams. She still had a trace of this feeling in her when she said, in order to banish it, "See what I brought you?" And she opened her straw bag, before she had even taken off her coat, and pulled out a bottle of Brazilian sugarcane brandy— "the last bottle of Pinga I had left. I didn't want to drink it alone."

Judith had to smile at how elegant Leo had made himself for her visit. He was wearing a gray flannel suit with a vest and looked like an old professor who had fallen into a fountain of youth but had not been able to rid himself of all the frailties of age. "Do you always dress this well when you're home?" Judith asked, stroking the lapels of his jacket. "Pardon?" Leo asked. "Oh, I see, no, I always get these suits from my parents, from my father's stock, remember—I don't have anything else to wear."

"And," Judith said, and like a magician pulling a rabbit out of a hat, pulled a pineapple from her bag, a real pineapple, "*abacaxi*," she said, "*fruta bem tipica brasileira*. I had such *saudades*, how do you say?" she said. "You'll see, Leo, this will do you good."

How touched Leo was!

"I saw it at the market and simply couldn't resist."

"Come in, come in," he said. He was full of polite touches, helping her out of her coat, bustling hither and thither, a steady stream of gracious gestures, "Please have a seat, make yourself comfortable, oh, I'm sorry," he said, and he removed the books lying on the easy chair, stacked them on the floor next to the chair, then picked them up from the floor and put them on the desk, stooped hastily to pick up other books, magazines, and papers that were lying around on the floor, also swooped up his briefcase, which was standing in the middle of the room, and carried everything to the desk. He seemed to be constantly stooping and bowing.

"Never mind, Leo, my place looks just like this when I'm working; it doesn't bother me."

"Do sit down," he said. "Wait, I'll get some glasses and plates," and he left the room.

A little daybed covered in a stained, primitive, brown material, and on it a crumpled brown blanket, like a hospital blanket; it looked as though Leo always slept there in his clothes and boots, ready at any moment to flee. All he would have to do would be to throw his books and notebooks into the suitcase lying on the floor to the right of the desk. To the left of the desk was the old leather armchair, which without the books that had been lying on its seat already looked as though it had been hastily abandoned. Next to the armchair stood a little table which held the telephone and a teacup. The cup was empty, with a hardened residue of tea at the bottom. Against the wall stood an armoire. It might contain underwear or books, or nothing at all. Perhaps the underwear was in the suitcase. In the corner of the room a little coal stove. It was still warm. Whoever lived here must have left just a short while ago. Nowhere was there any personal item to be seen, any object that would have allowed one to make inferences as to the personality of the tenant—his preferences, his tastes, his biography. Nothing that betrayed any desire to make the room feel lived in. As if someone had stayed here for a brief time, had read a couple of books and possibly taken notes in pencil. A pencil on the desk was the only writing implement she saw. If a pencil is left behind, it is easily replaced. There were no houseplants—those would require regular care, and would die anyway when one had to move on. There were no pictures—no, there was one, on the desk: behind the pile of books stood a photograph in a handsome frame of brazilwood. Judith picked up the photo; it showed a man in his middle years sitting at an outdoor café. It was—yes, no doubt about it—it was on the Copacabana in Rio. The man looked as bohemians in the Brazilian films of the forties and fifties always look, with a straw hat, a light-colored suit with a large pocket square, and saddle shoes. Judith had the impression that the man looked somewhat like Leo, especially around the nose and mouth, but she wasn't certain.

Where was Leo? Suddenly it felt as though he had actually fled and left her here alone. She put the photo back on the desk and listened. She was relieved to hear sounds coming from the kitchen. She was looking out the window when Leo came back into the room. She saw a few lit windows across the way, and down below in the courtyard the tarnished silvery gleam of the cobbles and the stonecutter's tombstone angels, and at the same time, reflected in the window, she saw Leo placing a tray on the desk; on the tray were two glasses, a plate with the pineapple, already peeled, and a large knife, which Leo was just now picking up. She saw Leo standing behind her with the knife, saw him looking at her, saw him standing there with the knife, maybe four paces behind her, but at the same time she was seeing him in front of her like a ghost, hovering outside in the darkness of the courtyard; it was as if she had eyes in the back of her head, but at the same time she was also looking at him face to face; he hovered rigidly before her and looked at her, and she looked at him. The Leo behind her put down the knife, the Leo hovering outside in the dark put down the knife, and from both sides, from behind and from the front, he came up to her, she didn't move, and he put his arms around her, kissed her on the nape of her neck and the side of her neck. Judith stood there rigid; she submitted and grew even more rigid; he kissed her with such fervor and at the same time as if it were so much a matter of course that she didn't move, neither pushed him away nor responded; he kissed her like a statue, his moist lips like moss on a stone sculpture. For a moment the thought crossed her mind that all the angels down below in the court-yard were Leo's victims, women he had kissed just this way, whereupon they had grown wings to fly away with, but too late: they had already turned to stone. And he had then lined them up down there.

Judith threw back her head and laughed. Leo floated out over the courtyard, Leo backed away behind her, she turned around, he was standing by the desk avoiding her eyes, he had the knife in his hand again and was sawing off slices of pineapple. "That was a wonderful idea of yours," he said. "It's been so long since I had pineapple, just once from a can, but that's not the same, fresh pineapples are so expensive here in Vienna, was this one very expensive? Now I forgot the silverware, wait, I'll get it—"

"Don't bother, Leo, we can eat it with our hands."

Leo licked his fingers, picked up the bottle of brandy, and looked at it helplessly. "Unfortunately I don't have any lemons," he said, "otherwise we could have mixed *caipirinhas*, but we could—"

"drink it straight," Judith said, "prefiro emoções puras."

They ate the pineapple and drank the brandy, standing at the desk as if it were the counter in a chaotic little bar on some streetcorner in São Paulo. Judith sipped the brandy appreciatively, then emptied her glass in one gulp. Leo watched her with feverishly glittering eyes and did the same, then another glass, and as they ate the pineapple they thrust their heads forward and held their hands under their chins to catch the juice. They looked at each other and giggled; it seemed to cost Leo considerable effort, even though he was giggling out of relief. Judith filled the glasses again, licked her fingers, and suddenly Leo had that serious expression again. He took her hand, raised it to his lips, and kissed the palm, his tongue darting over the pineapple-sticky surface. Judith withdrew her hand and shoved the last piece of pineapple into his mouth. "How good it tastes," he said, his mouth full, "but why are we standing around like this? Please sit down, don't you want to sit down?"

"Who's that in the photograph? Your father?"

"No," Leo said, "that's Uncle Zé, Löwinger, remember?"

"So that's how he looks. I had pictured him as older."

"That's an old photo. That's how he looked when I was a child. A really small child; in my first clear memories he looks the way he does in this photo."

"And why do you have it here?"

"Just because. Because I like it. Because I like him. Remember? My parents never made me feel they loved me. He did. Besides, he's a model of cosmopolitanism. With his success in business he could have afforded to remain as stupid and limited as my parents, for instance. But he's a sensitive, well-read man, extraordinarily knowledgeable about art and literature, the best interpreter of art I know. You'd have to see him stand in front of a painting and interpret it. Suddenly the world becomes orderly. The entire chaos of the so-called creation is chaos because it's merely random material for the real creation, which is art. Only art is true necessity. One can—"

"Do *you* think that only art puts the world in order? Or is that one of Löwinger's brilliant interpretations?"

Leo looked at Judith glassy-eyed, took a sip, and shook his head. "Like my mother, like my mother: she was here once and saw the photo, and she asked questions just like that. Why do you have that photo here? Oh, I see, you find this nonsense so interesting. One doesn't make daydreamers and scoundrels one's model, Leo! and so on. I felt as though she took it as an affront that I had Uncle Zé's picture here. It was funny, I don't know why. It doesn't matter, but if that's the way it is, the picture's going to stay right there."

"It was taken on the Copacabana."

"Yes."

"Are you feeling better now, Leo?"

"Yes," he said, and then he emptied his glass and gazed at Judith for a few seconds, during which Judith thought she could hear his heart beating, but perhaps it was her own. Then he added, "I'd feel even better if we were on the Copacabana now, lying in the sun on the warm sand, far from the cold here in Vienna—are you cold? I hope you aren't too cold?" Leo went over to the stove and added coal.

How concerned Leo was, so concerned about everything, so—worrisome, was that the right word? Judith lit a cigarette as she watched Leo fussing with the stove, a stoker in an elegant suit in primitive lodgings. Was it emotion, was it affection, the brandy or the glowing stove? She felt a rush of warmth, an inner glow in which her fear turned to ashes like a piece of white paper in a fireplace, so quickly and inconsequentially: in a flash the white sheet is black, and then it's gone. This afternoon she had been overcome by a sudden fear of being alone, fear of the long hours until night, when she would lie under a cool down comforter without being able to fall asleep, fear of death, which would not come and which she would watch for with eyes wide open in the darkness of her bedroom. And she had had a longing for brandy, a longing for the numbness and excitement it confers, and fear of drinking alone, the cold bed, the feeling of helplessness.

"Oh yes, an ashtray," Leo said after he had straightened up again, "I'll get you one right away."

"No, stay here, Leo; I'll use a saucer, is that all right?"

They drank more brandy, still standing, though now in silence. Judith noticed that Leo wanted to say something, but apparently did not know how to begin; but perhaps it was his cold that made him keep breathing through his mouth, so that it seemed as though he would say something any minute, but then did not. Judith found that comical and laughed, and Leo smiled in return. "Yes, you're feeling better, I can see that, " she said. "You took your medicine like a good boy. Now I prescribe a vacation by the sea. Copacabana for example. We're leaving at once. Come along."

Judith took Leo by the hand; he looked at her in confusion and yearning, she took another swallow of brandy and then left the room, leading Leo by the hand. That was the kitchen, as Judith could see through the open door. "But what is behind that door?" "The bedroom," Leo said, and he took two steps, but Judith didn't move and, pulling him back, asked, "Where's the bathroom?"

"Here," Leo said, "this door."

"Aha," Judith said, "ladies and gentlemen, we will be landing momentarily in Rio de Janiero."

She turned on the light: a simple bathroom, with white tiles on the walls and an old enameled bathtub on ornate little feet. "Is there heat in here?"

"Yes," Leo said, "here."

An electric heater was mounted above the door, and he switched it on.

"The weather is warm and summery, the relative humidity 90%. We wish you a pleasant stay," Judith said, and turned on the water in the tub. "Shall we swim in the ocean a bit?"

While the water was filling the tub, they undressed. Judith fetched the brandy and the glasses from the living room, and also the deskchair. She used the chair as a side table, placing the bottle and the glasses on it before she slipped into the hot water. She drank to Leo, who now also got into the bathtub. She liked his body: he was slim and firm, but without the stupid muscles of those body fetishists who are constantly playing sports and then strutting around the beach like peacocks. His chest was hairy, his male member indecisively aroused, *gostoso*, Judith said.

Again Leo had that earnest, fervent expression, and he wanted to put his arms around Judith right away, lather her with soap, touch her all over.

"Wait," Judith said, "relax."

They sat facing each other, leaning against opposite ends of the tub, nestled into the warm water, and drank brandy.

"Is the water too hot for you?" Leo asked, and he began to fuss with the faucets. A stream of cold water shot into the bath, Judith shrieked and drew up her knees, and water slopped over the edge. "Leave it be, it was lovely as it was," Judith said. Leo hastily turned off the faucet.

"Such a beautiful day, Rio é uma maravilha," Judith remarked. "Está melhor, are you feeling better?" she asked.

"Yes," Leo said, "I'm feeling fine now." And he told her how awful he had been feeling all day, actually since the night before, when Judith had disappeared at the demonstration. "That was stupid of us, to go out in the middle of it," he said. "We could have—"

"What was stupid about it? Do you want to let the fascists take over the streets?" Judith asked. "And anyway, even if people get separated for a little while, they find each other again if they just stay with the demonstration; you must have realized we went on to the Parliament."

"I noticed that, but there were those characters with chains and whips, and I got shoved to one side. Why should I let them beat me up? Besides, there were thousands of people there and police, too, so it's idiotic to say that we would have let the fascists take over the streets if we hadn't gone out ourselves."

"Leo, don't talk such nonsense. If everyone had said that, there wouldn't have been thousands of people there, and then it's very likely the fascists could have taken over without a fight."

"No," Leo said, "the fascists were in the streets because of the demonstrators; they wanted to disrupt the demonstration—"

"No, my good man, the demonstrators were in the streets because the fascists came out of the woodwork long ago, in the form of Nazis who make anti-Semitic speeches at the university, for instance, and students who cheer them on."

"Well, it doesn't matter how it started," Leo said. "What I want to know is, what does it have to do with me? With you? What does it have to do with us? We're Brazilians."

"Our parents are Viennese, and they were humiliated by these no-goods and driven away to Brazil—"

"Fortunately," Leo said. "Things were better for them in Brazil, and we'd rather be there, too—"

"Leo, you're out of your mind, and—"

"And anyway," Leo said, "things are different now—weren't there thousands of people out protesting against a handful of Nazis; our parents would never have been forced to escape if things had been the way they are now."

"No one said it was the same as in those days, but that's just the point, to make sure those days never come again."

"Those days won't come again anyway, whether I go into the streets or not, and if things ever get the way they were then, it certainly won't depend on whether I allow myself to be beaten up outside a café or not. Don't you understand—"

"Apparently you don't understand what you're saying—"

"Oh, yes," Leo said, and smashed his hand into the water, "you have a completely abstruse concept of history; don't you understand that these things, precisely because they are past, gone, over and done with, are allowed a few last twitches, but it doesn't mean a thing. You can watch from the window niches in the café. The police protect all the participants, and then the press has an opportunity to distance itself from the fascists again with all due ceremony. If it had really meant something, all the people in the café would have reacted altogether differently, but we were the only ones who rushed outside. It's like the hair or the fingernails of a corpse, which grow a little more even though the person is already dead: it doesn't mean a thing—the dead person isn't going to come back to life. All right, all right, it's good if people demonstrate when the Nazis dare to show their faces again, I agree, but what I mean is that these things will happen whether we get involved or not, and they'll happen the way they happen, whether we get involved or not, whether we let ourselves be beaten up or not, whether we catch cold or not, whether we let a car be smashed up or not, my car, to be specific!"

Leo told her what had happened to his car, and Judith asked sarcastically if he was going to hold her responsible for someone's jumping around on his car.

"No," Leo said, and then told her at some length how humiliating it had been to ask his parents for money to get his car fixed, and that he couldn't possibly ask them again—just imagine what his mother would say if he came begging for money twice in one week,

"What kind of problem do you have with your mother," Judith asked, "when Nazis who shout 'Heil Auschwitz' don't humiliate you? Besides, your car would have been damaged even if we'd stayed in the café, so please complain to the Nazis, not me."

"That's true," Leo said, "but why did we have to meet in that particular café? You intended all along to join in the demonstration, and I was there to fill in the time for you before the demonstration got to the Burgtheater."

"I suggested that café because I had a class, and the Landtmann is the café closest to the university. And even if I did mean to go the demonstration, I certainly assumed we would go together, because it affects you as much as it does me, what with your family history and your consciousness."

"All I'm conscious of," Leo interrupted her, "is that I despise sacrificing oneself totally for something that's going to happen anyway. A person should concentrate on those things only he can do."

"Such as?" Judith asked. "Wait! I know. Straightening out the world all by oneself, right? Like that—that—what was his name, the one you were so enthusiastic about, who destroyed the Rubens painting?"

"Walmen."

"Right, him. Like him, right? Thinking philosophy through to its ultimate conclusion. That was something only Herr Walmen could do. And destroying a Rubens painting. That only Herr Walmen could do. Of course he had no time for demonstrations. And that's why the world is in such great shape now, thanks to our dear Herr Walmen."

Leo smashed both hands into the water and shouted that it was absurd to make him out to be a nut just because he didn't consider it necessary to trot along with every demonstration, since in that case all philosophers would have been nuts, Hegel and—

"Could it be you're comparing yourself to Hegel just because you're afraid of a couple of Nazis, and for that reason you don't want to go out into the streets?" Judith shouted.

"You're the one who's making the comparison! With Walmen, to be specific, and you're the one who's afraid of a couple of Nazis! If a couple of Nazis show up anywhere, you have to have a huge demonstration."

"Please calm down."

Judith tried again to explain her point of view to Leo, very calmly, and Leo withdrew scornfully to the frosty position of the intellectual, who is by nature solitary, who at the very most would glance out the window of his study to watch a demonstration. "Ah, yes," Judith said, "what kind of demonstrations do you have outside your window? A demonstration by cemetery statues, angels of death, fallen angels, or what? And when you've observed them, you sit down at your desk and go back to thinking your philosophy through to its ultimate conclusion, right?"

Leo jumped up. "All right, just follow the herd," he shouted, "follow those fools, who feel so strong and self-important in a pack, but, but"—was Leo crying? Or was it only drops of bathwater running down his face, like the water running down his body? Judith filled her glass to the rim with brandy and downed it in three large gulps. She looked at him with icy coldness, as if through a filter. She narrowed her eyes: this was a filter, it filtered out every trace of illusion that one human being can have about another; she suddenly saw him with perfect clarity, slippery and pathetic, with his banal attitudinizing; he trembled with agitation if his attitudinizing was rejected, but then who would be fooled? Hence his obsession with taking cover, like a snail, his flaccid penis before her eyes like a snail without a shell, crying out to be picked up carefully in two hollow hands and protected against the stupid world, which has no understanding of snails, this obsessive longing for an accomplice to whom he could portray his taking cover as a heroic act, and in addition one was supposed to mistake this for love; he stood there wet and trembling before her, scrambled out of the tub, and only then did Judith notice Leo's bluish gooseflesh, notice that the bathwater had meanwhile become ice-cold, and that she was freezing. They had argued until they were sitting in cold water, and now she couldn't help laughing.

"Judith," Leo said.

They quickly rubbed each other dry and ran into the bedroom and jumped into bed to get warm, but now it was impossible for them to muster any trust or tenderness.

THOMAS FEIBEL

Gefilte Fish and Pepsi
A Childhood in Enemy Territory

> Reason is neither German nor Jewish; both the German and
> the Jewish people would do well, especially today, to bring
> their Germanness and their Jewishness into conformity
> with reason; to get off their German and Jewish hobby-
> horses, and, instead of these humble steeds, mount the
> high horse of true humanity.
>
> —Mynona (Salomo Friedländer)

"**D**ON'T EVER SAY YOU'RE JEWISH!" my mother whispered
to me urgently. I held on tightly to the cornucopia of goodies
with which German children are always sent off for the first day
of school. At the age of six, of course, I had no idea what it
meant to be a Jew in Germany.

A few years later, we Jewish kids could be found hanging
out in the Jewish community center's multi-purpose room, while
our classmates chugged around town on their mopeds. Our
religious instruction took place once a week in this grungy basement. After the Shabbat service, a little snack was served: half a
fillet of herring, a little challah, and sweet Carmel wine. A stereo
system and a pool table had been provided for us young people,
as well as a little stage, used only once in all the years I went
there. A small, locked cabinet with a roll-back front held our
entire library.

It was in this room that we spent our free time. We listened to the Stranglers or Patti Smith, and were bored out of our skulls.

Every year after Yom Kippur, one of the adults (all purged and purified after the fast) would get fired up with the idea that Judaism might be dying out. So the grown-ups would make a special effort to pass on to us youngsters what little they knew about their heritage. One day they dubbed our dim basement the Jewish Youth Center. To celebrate the grand opening, they threw a party. Like all our parties, it fell flat. As usual, hardly any girls came. The few who did show up were soon scared off by our display of pubescent charm.

At first, activities at the Youth Center were limited to soccer, for which we could barely muster eight or nine players. Besides: what other team would we have played? That question hardly concerned our ever-changing youth-center leaders. They gave our club the unassuming name of The Maccabees, and after that didn't give a shit about our listless attempts at kicking the ball around.

Then the solicitous adults made a mighty effort to pull together a cultural program for us. They also arranged discussions on Nazism, the persecution of the Jews, and mass extermination. Genocide remained for us young people incomprehensible, abstract, unreal. Yet these discussions always brought home to us one idea: We were living in enemy territory. We slid into a kind of paranoia, which our childish megalomania only reinforced. If the talk turned to famous Jewish figures, we would say "we," as if Marx, Freud, and Einstein were our older brothers. Anti-Semitism puzzled us. Didn't the anti-Semites know that "we" had discovered the theory of relativity, that "we" had achieved extraordinary things in many fields of intellectual endeavor? At that time all we could think of was growing up as quickly as we could, so as to come into the inheritance of the Chosen People.

Geri wanted to be a doctor and to practice in Israel. Joe kept working on his Elvis impersonation. Michael was the math whiz of the group. Ari wanted to tear down his parents' snack bar

and rebuild it brick by brick in Tel Aviv. I wanted to be a writer.
I would, of course, have to show myself worthy of my famous
Jewish forebears. After indulging in these vocational flights of
fancy, we would usually come down to earth at Joe's parents'
snack bar, where we would stuff ourselves with hamburgers.

Our weekly attendance at Shabbat services happened to do
good things for our grades in religious school. A few years later,
our Shabbat evenings became somewhat livelier: we had visitors
from the Society for Christian-Jewish Cooperation and from a
number of schools. The way these visitors looked at us while we
were praying made us uncomfortable. In one respect, the goyim
were a pain. As we saw it, they came not out of friendship but
out of guilt, which they were welcome to, as far as we were
concerned. On the other hand, the Shabbat meal seemed more
exalted on such evenings. In a festively decked-out room we had
gefilte fish with challah and chopped eggs, served with Pepsi-
Cola. The girls never ceased to fascinate us. Beautiful, blond, and
desirable. It was clear they would never belong to us. The most
beautiful girl in the world did us no good if she wasn't anchored
in the Jewish faith.

Jews everywhere have specialized in keeping an ear to the
ground. Yet they have failed to note the difference between
hypersensitivity and delicacy of feeling. We, too, considered
ourselves active and alert, and we kept a sharp eye on German
life around us. In each other's presence we always emphasized
that what had "happened" to our parents would not happen to
us. After all, we always kept the Promised Land in mind, and
we could hardly wait to dedicate our lives to the Jewish state.

The arts were a closed book to us. When it came to painting,
we could, if pressed, come up with the name Chagall. Hardly
any of us had heard of Arik Brauer. We paid no attention to
literature, yet each of us had Leon Uris' *Exodus* and Ephraim
Kishon on his bookshelf. The only movies that appealed to us
were Woody Allen's (I would rather not mention the James Bond
films). We followed *The Holocaust* on television with great
suspense. It gave us quite a few nightmares. The abstract became

a bit more concrete. We didn't go to art galleries, museums or, heaven forbid, the theater.

The only thing we were interested in was Judaism. Yet we developed a culture of our own. In our formative years, it consisted exclusively of the study of our enemies. The Germans (what an over-simplified concept!) no longer offered a worthy adversary. They were intent on fostering dialogue. This was not the way an enemy was supposed to behave. An enemy does not want discussion. An enemy has rigid positions from which nothing can budge him. An enemy is consistent and unrelenting. An enemy had to be like us.

To work up some real hostility, we would talk about the threat from the radical right, and if that topic was exhausted too quickly, about the Palestinians. Thus we built up an inexhaustible reserve of enemies, all of whom were surely out to get us. During the summer and winter vacations we reinforced our sense of community at camp, which provided a sort of breeding ground for paranoia and separatism. There was kosher food, with milk and meat utensils meticulously separated. We warbled nothing but Jewish songs, played Jewish games, untiringly danced Jewish folk dances to Jewish folk music, and during those three or four weeks of vacation we lined up Jewish girlfriends. It was assumed that this was the best place for us to meet our Jewish brides, who would bear our Jewish children so that the Jewish race would never die out.

Once, during camp, we went to a restaurant, where we had an opportunity to demonstrate our political savvy. A young Tyrolean was selling buttons, among them one with a swastika. The older members of our group, of whom I was one, surrounded the guy. He was no older than us, wore a red ski jacket and a ski cap, and had a peach-fuzz mustache. More and more of us gathered round. We greedily drank in every detail of his appearance. We had finally come face to face with the prototypical fascist. So *that* was what they looked like.

We jabbered at him incessantly. The scrawny fellow tried to make a break for it, but we managed to stop him. Taunting him gave us a heady sensation. Finally we were generous enough to let him go, but only after we had confiscated all his swastikas. That was our heroic deed.

We were neurotics in a marinade of Jewishness. I was slowly beginning to drown in it. We never really experienced persecution like our fathers and forefathers. At sixteen I already knew that my parents' tale of horrors could never be mine. But such a thought could not be broached, even with your closest Jewish friends. It was a touchy topic. Once, in one of many discussion sessions, I asked whether Jews would have voted for Hitler if he'd persecuted only Communists and Muslims. That was the beginning of the end. Instantly I was labeled a "Jewish anti-Semite."

Jewish anti-Semites were the lowest of the low. They were thought of as scum. You couldn't get any worse. One guy threatened to kill me. It took four others to restrain the enraged attacker. In the last few days of vacation, I had to put up with a lot of beatings. Things went no better for me at home. Finally I decided to stay away from my old friends. I stopped going to religious school, and didn't set foot in the synagogue. At last I could breathe.

At school I stopped being secretive. I no longer refused to answer when my Christian classmates asked why I didn't attend religion classes with them. My classmates now talked about the "Jew boy" and teased me during recess. I realized that my Jewishness just provided them with an excuse to rib me. It was like Peter's incredibly thick glasses or Dirk's little potbelly. This wasn't fascism, as far as I was concerned, so I accepted it calmly.

History was taught by the principal. He would swagger up to his desk. With his briefcase, an arsenal of ballpoint pens and pencils, and a sponge he would portray for our benefit the tragic course of the Russian Campaign. This armchair soldiering was based on his personal participation in the Second World War. He would imitate the noise of the tanks' engines, the machine-gun fire. His voice would grow louder and louder, his face would flush. We got the impression that at home he must have a scale model of the entire theater of war. He'd been mentioning Hitler's Russian campaign ever since we did the Etruscans. Through skillful maneuvering we managed at least once a week to get him to put aside the material on the syllabus and let the German Panzer sponge sink in the Russian mire before our eyes.

Although acting all this out gave him great pleasure, he never failed to urge the cause of peace. "This campaign, in the depths of winter, dear children—and you can't begin to imagine what a winter!—was the worst thing Hitler did to us Germans," he would say after the little battle. Then his glance would catch mine out of the corner of his eye. I had followed his antics with as much fascination as my classmates. "Except of course for that business with the Jews," he would add, as if on command. Two years ago, I thought with amusement, I would probably have tried to report him to the U. N. Security Council.

I enjoyed my freedom to the hilt. At last I had found my way to people who could talk about the most ordinary things. My new friends took bicycle trips, smoked joints on the sly, and lived with all the bravado of carefree youth. I felt terrific, but I had not fully shaken off my old habits. I would thrust my Jewishness under people's noses, whether they were interested or not. Most of my new friends saw nothing special in it. After my disclosure, which was always made awkwardly and at a completely inappropriate moment, they would simply go back to the matter under discussion.

Soon I dropped my standoffish behavior among non-Jews. We went to rock concerts at regular youth centers, and I finally had a steady girlfriend (not Jewish, of course). I had a lot of catching up to do. One evening a nice guy at a youth center casually struck up a conversation with me. He'd spent the whole day at a demonstration against fascism in Chile. Of course I told him right away that I'd been born in Chile. He immediately got me a beer and wanted to hear more. I had this conditioned reflex: confronting new acquaintances with my Jewishness. He seemed delighted with me, and kept slapping me on the back. He was combating fascism on purely humanitarian grounds, he said, but

I was the quintessential victim. "The only contact I've had with victims is through photos," he said, and he scrutinized me just as we had scrutinized the Tyrolean. He harangued me all night. After several more beers, he wanted to recruit me into his party. "You must join up. With us, you can actively resist the repression you've experienced personally in this country," he declared. Later, somewhat the worse for wear, he reproved me for Israel's inflexible posture. Get me out of here, I thought. Nevertheless, a few days later I found a party membership form in my mailbox.

By the time I'd completed my education, I considered myself fully emancipated. I lived harmoniously with a non-Jewish woman, a social worker, and I viewed myself as a normal West German. Only the entry IB (Israelite Persuasion) on my tax form occasionally made for confusion in the personnel department. No one reminded me of my childhood desire to emigrate to Israel like the others. I liked the city where I lived; I liked the German language, and German literature even more. I wanted to write.

My first contact with a daily newspaper came about, ironically, through my rabbi. On his say-so, I was assigned to cover nearly all stories involving the Jewish community. I was regarded there as "press," and I attended events as a guest. That put a pleasant distance between me and the others. Reporting on the meetings of the "Christian-Jewish" organizations bored me to tears; I just let the lectures wash over me. When is a Jew still a Jew in the twentieth century? What does intermarriage signify, and is the Jewish race dying out, statistically speaking? It didn't want to die out, and I didn't want to report on it anymore. I asked at the office for new assignments. They had been delighted to find someone "with the necessary sensitivity." So we came to a parting of the ways. Every time I offered my services to another paper, my portfolio drew the editor's attention to the specialty I was trying to escape from.

Toward the end of the summer I got a telephone call from my old religious school teacher. That in itself was nothing

unusual. We spoke fairly often, in connection with my work for
the newspaper; some characterized our relationship as respectful,
others as icy. "A Jew can't drop out—because he will never stop
being a Jew," he said by way of introduction, and laughed. "I
never intended to drop out of Judaism," I replied. "I simply
stopped going to the community center." He dodged the argument that might have flared up and worked his way around to
the real reason for his call. The Society for Christian-Jewish
Cooperation—I shuddered in anticipation—was planning a
memorial expedition with the Jewish community to the former
concentration camp in Gurs. I refused, wanting nothing more to
do with the people from the Jewish Youth Center. Until this
telephone conversation they had been at a nice remove, and that
was where I wanted to keep them. "I have no money," I offered
as an excuse. "No problem," my teacher replied; "you're to come
as our guest." He was calling, he admitted, because he was in a
jam. Almost eighty percent of those who had signed up were
not Jews, and there were almost no Jews from the local community. That would cast a pall over the whole undertaking. With
the practiced persistence of a salesman he extolled the attractions
of the trip: four days near the Pyrenees, hotel accommodations,
and at least one hot meal per day. I remained skeptical. But
when he launched into praise for my articles, I gave in.

The Gurs group consisted of Gurs survivors, local politicians,
three clergymen, a journalist, numerous members of the society,
and seven Jews about my age. During the day we inspected
various sites of horror. When we got off our bus with German
license plates in Oradour, French residents hurled insults at us.
The city had been leveled by the Germans. My teacher positioned himself protectively in front of the Christians in the group
and announced to the angry little mob that we were Jews, and
thus also victims of Nazi Germany. That did nothing to improve
the situation.

After Oradour, we drowned our sorrows in French red wine,
accompanied by superb steak and *haricots verts*. Frau Grün had
been deported to Gurs as a young girl. The sight of the camp

brought a lump to her throat. Weeping, she described what she had suffered. Again and again she complained that she had been fed nothing but hot water with two or three grains of rice. In the various restaurants where we ate, I often glanced at her, and one time found myself wondering how she must be feeling as we wolfed down the delicious food. At that moment she helped herself to another piece of bread and then expertly dissected her trout.

The hyphen in the Society for Christian-Jewish Cooperation separated more than it connected. The Jews and Christians sat strictly apart. Neither group wanted dialogue. The non-Jews set great store by certain events they staged. A minister gave an "impromptu" speech, in which he spoke in solemn tones of his father: "My father, dear friends, my father was what was commonly called a Nazi bigwig." There followed a one-and-a-half-hour monologue on how the son had confronted this problem, no holds barred. Another time, a city council member made a sincere effort to sketch for the benefit of us ignoramuses the rise and fall of the Third Reich. Not infrequently, the chief emphasis was placed on those brave Germans who had stood by various Jews. We were all sick and tired of solemn admonitions and remembrances. No one wanted to hear any more of this hogwash. At the beginning the young people were put off by the sight of the graves. Yet nothing really got to them except a bad meal. The former camp inmates were our guides. They could remember the smallest details, the individual stations of their torment. But for the most part they remained calm and answered even the stupidest questions with equanimity ("As a wife and mother and a good Christian, I have a question for you, Herr Goldmann"). Only once did they get upset: when they noticed a statue of Jesus in front of a Jewish memorial tablet. The minor uproar that ensued brought us to the doorstep of this French town's mayor. The official pronounced himself devastated, and invited the group to join him at his regular hang-out.

In the evening the Jewish teens played pool as in olden times, as though this were a noble obligation going back to

Moses. A city councillor played pinball, three others from the Christian league played cards or chatted about summer cottages in Southern France. On the fourth evening I joined a group of Christians, thinking with my chronic naïveté that they were interested in dialogue. Instead, heated arguments broke out. I was filled with the spirit of emancipation and eschewed dogma. The last thing I wanted to do, I assured them, was to rub salt in the wound. But I had unknowingly broken a taboo. Publicly everyone deplores the Third Reich, but only for himself. One mustn't stand in the way of penitence.

Starting with this all-expenses-paid excursion, all lines of communication between me and the Jewish community were cut. I used the time for myself, and worked on stories. My greatest desire was to write a novel that would have nothing, absolutely nothing to do with the Third Reich or Jews. In my work as a journalist I continued to be expected to treat Jewish topics; I confined myself to doing interviews. After every article I would swear it was the last. What it boils down to is that authors who happen to be Jewish are not allowed to concentrate on their own writing. Someone always comes along and calls for Jewish topics. One of my best friends had been giving talks on the Warsaw ghetto for years. He appeared on television, wrote articles, and gave readings at night school. One evening he told me, "I'm so sick of being trapped. I earn my money by baring my concentration-camp soul over and over again. I'm like some junkie who has to keep going cold turkey in order to hang onto his job." After a sip of red wine he added, "If you're witty, they call you 'typically Jewish,' and if you dramatize it, you're conjuring up the spirit of the Wandering Jew." Sadly he showed me a letter from a radio producer: "But I am convinced that your broadcast by its very nature will be a plea for an end to xenophobia. Please describe your childhood in the concentration camp, and talk about what makes you so mournful. But don't let me second-guess you. Feel free to do whatever seems right." "Feel free, but hop to it," my friend remarked bitterly.

I flew to Berlin to give a lecture at the Jewish adult education program. The organizer had instructed me to go to the community center as soon as I got in. I arrived with my two suitcases at 79–80 Fasanenstrasse. More than a dozen heavily armed police were swarming around the door. The picture reminded me of synagogue visits in the seventies, and I couldn't help laughing. I made my way past the policemen, who took no notice of me, and went into the lobby. The Jewish doorman flew into a panic. He jumped up and hurried toward me, shouting at the top of his lungs, "Where you going wid dem suitcases, for God's sake, where you going wid dem suitcases?" Hearing his shouts, policemen burst in, released the safety on their guns, and aimed. My smile vanished from my lips.

MAXIM BILLER

Finkelstein's Fingers

1.

WE SAT WITH OUR BACKS to the street, on broad, comfort-able leather stools, and over the bar hung a mirror. In the mirror one could see Broadway, which down here, near the World Trade Center, at the southern tip of the city, with its empty warehouses and discount outlets, seemed cold and mean. It was getting dark, and as the streetlights came on, one after the other, I was stirred, as someone else might have been at the sight of a particularly well-turned sunrise.

The woman with whom I was talking had approached me a few minutes earlier. Suddenly she was standing there, her lips quivering in a foolish and uncertain way, and then she said, out of the blue in German, that I looked just like the Hungarian poet Miklós Radnóti. But of course, she continued, she knew who I really was, and she said it in the tone of those people who think they have an undeniable claim on anyone whose photo they've seen in the newspaper.

She was old, and although older women don't interest me much, I took a good look at her. I liked the roundness of her eyes and the fluttering of her false eyelashes. I liked the way her pouting lips quivered whenever she fell silent or was pensive. And her white, nearly skinless face with two long furrows around the mouth reminded me, in the halogen lighting of the coffee shop, of a beautiful Etruscan death mask.

I had offered the woman a seat, but she didn't want to talk about me at all. She merely inquired politely how large a printing had been done of my last book, and remarked contemptuously on the controversy that had erupted over it. Then she said, just as out of the blue as before, that I did not deserve Radnóti's face and eyes; I, the child of prosperity, had no idea what Life and Literature were really about. Finally she began to talk—about herself, about Miklós Radnóti, and Professor Finkelstein.

Who was she? The wife of a Hamburg attorney who had one day simply gone off the deep end.

She had three children, a dog, and a master's degree in American literature, and one evening a month she had an open house in her large apartment on Klosterstern, with food and live music. She was friends with young artists, whose paintings she bought. Her familiarity with the cultural sections of the German papers was matched only by that of the people who wrote for them. Apparently she had read every line ever written by Updike and Nabokov, Faulkner and Henry James. When she became pregnant the first time, she had given up everything for marriage and family, and now she was finally fulfilling her old dream: taking a course in creative writing at Columbia University.

And who was Professor Finkelstein? To her, a monster, a sadist, a tormenting spirit, who had decided from the outset to show his student from Germany what the score was.

"A person can speak frankly with you," she said to me. "You don't give a damn about taboos and sensitive subjects."

"You bet your life."

"Then listen: Finkelstein is small potatoes in America. I know that for a fact—the other students told me. He got his teaching position only because of his race."

"You mean—"

"Of course. They all stick together, most of all here in New York. I've heard there are actually people who pass themselves off as Jewish in order to have a chance at making it professionally."

"That's pretty funny, isn't it."

She looked at me amiably and smiled. "Well, if you want to call it that . . ."

I looked into her white face, then raised my eyes. In the mirror over the bar I saw a man get out of a taxi and lean in the window on the taxi's passenger side. His body jerked nervously, and he was waving his arms. Suddenly the driver jumped out of the car, tore open the trunk, and began throwing newspapers, books, and clothing onto the sidewalk. They wrangled with each other a little longer, then the driver drove off in a rage, while the man gathered up his things. He leaned against the plate-glass window of the coffee shop. He was breathing heavily, and his glasses were bent. As I observed his face, I was startled—he looked so much like me. The same small face, tangled red hair, broad, heavy jaw with an overbite and a scar on the lower left. He even wore a jacket similar to mine, and he seemed to have the same small, somewhat squat build . . .

2.

"You aren't listening to me at all," said the woman next to me, offended.

I looked at her hard, and made an effort to appear focused and polite, but suddenly I couldn't remember who she was or why I was talking with her.

"May I go on?" she asked sharply.

"Yes," I answered slowly, "of course . . . "

"All right . . . The second time the class met, Finkelstein stood up in front and read one of his own short stories," she said.

Again I looked in the mirror. It had gotten dark in the meantime, people were rushing back and forth, cars glided along Broadway, red and yellow lights turned into sparks, threads, and exploding points, and for a moment the nighttime image in the

mirror froze into a photograph. There was nothing more to be
seen of my double.

"Excuse me," I said, "I'm really listening to you now."

"Do you know what the story was about?" she said.

"Haven't the faintest."

"Guess!"

"Sex?"

She shook her head.

"Love?"

"No."

"Betrayal?"

"No."

"The city?"

"No, not that either."

"Then what?"

"Come on, you'll get it."

"The Holocaust?"

"Exactly!" she exclaimed cheerfully and loudly. "The Holocaust!" Then a shadow passed over her Etruscan face, and she
said, "Finkelstein's story was about a former Polish partisan who
trades her New York apartment for a country home in Connecti-
cut and from then on is pursued in her dreams by SS-men."

"Not bad."

"In the end she wakes up in the middle of the night, shouts,
'They're coming, they're coming,' dashes to the kitchen, and
smashes all her dishes to smithereens."

"I've heard worse."

"You may be right, you're the writer," she said, and then she
leaned her shoulder against me. The pressure grew as we talked
on, so much so that I began to wonder about her.

"After Finkelstein finished reading it," she said, "he melo-
dramatically laid the manuscript of his story, which has of
course never been published, on the lectern. He paced back and
forth across the seminar room like a trial lawyer in a Hollywood
film, as if we were the jury, and then planted himself smack in

front of me and said smugly, 'So, Anita, how do you like the
story?'"

She looked at me expectantly.

"You should change professors," I said, "if Finkelstein doesn't
appeal to you."

"Of course, no problem. In the end, one can change everything: professors, history, your father, your mother, even the
country you come from."

"What do you want from me?" I snapped at her, and her old
white cheeks immediately filled with blood. They turned red and
firm and hard; and suddenly her face looked green, then yellow,
no longer like a beautiful death mask. It was like one of those
hollowed-out pumpkins Americans spook each other with at
Halloween.

She pulled her shoulder away, stood up, laid a five-dollar bill
on the counter, and left without a word of farewell. In the mirror
over the bar I saw her linger in front of the subway station,
loiter around a newspaper stand for a while, take a few steps in
the direction of Midtown, toward Chambers Street, then turn
back and go down the steps to the subway.

3.

I kept looking outside; I gazed into the mirror above my head.
I was glad to be rid of the German woman, but I found it even
more reassuring that my double had not appeared again. Finally
I pulled my book out of the inside pocket of my jacket and
opened it. I had brought it to New York because I had been
hoping to find an American publisher, but I had soon given up;
two telephone conversations with agents who'd been recom-
mended to me had drained me of my courage. I was reading my
stories again now, for the first time since they had appeared in
Germany six months earlier, but I didn't understand them. I

skimmed over words and sentences as though they were just
pretty geometric patterns and lines. Then the door to the coffee
shop opened, I heard soft, dragging footsteps, I heard a gentle
sigh, and Anita from Hamburg was sitting next to me again and
pressing her shoulder against mine.

"You have to help me," she said.

I quickly put the book away. "What's happened?" I asked.

"I have to hand in my term paper by tomorrow . . . "

"What is it?"

"A short story."

"And what am I supposed to do?"

"Write it."

"My English is atrocious."

"I could translate it."

"In one night?"

"In one night."

"How much have you written already?"

"Not a line."

"A nice little victory for Professor Finkelstein, right?"

She took the five-dollar bill from the counter and rolled it up.

"The topic?" I said.

She slid the bill back and forth between the palms of her
hands. "Guess!"

"Sex, love, betrayal?"

She smiled, and now she was as beautiful and striking as at
the beginning, and then I smiled too, and we said in unison,
"The Ho-lo-caust!"

"Here." She laid a black-and-white photo on the counter. The
photo showed a young man with eyes half closed and a cigarette
in his mouth. He had a small face, a broad jaw with a scar on
the lower left, freckles, and light hair, probably red. "Here," she
said, "this is Finkelstein's topic. We're supposed to write about
Miklós Radnóti. Three thousand words."

4.

I glanced in the mirror. Nothing, not a trace of my double. Broadway was emptying out, and the façades of the buildings, with dark, barred windows above the stores, were gradually acquiring that nocturnal shade of sepia.

"I don't know," I said.

"Please!"

"Tell me about him first. Maybe something will come to you."

"Nothing will come to me. I can't do it, I simply . . . You're the writer."

"Come on now! Get started!"

"All right, I'll try," she said, and then pressed onward, rapidly, breathlessly, without hesitation: "Miklós Radnóti was born in 1909 in Budapest. He translated Apollinaire and Hölderlin into Hungarian. He was a poet himself. A good poet. He had a chance to escape from the National Socialists, but in the summer of 1939 he returned to Hungary, after a trip to France. He thought Admiral Horthy would never allow anything worse to happen."

"And what's the story?"

"The story is his death. What else would it be?" said Anita. She hissed at me, "I'm sure Finkelstein, that Holocaust worshiper, thought this up just for my benefit."

"You're paranoid," I replied with a quiet, sadistic smile. "So, how did this Radnóti die?" I asked her.

"They found him a year after the war."

"Where?"

"He was halfway between Budapest and Vienna. In a large pit. He had had to shovel it out himself, along with some other prisoners."

"I see. So how many corpses were there?"

"Twenty-two," she said.

I beckoned to the waiter. He leaned over the narrow stainless countertop and filled our coffee cups. I liked the sweet, weak

New York coffee. I drank it constantly, five or six times a day, and with every sip I thought about having to go back soon. I had only a week left.

I offered Anita a cigarette, and she stuck it behind her ear, to be precise, between her ear and the thick, quilted edge of her wildly patterned cap, which she'd probably bought in a second-hand shop on St. Mark's Place. Then she ordered a doughnut for each of us.

"What did they do to them?" I asked.

"During the last autumn of the war, the SS marched them for months through Wallachia. From Heidenau, near Bor, by way of Belgrade and Novi Sad all the way across Hungary to Györ. Anyone who couldn't keep going was done for."

"And Miklós Radnóti couldn't keep going?"

"No, apparently not."

I felt the pressure of her shoulder, and then I noticed that she was inching her foot along the footrest. She brought her foot up and finally pressed it against the inside of my shin. She turned her face toward mine, and she came so close that I could see little red and blue veins in her temples. Her negroid lips had a smoky flavor, she was sweating very slightly on the back of her neck, and I think she had on that rare, old-fashioned Chanel scent that always gives a suggestion of grass and gasoline.

It was just a short kiss, very short and very hard.

"And what's the twist on the whole thing?" I asked afterward.

"When the mass grave was opened after the war," she said in a friendly tone and then brushed the back of her hand over her wet lips, "they found a sheaf of poems in the pocket of Radnóti's windbreaker. He'd written them in the camp at Heidenau and also on the death march to Györ. So Finkelstein says. I have no way of checking. It wouldn't surprise me if this was just one of his hoaxes."

"A nice little Anne Frank story . . . Are the poems any good?"

"Finkelstein says Celan couldn't hold a candle to Radnóti. But no one ever undertook to disseminate his work."

"I don't know if I can do anything with this," I said softly.

"Of course you can," Anita replied. She took Radnóti's picture from the counter and stuck it in my jacket pocket, next to my book.

"I really don't know . . ."

I was still wavering, but she paid no attention. She took my fingers in hers, squeezed them until they hurt, and then said, "Tell me where you live."

"Right around the corner."

"Right around the corner," she repeated. Then she put another five-dollar bill on the counter, pulled the cigarette I had given her out from behind her ear, and lit up . . .

Once outside, before we turned onto Chambers Street, I glanced into the coffee shop. There he sat in the window, at a small table—my double. He was drinking tea and sorting his newspapers and books. He had laid his clothing, in a bundle, next to him on the floor. He seemed agitated, distraught, but not at all crazy, and I suddenly had the impression that he and Anita had secretly smiled at each other through the plate-glass window . . .

"OK, Anita," I said to her, "we'll show your Finkelstein."

5.

I've been to New York often, but every time I leave it's as though I've never been there. And that's why every time I go I hardly remember it, only the light, which is entirely different from ours in Europe; all I know is that if you take the highway to Long Island, past the huge white cemeteries of Queens, you can see even more distinctly that the light in America has something subdued and tender about it, as if a huge red filter were suspended over the country . . .

This time I was staying with a friend on Chambers Street,

between Broadway and Church, and, except for the first couple of days, I was there alone, because soon after I arrived he flew to Munich to visit his parents. I fed his two cats, brought in the mail, and checked the answering machine. Now and then he would phone from Munich to see if anything was new. Otherwise I had nothing to do, and I decided right at the beginning not to bother anymore about placing the American rights for the book. And then I fell into that mixture of restless curiosity and constant fatigue that takes hold of me in almost every foreign city. I covered TriBeCa in all directions, went down to Wall Street, and from there to Battery Park, where I stared at the Statue of Liberty for a few minutes. I walked to SoHo every day, went to the galleries and boutiques, ate lunch at the vegetarian restaurant on Greene Street, and then took the subway home, to sleep or watch television. In late afternoon I would often go out again. I would sit for a while in the coffee shop on the corner and then take the subway wherever I felt like; I would decide on the platform or on the train . . .

I still recall vividly how two days before leaving, I stood on the riverside promenade in Brooklyn Heights and looked across the East River toward Manhattan. I saw the island with its densely crowded skyscrapers, and then I turned around, and there were these little Brooklyn townhouses behind me. I still recall wandering through the Lower East Side afterward, eating blintzes with sour cream in a Jewish cafeteria and overhearing the owner firing his Vietnamese cook. And most of all, I recall how I stopped in front of a bookstore to look in the window, and the owner came out and had *payes* under his black hat and was wearing Hasidic garb. He closed the shop, pulling down the metal shutter, and as he hurried away it occurred to me that it was Friday noon and Shabbat would be beginning soon, and then I noticed that all the streets around me had suddenly emptied out, and that was certainly the most beautiful moment I have ever experienced in this city . . .

6.

Two months after my return from New York, I came across an article by Anita in *Die Zeit*. It was called "In the Labyrinth of the Past," and it was about Professor Finkelstein, his Jewish origins, and Anita's experiences in Finkelstein's creative writing class. I was thrilled, and I read the article straight through—as I always do when a topic discussed in a newspaper or magazine is something I know a lot about. Anita first described the torments and self-doubt she had had to endure as a German in Professor Finkelstein's class, and at this point she twice referred to him as the "great, wise, and understanding American of Polish-Jewish extraction." She wrote that it had been a brilliant piece of strategy the way he had sharpened her historical consciousness through circumspect inquiries into her biography. But of course she had had to work through the entire grieving process alone; she would never forget the day when Professor Finkelstein had sent her to a seminar on Holocaust literature. There, when she was in the middle of reading the gripping poems of the unknown Hungarian-Jewish poet Miklós Radnóti, a dam had suddenly burst inside her, whereupon she had dashed all the way across the campus to Finkelstein's office to make her confession at last. Weeping, she told of her mother, who at every parade had elbowed her way to the front to be kissed or hugged by the Führer. Raging, she talked about her father, who had first worked at IG Farben in Ludwigshafen, later at the plant in Auschwitz. Yes, and then she described to the professor her own personal postwar drama, the silence at home, her father's drinking, her mother's depression, and her own craziness during the student revolt of the sixties. Finally she kissed Finkelstein's hand to beg his forgiveness for everything her people had inflicted on his. "And thus," Anita concluded, "began my friendship with Professor Finkelstein. We exchange letters, we telephone each other sometimes, and he has promised he will spend Christmas at our house on the Lüneburg Heath."

I smiled. Once again I smiled my conceited Jewish sadist's smile, and then I noticed the photo next to the article. According to the caption, it was Professor Finkelstein, and it was the very photo that Anita had laid on the counter that time in the coffee shop.

I stopped smiling. I folded up the newspaper and looked around me. I was sitting in an Italian restaurant on Isestrasse. It was Saturday afternoon, the last weekend before Christmas, and there was no one in the place except me and the waiters. I had got up late and was only now having lunch. Just as I was about to order coffee, I felt a cold draft hit my legs. The door opened, and in came Anita, accompanied by two very handsome young men. Both had short black hair and lean, bright faces, and surely they were terribly in love with the older woman at their side.

Anita didn't see me. She sat down at the bar with her back to me, and not until twenty or thirty minutes later, when she had already paid and was getting ready to leave the place with her two friends, did she turn around. She recognized me at once. She took a cigarette, stuck it behind her ear with a smile, and all at once everything was as before, in our coffee shop on Broadway . . .

Of course Anita was no longer wearing her New York cap. Her hair was pulled back tightly and smoothly, she wore a string of pearls around her throat, a cashmere sweater, and gold earrings. She looked spirited and youthful, not crazy and lonely as I remembered her.

So we meet again for the first time, I thought, and now, seeing her so rich and vital and contented, I didn't regret a bit what had happened on that fall evening in New York . . . First we had talked a bit about literature, and then, after I had written her paper, had spent half the night fucking . . .

I got up and went over to Anita. "So," I said, "how did Professor Finkelstein like our story?"

7.

Aha, he thought, aha . . . This crazy German has actually fallen in love with me . . . Finkelstein got up from his desk, took off his reading glasses, and laid them on the manuscript of Anita's story. All through the course he had been waiting in suspense for her final paper. He didn't care if she had talent; he just wanted to know if she would write about him, whether she might even declare her love, and now it had happened exactly as he had pictured it.

Finkelstein had always hated his German student, because of her enraptured gaze, because of the pushy way in which she leaned on the lectern during breaks. He found her unattractive and too old, and even though he had thought a few times about tying her hand and foot to a dirty, wobbly hotel bed, he always pushed the thought aside as one of his more aberrant fantasies about the Nazis. Finkelstein hated the Germans; he would never travel to their gloomy, idiotic country. He understood their problems, but he simply wasn't interested in them, and several times he had had to restrain himself when Anita posed her stupid, woeful, German questions in class, in that weak, whiny, woeful voice of hers.

Now Finkelstein was standing in the bathroom. He looked in the mirror at his little Yeshiva student's face with the broad, heavy jaw and the scar on the lower left where the neck began. He ran his hand through his crisp red hair; it feels like wire, he thought, and then it occurred to him that he had actually seen Anita at his coffee shop that evening when Ruthie had kicked him out once and for all. She had been talking to an odd-looking foreigner at the bar. Suddenly he found himself thinking only one thought: One must be fair!

He rushed into his study, turned on the computer, and went to work. "Your text, Anita," Finkelstein began his comment, "is fluent, readable, and at times cleverly constructed. You have apparently attempted, through the use of a split character, to convey the real and simultaneously paranoid element in the Holocaust experience of the descendants on both sides, the side of the victims as well as of the perpetrators. In the process you lose your narrator in the labyrinth of your character-duplicating machine . . . "

Finkelstein jumped up, making, as he always did when he was writing and a word or phrase didn't come to him, furious chewing movements with his mouth. He started to whistle something, he thrust his hands into his pockets, pulled out a few coins and began counting them absentmindedly, but the next moment he was sitting on the chair again, pounding the keys of his computer.

"Even if one can surmise," Finkelstein wrote, "who the narrator, his double, and the (fictional?) poet Miklós Radnóti are, and how these emanations are related to each other, in the last section only confusion and misunderstanding result when you make 'Professor Finkelstein' (I'm a good sport!) the double of all the previously introduced figures. What are you trying to say? And what, by the way, was your point with the little obscenity in the last paragraph? I know it is fun to write such things—but despite Miller, Bukowski, and Roth (all of whom I consider imposters, by the way), the world is not yet ready for this . . ."

Was that too harsh? Finkelstein wondered. It didn't matter one way or the other to him. But then he hunched over the keyboard again. "You have talent, Anita," he wrote. "You have a good control of language and a knack for creating atmosphere, and if you keep working at it, you can become a real writer some day. There are many writers who have started out at a more advanced age than you. So, good luck for the future, and if you come to New York again, stop by and see me; we could have dinner together. —Sam Finkelstein, Ph.D., Department of English, Columbia University."

The professor crossed his arms behind his neck, scratched himself vigorously behind both ears, and read through what he had written. But when he was about to turn off the computer, his fingers jerked back to the keyboard, as if of their own volition. "Wait, dear Anita," Finkelstein's fingers wrote, "how about tomorrow night? There's a little Japanese place on my block, clean and cheap. We could go there and talk about literature a bit, and later . . . A little joke between writers, Anita. Which of us knows if what we write is really true? So I will call you tomorrow morning, you wonderful German weeping willow!"

Finkelstein smiled. That was really a good idea he'd come up with.

And so simple! He'd been masturbating every night for months, conjuring up images of Ruthie, and he had finally earned himself a little real sex.

He stood up and looked out the window. He saw the two blinking towers of the World Trade Center. To the left, in a long, deep, straight line, Broadway's dim tail of lights stretched through the dusk. Damn it all, the little weeping willow was right again, Finkelstein thought. In this part of town Broadway really did look pretty cold and mean.

RAFAEL SELIGMANN

from

Rubinstein's Auction

The Auction

"GOOD MORNING. My name is Taucher. Some of you already know me. I'll be substituting for Herr Faden in German class until further notice."

Know you? You can say that again!

"Gentlemen, I find the arrangement of this classroom too military, too rigid. We're not here to drill but to discuss and learn from one another." She looks straight at us—and that includes me. "So I'd like to ask you to form a half-circle."

A few of the guys sulkily nudge their desks away from each other.

"Don't be bashful. Discussion can take place only when everyone is on the same level. Don't expect any pronouncements from on high. I want my desk to be part of the half-circle. Thus far only a faint halo has formed around my seat." With short, brisk steps she goes to the first unoccupied desk, seizes hold of it and the chair that belongs with it, and pushes them snugly against her desk. "So, who's going to sit next to me?" She smiles.

Why not me? My temples are pounding. What is it about this woman that drives me crazy? She's not even especially good-looking. Fairly tall, small bust, broad butt, long, muscular legs. At first I hardly noticed her face, only her full, pale pink lips and her high cheekbones. But then about six months ago she asked me something or other in the hall. She looked at me so warmly that my heart began to thud. That hasn't changed. And now I'm supposed to see this woman almost every day.

It's now or never. "Me!" A crow would be proud of my croak.

"That's more like it! Come right up here, Rubinstein."

I stuff my books and papers into my briefcase and head for her desk. I even manage a grin.

No sooner am I seated than the burning in my head gives way to a sense of delicious warmth. Behind me I hear pushing and scraping. Now she's right next to me! She's wearing flat sandals with narrow thongs. Pale pink polish on her toenails. The naked look.

Suddenly she gets up, comes over to my desk, and takes up a position beside me. Her warm, firm fingers casually reach for my left hand, and slowly but surely she pulls my hand up in the air. The blood rushes to my face. Before I or anyone else can react to my being hand-picked this way, Hilde Taucher delivers her little lecture in a quiet voice: "Yes, fellows, having the courage to be a non-conformist can have its rewards, as you see."

With that, the general paralysis vanishes. The noise mounts in waves. Shouts, whistles, stamping of feet. Cries of "Me, too!" "Move over!" "Time to change partners!"

She gently lowers my hand and says in that quiet voice, "Sorry, gentlemen, you missed out on the historic moment!"

I'm intoxicated. Confused sensations and scraps of thoughts go shooting through my head. "Hey guys, listen to this. If any of you are really so wild to sit next to our instructor and hold hands with her, be my guest. I'd be happy to change places," I shout. At this moment I'm the uncontested star of Class 13b, for the first time ever. How did this come about? No matter! I've got to stay ahead of the game! I've got to!

"Me!" "Me!" "Me!" "No, me!" come squawks from the class.

"Listen here, fellows," I hear myself saying hoarsely. "If there's such demand, I'll have to play King Solomon. I'll auction off my place."

Wherever did this idea come from?

"Five marks!" bellows Schön.

"Ten!" shouts Kleiner.

"Twenty!"

"Twenty-five!"

"Twenty-five! Going . . . going . . ." I answer shrilly.

"Forty!"

"Fifty!"

"Fifty marks twelve," says Bergmann, the class clown.

"That's it, you sissies! A hundred marks!" Kraxmayer says firmly, putting an end to the auction. Without undue haste he pulls the blue banknote out of his wallet, takes his briefcase, and strides up to me. He presses the banknote into my hand, which automatically reaches out to take it. I have to force myself to get up and turn over my seat to him.

Silence.

"Well, look at that, will you! A German woman gives him her hand, and Rubinstein promptly auctions it off to the highest bidder! Now I see how you people get so rich!" I hear Franz Bauriedl's drawling voice behind me.

You've got to do something, no time to lose! Otherwise it'll be all up with your role as class hero. You've got to punch that Bauriedl in the face! True, he's half a head taller than you, but he won't hit back—he can't afford to in this situation.

But I don't have the courage. In the past few minutes my nervous energy has drained away. I'm scared. You've got to do something! I can't, I just don't have the strength to hit Bauriedl. What am I supposed to do, damn it?

"I'm going to donate the money—to a good cause." My voice cracks. You miserable coward!

"To the synagogue, I suppose?" Bauriedl inquires.

"That will do, fellows!" Frau Taucher firmly exclaims.

Instantly the racket subsides.

I've lost! I still have Kraxmayer's hundred marks in my hand. My eyes fill with tears. Out of here! I've got to get out! I can't let them see me blubbering. I'm out of there. Slam the door behind me. Dash to the bathroom, into the first stall, bang my head against the wooden partition. Crying, crying. Fucking Germans!

In the Whorehouse—for Nothing

I can't stay in the bathroom forever. It'll be recess soon. I can't let the guys see me bawling. I've got to get out of here. But where to? Stop blubbering and use your head! You can't go back to class. They'll see I've been crying, and they'll laugh at me. I tear off a long strip of toilet paper and blow my nose. You've got to get out of here!

I dash out of the building, cross Lerchenfeldstrasse, vault over the barrier into the English Garden. They're having recess now. What if I just go back and act as though nothing happened? "Couldn't find anything else to sell off, Rubinstein, huh?"

I can't spend the whole day in the English Garden. Home? "Why are you home so early?" That's out of the question. Let's think this through, Reb Yid. First of all, what about the money? The Red Cross? The Humane Society or that sort of shit? Should I really donate it to the Jewish community? Nah, they have plenty. Just pocketing it would be dumb, too. I know, I'll go to a whorehouse. You're nuts! What do you mean? I don't know the first thing about sex. I did go to the whorehouse a couple of times with Itzi and Heini, but of course none of us dared to go with a whore. Besides, it's pretty expensive. All right, that's it! Krax'll pay for it, without realizing it!

The thought of sleeping with a woman excites me. Damn it all, I *am* going to the whorehouse!

Half an hour later I'm standing outside "Imex House." On the way here on the streetcar my pulse kept going faster and faster. You can still turn back, Rubinstein. Scared shitless again? You can't keep running away from things.

I push open the glass door. It's true! Even on a Monday morning the place is open.

The black-haired one in tights isn't bad. She looks at me and smiles. "Coming with me, sugar?"

"How much?"

"Thirty, rubber included."

Not all that expensive. I'd have seventy marks left over. I follow her up the worn wooden stairs.

On the second floor two women are standing around. The blonde is kind of fat, and besides it's been a while since she saw forty. The one in the wig next to her is about ten years younger. Keep going! On the next floor are three women. Two in black tights, the third in a miniskirt. She really looks nice. A bit plump, calm gray-blue eyes, hardly any make-up. She looks about my age.

"How much?"

"Thirty marks, because it's you."

"Good."

Now there's no turning back. I have to follow her.

"Come this a-way," she says in Bavarian dialect. She goes on ahead to the corridor. I stare at her bare legs. A few steps and she opens a door. The room is small and poorly lit. I see a couch covered in gray, an old red easy chair, and in the corner a tiny sink.

"You like threesomes, sugar?"

"What does that cost?"

"Sixty."

"No."

"How 'bout somethin' to drink?"

"No."

"All right. Then gimme the money now, please."

I hand her the hundred-mark note.

"You like it French?"

"No."

"Hey, you're no big spender."

"Well, the money's not all mine, you know."

"Aw, come on, tell that to somebody else."

She sticks the money in a little patent leather bag and fishes out two bills. "Here, take your seventy marks." Then she fishes a condom out of the same bag, sits down on the couch, and pulls up her skirt. She has nothing on underneath! I've never seen a woman naked. And this broad simply pulls up her skirt— without batting an eyelash!

"Come here. Get undressed. Not your shirt, just your pants."

I obey. Lay my pants and briefs on the easy chair and sit down next to her on the couch. My hands and feet are like ice. I feel stabbing pains in my elbows and the hollows of my knees.

Her short, pudgy fingers are already reaching for my shmuck. Rubbing and pulling—ouch! Should I tell her I've never been with a woman before?

No! I'm not going to play for sympathy!

"Ain't nothin' happenin'."

She's right, not a thing. I'm getting out of here. No! Damn it all, I can't run away again!

"Well, what should I do?" Typical Jonathan Rubinstein.

"We can do it French, sugar." She smiles.

"Fine."

"Yes, but you have to pay twenty more."

I give her the twenty. She gets up, the skirt slides down, she pops the money in her bag. Then she sits down on the bed again, pulls up her skirt, grabs my shmuck and rubs it with short, jerky strokes.

"Hey you, still nothin' happenin'."

"Isn't there something you can do?"

"Sure there is. But *that*'ll cost you another fifty."

Are you totally out of your mind? The moment the broad pulled up her skirt, the last flicker of lust died away. You don't feel the slightest bit of desire, only fear and disgust. You know all this whore is interested in is taking all your money, and you're just going along with her so as not to disgrace yourself completely.

I give her the money.

Now I'm rid of all my ill-gotten gains.

She sticks the money in her purse and bends over my shmuck. Again that painful pulling and rubbing.

"Hey sugar, nothin' happens, no matter what I do."

"That's all right."

"Whatever you say." She gets up, hands me a paper towel. "Please throw the rubber in the garbage pail." I do as I'm told and slip quickly into my clothes. Meanwhile she's washed her hands and hurries on ahead into the corridor.

"Bye, sugar."

I don't reply. I hurtle down the stairs.

You dummy! You fuck-up!

On Hohenzollernstrasse the heat's oppressive. I have a nasty taste in my mouth. I run in the direction of Leopoldstrasse. Pull yourself together! You're going to walk home now; otherwise you'll go off the deep end.

It takes me almost two hours to walk home through the English Garden and along the Isar. That gives me time to calm down somewhat. In front of our building on Ländstrasse I hesitate briefly. Then I push open the heavy door and climb up the worn wooden stairs. I stick my key in the lock of the door to our apartment.

Jackass

"Shalom, Jackass."

"Why are you so late?"

"That's none of your fucking business."

"Is that any way to speak to your mother?"

"Sure is! How often do I have to tell you it's up to me if and when I get home."

"But I have to know when to heat up your dinner."

"When I tell you to!"

"Excuse me, but have you lost your mind? What gives you the right to talk to me like that?" She gets up from her seat at the kitchen table and confronts me, all five feet of her. "Don't you have the slightest respect for your parents? Aren't you at all grateful to Friedrich and me? Since you were born we've done everything for you."

"Am I supposed to be grateful that you took me away from Israel and brought me to this Nazi country?"

"There are other kinds of people here, too. Besides, in a few years all the Nazis will be dead."

"So will you!"

For a moment her light brown eyes open wide. But Jackass quickly gets a grip on herself. "You've forgotten what it was like for us in Israel, Jonathan. I was sick, Friedrich had no job. How would we have provided for you?"

"Right-o! Now it's all my fault! To save me from starving to death you had to come to Germany. Isn't it strange, though, that not a single person has starved to death in Israel—which you can't exactly say of the Jews in the German concentration camps!"

"That's all in the past!" she shouts.

"Nothing's in the past! The old Nazis are still alive and well and raising their children to be new Nazi swine!"

"Something must have come up in school again!"

"Damn right it did!" I bellow.

"I don't understand why you always get so worked up over it. Aaron Blau and Herrschi Bierstamm live here, too, and they don't have any trouble."

"You mean Arthur and Heinz? Those cowards are so chicken they won't even use their Jewish names. You just wait: soon they'll be calling themselves Adolf and Horst, to make absolutely sure no one would ever suspect they weren't Aryans. But it won't do them any good! Don't go thinking they get picked on any less than I do. When they're older they'll probably get their hooked noses fixed. Maybe that'll help."

"You sound completely anti-social!"

"That's what I am. As a Jew I don't belong in this society."

"And besides, you sound like a Nazi. As if all Jews had hooked noses! Just look at your father! Blond and blue-eyed."

"And with a nice streak of Germanic stupidity."

"Lord of righteousness, is that any way to talk about your father?"

"He deserves it! Most of the Yids here make money at least! That includes the Blaus and the Bierstamms. But our Friedrich works himself to the bone ten hours a day at Silberfaden & Ehrlichmann's warehouse, and brings home beans. A fantastic job like that he could have found in Israel, too. Though there he would never have been able to buy his own car, not even one of those Volkswagens the Führer loved so much. Not that it does him much good—our Friedrich can't even drive right. He always gets red as a beet when he's behind the wheel, the runt."

"God in heaven, is that any way to speak about your father? Has it ever occurred to you that the 'runt' has provided for you for more than twenty years? That he knocks himself out every day so you can have food, clothes on your back, and a roof over your head?"

"Spare me the broken record. I know, I know, I owe you eternal gratitude. I don't owe you a fucking thing, if you really want to know. It's expected that parents will provide for their children. Your parents provided for you, too."

"But we were grateful."

"I've heard enough! If you don't shut up, I'm going to get nasty!"

"I'd like to see that!" Her eyes are blazing.

"You will, too! I'm warning you, Jackass. If I hear another word out of you, I'm going to explode!"

"Well, go ahead and explode! You think I'm afraid of you?"

"I don't give a damn. I'm going to submerge myself." I push her aside and go into the bathroom.

"But your dinner will get cold."

I lock the door and run water into the tub while I undress. Yelling made me feel better. Now for a hot bath. I have to wash off all the filth, from school and from the whorehouse.

I get into the tub. The hot bath calms me. I turn on the shower for more hot water.

"Why are you showering in the bath? You're going to flood the whole bathroom."

"If you don't shut up this minute, I'll come out just the way I am and throw you in, clothes and all."

I heave myself out of the tub.

"Don't splatter water all over!"

"I'll splatter if I feel like it." And with whatever I feel like.

"But I expect you to mop up the bathroom."

"I'll mop you up, if you don't shut your trap."

"Is that any way to talk to your mother?"

"Just you wait!" I throw open the bathroom door and rush at my mother, dripping water everywhere.

"Are you meshugge? You'll catch cold. Dry yourself off this minute!"

"On the contrary. I'm going to get you wet, too!"

"Gevalt! Nebbich my son's completely meshugge."

She flees to her kitchen and locks herself in. I stomp to my room, throw myself down on the bed, and pull the bedspread up over my ears. After a while I feel a pleasant warmth spreading through my arms and legs.

*

Why did I let Bauriedl get under my skin that way?

Why does this keep happening to me?

Because I'm a softy and a cry-baby. But no more. Instead of tears and hurt feelings, nothing but icy hatred—for the Germans!

All right, I've been lying around enough now. I pull on my clothes and storm out of my room.

"Where are you going? You can't go out with wet hair! You'll catch cold."

"So what if I do? Then you can fuss over me." I slam the door behind me.

Class Boycott

You've got to go in eventually. If you stand out here in the hall, everyone who goes into the classroom will see you. Then they'll all know that you're scared to go in. Why do I keep running away? What can these creeps do to me anyway? Nothing!

I open the door. Most of them are already there. The minute they catch sight of me, they stop talking. Heavy silence surrounds me. I go to Kraxi's old seat, drop my briefcase on the desk, and collapse onto the wooden chair. It's easy to imagine what happened after I left yesterday. Doubtless Frau Taucher felt called upon to expatiate on the "reprehensibility of anti-Semitism." When will she and her well-meaning colleagues realize that these idiotic lectures achieve just the opposite of what they intend?

The standard-issue indoctrination on the Jewish Question has been dished up so many times that no one listens anymore. What I really can't stand is when they take up the "Final Solution" in history class with good old German thoroughness. Many students feel ashamed, and everyone's embarrassed by the whole thing— except me, it seems. None of them realize that I'm always asking myself: Would you have acted any differently if you'd been a German? How can you be sure you wouldn't have joined the Party or the SS?

The guys haven't the slightest suspicion. On the contrary, they think I'm arrogant because I don't discuss it with them. But what should I say when I'm asked for the hundredth time if it wasn't "only four million" after all?

Or whether "the whole business with the gas chambers" wasn't a "Jewish scam to get money out of Germany?" Will the Germans ever forgive us for their guilty conscience?

During recess my feeling of being ostracized gets worse. Even Klaus Winterer, a guy I usually shoot the breeze with, turns away. My hatred, which gave me strength last night, has turned to weakness. I have a tingly feeling in my elbows and the hollows of my knees. If only one of the fellows would at least look at me. Nothing. As if I didn't exist. Yet I'm standing only five feet away from them in the schoolyard.

Suddenly Wolfgang Pauls yells out in Bavarian dialect, "Who's got fifty pfennig?"

Involuntarily I reach into my pocket, fish out a coin, and toss it to him. You idiot! Must you suck up to them at every opportunity?

Pauls actually catches the coin, a reflex action. But the second he realizes it came from me, his mouth and eyes widen in dismay. He catches himself instantly, presses his lips together, and frowns. With a swift movement he hurls the coin down at my feet.

You couldn't have offered him a better opening to make a fool of you. Everyone in the class knows how embarrassed he is about our earlier friendship, now that he hangs out with National Democrats and other neo-Nazi groups. The "National Socialist" Wolfgang Pauls, for years the inseparable friend of Jewboy Rubinstein! No wonder Wolfgang's "political activism" has been smirked at by the rest of the class up to now. And you, dummy, have to go and give him a chance to show all of them that he's broken with his "Jew-lover" past. No need to even say a word—he can demonstrate his contempt in silence.

Are the anti-Semites poor devils themselves, as my friend Peter always claims? Or are guys like Franz Bauriedl and Wolfgang Pauls really superior to me? In any case, they manage to hurt me whenever they feel like it. And why? Because they're at home in this country, and we, no matter what they may say, are foreigners.

ROBERT SCHINDEL

prolog from
Gebürtig

Two-Headed Lamb

> You can't get out of your head
> You can't get into the dream
> Your heart goes out walking
> You can't get out of your heart.
> *Jakob Haringer*

1.

THE CHILDREN OF THE TWO-HEADED EAGLE were for the most part sheep, who spent their lives wallowing in blood and shit, so that their eventual slaughter satisfied no one, except God. And we are their children, literary editor Demant told his heart as he was trotting one April evening around eleven to his favorite pub. These lambs are occasionally medium-wild, and on most of them two heads sprouted from their wool a good while ago. One head bleats, the other one munches the bleating. Around one neck hangs a goitrous bell, around the other a clapper like a necktie.

Demant took a long stride in order not to step in a woman's laugh, the vomited remains of which were lying on the sidewalk, and his thoughts worked their way up from there to Christiane, his girlfriend during February, July, and November of the last two years.

Christiane was sitting in the pub, considering how she could communicate her fantasies to her girlfriend without vacuuming her up from the conversation carpet. Finally a laugh welled up from her belly, floated awkwardly through the pub, and slowly dripped down on the people sitting around. No one could describe these fantasies, outside it had cleared up, up front by the bar stood the unemployed sociologist Masha Singer from Ottakring and the designer Erich Stiglitz from Mauthausen. A snowdrifted hamburger with ketchup formed as much a part of Christiane's fantasies as the sounds of shoulder-bites in Yesterland, which is perhaps in Lilienfeld on the Traisen. Christiane Kalteisen began working as a psychotherapist last winter. Now she was sitting next to her girlfriend, but she was looking among her own faces for one with which she could greet the approaching Demant.

Otherwise, in addition to me, there were half a hundred people in the pub, so that except for Danny Demant everything was all set. But until he gets there, the stories take place behind my back. I, by the way, am fairly well distributed around the pub, for I write down whatever comes my way, so that the various wordlessnesses leave traces. I'm Sasha Graffito.

Demant entered his pub. Christiane raised her head, shaped with the corners of her mouth the mockingbird face she had prepared, such that Demant brought to a conclusion the conversation he was having with his heart, saying:

These lambs, you know, the grandchildren of the two-headed eagle, are very inward human animals at certain levels, gutshot in their body languages, positively charged step-poles in their pupils, but perdominated by a solemn sensuality. When they raise their heads and look into the good Lord's open heavens, from thence comes their fear of bombs and poison rain, causing them to ring bells, sing slogans, while from their innards life-lust and love-guile make their wool moist. In their hearts and lungs lurk faith and superstition, which express themselves in their brains as I-DENTITY and I-NESS. In case the lambs then name themselves, each has before its own name a HEAR HEAR or a RELATED NEITHER BY BLOOD NOR MARRIAGE as a title.

Lookahere, he greeted Christiane mockingly, and since he just managed to trap his depression behind his teeth, he kissed her elegantly and light-lippedly but not hastily between her restless mouth-corners, pulled his pullover over his head, and sat down.

> The two-headed lamb of innocence
> Nibbles down the inner turf
> Shaped from the temporal slime
> Each head must want itself in the other.

2.

What is this thirty-five-year-old Stiglitz, blond and from Upper Austria, supposed to talk about with this Jewish-Viennese Singer woman from Ottakring, I ask myself, and surely Stiglitz is asking himself the same question. Yet the two know one another. They have friends in common, Danny Demant and me, for instance, and they see each other at parties now, as before at demonstrations and always in pubs. They know such and such about each other. Stiglitz is standing here because he has no one at home, and he looks into the women's eyes and drinks wine. Masha is waiting for friends and acquaintances and letting herself be looked at. Out of the corners of her eyes she has noticed Demant and will exchange a few more empty phrases with Erich and then go to Danny's table. Erich nods to Demant but will stay where he is, because at Danny's table they talk talk talk, and you can be sure of going home alone.

Because Masha is making the transition from the empty phrases to the pauses between the empty phrases, Erich notices that she will be leaving in a moment. He feels stomach acid welling up, he looks into the eyes of this dark-haired woman and says:

Mauthausen is a lovely area.

Masha nods, then stops nodding. Now I should be unable to

breathe, she thinks to herself, for remarks like this have always made her go rigid. She's never been able to discover whether such things actually upset her—she simply gets upset.

Hey, listen, she said, that was a tasteless remark. Come on, he said, I grew up there. I should know. The area's very lovely. As a child I always played in the concentration camp. An incredible playground. Do you think I thought anything of it when I was ten? I was twenty when I found out that my uncle was a prisoner there.

All right, Masha gets upset, all right. Children will be children. But now you're three times that age. How can you rattle on in such blue-eyed innocence?

For miscegenation, by the way, Erich continues. Well, because I'm innocent. Stiglitz puts the glass down behind him. Now he sees there's no question of leaving. The supercilious sociologist is standing transfixed on his playground. The butcher who provided the SS with meat may be retired, but Erich knows him well. He grew up with Murner's son, and Murner was SS in the camp.

Well? Masha shoots sparks at him: You think it's not your fault.

How can it be my fault?

Because you talk about it so calmly. You talk in such a blue-eyed way.

While little Erich clambers around on the death steps of Mauthausen, time passes as though Masha were being thrown into the quarry again. In the cold metropolis of Vienna she wants to darken the filthy sky even more for him. He sees clearly that she's mocking him with her indignation; calmly she pulls one dead relative after the other out of her womb, without saying a word, so that the marbles roll out of little Erich's hand, but instead of bouncing down the steps of the quarry, merrily, they disappear into the wide-open mouths of those smashed cadavers.

Masha sees nothing of the sort. Once again she's simultaneously beside herself and sunk deep into herself, as if her sandbox were filled with ashes. Before she can raise her hands in self-defense, little Erich leaps into big Erich's belly with Karacho, and Stiglitz narrows his lips into a thin line:

Asshole, he says, beat it! I'm never talking to you again! You want to make me out to be a fascist? Get the hell out of here!

> There stands the lamb with two heads
> Wants to go pale, at the same time red
> In order not to exhaust itself thereby
> Both heads are necessary

3.

While I empty my glass of wine, I see Masha hurrying with hunched shoulders to the table where Demant and Kalteisen are sitting. Erich Stiglitz stares at her back before he drops his eyes to the floor, reaches behind him, looks at the empty glass, frees himself from the wall, and goes around the corner to the men's room.

Masha is sitting next to Danny now and reporting to him: as she does so, he isn't looking at her, is only an ear to her. Christiane Kalteisen is talking and laughing into her girlfriend; the latter is merrily woven into the carefree exchange, so that for me this table breaks into its two halves, as if between the twos a glass wall were going up, silent, invisible, hermetic. Stiglitz comes back and takes up his position again, orders another glass and, like me, observes this quartet.

Masha's eyes are moist, but Demant has gone outside of the room with his eyes and perhaps outside of time; his ear seems to be representing him completely. Even during the pauses that Masha now interpolates and into which Demant plunges his face, none of his spiritual presence can be detected. His ear disappears behind his cheekbones, his eyes register the gradual transformations in Masha's face as nothing but a random face, the passage of time in another face.

Of course, now she's going to weep on the shoulder of her Jewish friend, Stiglitz thinks. The Viennese are sitting there and shitting on him, while he can do nothing but drink wine and stare at the floor. He cannot deny that Masha exerts an attraction on him, in that his obscene birthplace has linked him with— what he considers—her Jewish posturing in the crudest way. This attraction leads him to come up with evidence, since he has long since gotten over his provincial status. But the very same attraction seduces him into insisting on his origins and conducting himself accordingly. He feels it has to be intellectual women who must accept him as a man, preferably even ones whose broken pride makes them appear desirable. On the other hand, it strikes him as ridiculous that after ten years in Vienna he still feels like a social climber from the country, without fitting in effortlessly, as he long since earned the right to. One would like to assume that the Jews of all people have developed sensitivity to discrimination, but instead of joining forces with him because his foreignness might mirror their own foreignness, they fancy themselves the quintessential urbane intelligentsia. They of all people, as if back then, not without further ado, they hadn't been humiliated in the most ridiculous fashion before they were hauled off.

Masochistic to the point of asphyxiation, but playing up her victim status vis-à-vis him. Then abandoning him there. In Masha's eyes (Stiglitz drills this thought into his soul) I belong to the eternal victors in this country. That's why I'm doomed to be an eternal loser in this city.

But Masha talks for a while in the direction of Demant. At the moment she doesn't even want to know what he thinks, but she's speaking against her sinking feeling, out of uncertainty. It doesn't matter whether justifications plough through the mounting sadnesses. At each of the words, as well as at the penultimate syllables, vague sensations of failure overshadow them.

This makes her speech more and more ambivalent and makes it pull out of itself fragments of pauses, while her eyes grow moist.

It seems as though she could be provoked by this Stiglitz without having been personally affected for even a moment. Not that he interests her, but even so she was able to read from his movements the attraction she exerted on him. But as she now notices again, her Jewishness has taken on a haphazard existence uncoupled from the rest of her expressive capability; by virtue of this uncoupling, those movements of his that refer to her interrupt themselves and continue, so it seems to her. The independent existence of her breasts and legs, her voice and her eyes, is already so familiar to her and altogether a woman's thing, but such separate attributes affect blond mama's boys like Stiglitz like specially handled sedimented charnel-Hebrew, that's how it feels to her. They have long since broken out of Masha's time and are making Upper Austrian landscapes truly Upper Austrian. Without its accidental Jewish vagina, the lovely landscape of Mauthausen is completely uninteresting to Erich Stiglitz. Since Masha sees herself as excluded but because of that as desired and coveted, she must at least be allowed to produce a little fluster.

When he talks about it so calmly now, he's actually deporting me; he's forcing a heritage on me that I haven't assumed, and calmly assuming possession of his own.

All of them, all, calmly and innocently left behind the Jewbeating and all the other feelings of homeland, they're standing around with a naturalness that resembles the area where they feel so cozily at home.

He says quite simply, Masha tells Demant, that I have to go to bed with him, because Austria's deeply involved in foreign affairs.

Come on, come on, goes Demant.

In any case he doesn't care a bit about my sensitivity. I'm not going to put up with it. Nothing has changed. Their fathers stuck ours in the furnaces, their mothers said the Rosary, and the sons broadmindedly want to include us and in the meantime ignore us, even want to be victims themselves.

Aren't they? Demant asked, from across time and space.

They remain the locals. The victors. And they chop me up. And I exist in pieces. And what I am is foreign to me. That's what they want! And I'm not putting up with it anymore!

He, too, consists only of pieces. Demant dips his face into a long pause before he says this.

Masha stares at him, full of emotion: But the Danube connects them, she hisses bombastically. You know, Danny, his pieces are what make up this country. I'm supposed to drown in something like that. That would suit them fine, those blue-eyed mama's boys.

It would suit me fine, too. I mean, they're drowning in it themselves. Shouldn't we all drown in it together?

Masha Singer now answers softly, and once again the end syllables darken:

I know I'm incomprehensible to you.

Demant smiles. What good does it do if I understand you precisely? If he considers Mauthausen a pretty area, at least you can leave that be. Oh, you just want to be like him. Again. Or like her. And Masha stares with an impenetrable face at Christiane Kalteisen.

Demant throws back his head, his voice hisses a little at the beginning of each syllable: Aren't our Jews allowed to be a little dead occasionally, or must they always remain alert, even in the form of bonemeal?

Masha shakes her head and opens her lips, but instead of dark-syllabled words nothing comes out; instead, her tears fall back into her mouth.

> Far off in heaven the airy grave
> Of the six million lambs
> The two-headed lamb now seeks counsel
> From the land of the sons, land of the hammers.

BARBARA HONIGMANN

Novel of a Child

D EAR JOSEF,

I would like to write you a letter. A long letter, with everything in it. As long as a novel. The novel of a child.

You will doubtless say that a person would have to be in
pretty bad straits to resort to such things as long letters and
novels. I know you think none of this helps, but you know that
I think it does. How does it happen that we are all so forsaken
by God? Sometimes I'm afraid there *is* no real redemption, for
it would have to come as a gift, and we always have to buy
everything, buy, buy, buy.

Dear Josef, I hope our friendship never ends, ever; I hope
there will always be at least something—I don't know what—
between us. In all these years of our not seeing each other things
have gotten easier between us, haven't they? I mean, easy-diffi-
cult, as opposed to difficult-difficult, because everything else is
so difficult-difficult. I think of you so often, and often I'd like to
ask you what to do. I'd like to write to you and tell you how I
am and what's been happening and how everything turned out.
Sometimes I'm afraid you're angry with me. I want to tell you
so much—everything—and you never want to say a word. Why
is that?

Can you see me? I'm lying in bed, sick, and I've been in bed
so long that sometimes it feels as though I'll never be able to
get up again, and will never be well again. Of course I don't
have a real illness, and it's silly to think a doctor could help.

Just once I'd like to hold a feather in my hand, or a golden ball—if I touched myself and you with it, we'd be redeemed—or a magic word, but no one knows the word. There may be one person who does. First one would have to find him, however, and find the way—but no, no one knows that.

Occasionally, when I fall into conversation with people I don't really know, on the street or at the greengrocer's, and we compare notes on shopping and then move on to this or that, and they tell me something about their family, there sometimes comes a moment, I don't know why, when suddenly I feel so lighthearted, so relieved, and I'm hopeful that I can pick up something from them. At times like this it no longer seems to me as though nobody knows anything, but as though I'm the only one who doesn't. Maybe they know everything, and everything's really very simple; I don't know, but maybe I can learn it from them. Sometimes you get a feeling like that when you look at night into the brightly lit windows of the house across the way, or when you walk down streets in an unfamiliar part of town, past houses and gardens. Everything looks so peaceful and happily self-sufficient, and I'm filled with longing and think, there, behind that window, in that house, they know how to do everything properly. And I feel like going up to the house and knocking and asking whether I may come in, and whether I may live there, and I'd like to stay with those people forever.

Oh, Josef, I really would like to see you. Sometimes I think: if only I could see you just once. We could play Chinese checkers or Hangman, and we could discuss everything.

Do you remember the time we went out to Sagorsk, taking the little suburban train and disobeying our instructions to stay within a thirty-kilometer radius of Moscow? How we passed the gardens and dachas and the large and small villas, and everything looked just the way it's described in Russian novels? There was deep snow in Sagorsk, and we held hands and walked down the road that ran through the village, with narrow little wooden houses huddled in the snow on either side. The road

led farther and farther downhill, and the monastery seemed to
rise higher and higher in front of us. Way up above, we saw its
little forest of gold and bluish-purple domes and turrets and
crosses. When we finally got there, we didn't know what we
were supposed to do, and opened the first door we came upon.
Inside was a vast space with many people praying and lighting
candles, and so many beggars and cripples followed us around
and plucked at our coats. It all seemed so uncanny that we
wanted to leave at once. Do you remember? Then many other
churches, all dark, always with icons, always with candles; we
couldn't stand it anymore and ran outside and found ourselves
in the snow again, and it was so cold. But then we came upon
a little chapel, like a small child among all the grown-up
churches. Many people were pushing to get inside, and we
heard that holy water flowed there. That made us want to go
inside, too. The holy water was flowing from a beer tap mounted
on a crucifix, and people were standing in line to fill bottles.
Most of them were vodka bottles, wrapped in a copy of *Pravda*.
Suddenly a fat old woman pressed a booklet into my hand and
said I should open it and read. It was in Cyrillic from beginning
to end. No, not to myself, but out loud, the old woman said; I
should read it aloud for the others. A cluster of old women had
already formed around me, waiting expectantly. They said the
booklet contained the revelation of a forgotten saint, but they
couldn't read. I was supposed to proclaim the revelation, yet
could barely decipher it. But the old women helped me—they
knew the text by heart. I wasn't allowed to stop until the entire
booklet had been read. It took a long time, and suddenly I realized I had no idea where you were and was afraid I'd lost you,
but I couldn't go and look for you, for the old women were
holding onto me tightly. When they finally let go, I lingered to
drink a little glass of holy water, already afraid I'd never see
you again, but then suddenly I saw you, right there in the corner
close to me, leaning against the wall, and you'd been standing
there the whole time watching me.

And do you remember how, very late that evening, when we

were back in Moscow, you asked me, "And what if it helps, drinking that holy water?"

But it didn't help; we didn't stay together.

And what was it that drove us apart? Did I hurt you somehow? You hurt me badly, too, you know.

I often find myself wondering just when it was, on what day we lost each other. On what day were we still together, and on what day were we alone and on our own again. I wish I could at least pinpoint the moment of transition, when we crossed the dividing line and everything was different. In the beginning, when a person comes into the world, there's a clear transition, but then, after that, later, one thing always flows into the next. I want to tell you what it was like when my son was born.

On the morning of September 30 I went to the hospital in Berlin-Buch to be examined, but nothing was happening yet. I took a walk in the woods in Buch, even though it was raining, and I walked a long distance, until I was utterly exhausted.

Coming home on the municipal railway I ran into a friend of mine, and she came back to my place with me. We had tea and talked, and she told me about her father's dying when she was still a child. She had never really spoken about it, even though we'd known each other for a long time. Then another friend came by and brought a few baby things, including a cap his wife had knitted specially for me. Then I left the house again, because I was supposed to meet another friend; she'd been collecting baby things for me, too, and I wanted to pick them up. I took the municipal railway out to Karlshorst, where I'd lived for a long time and she and I had gone to school together. Just after I got there I felt a stabbing pain in my big belly, but I didn't want to mention it. I felt awkward with my friend, because she's a doctor and I didn't want to seem to be taking advantage of her. But it was definitely labor pains, and we had to order a taxi in a hurry and go to my place and get my bag packed. And then the long ride back to the hospital. There they told me I was already very far along and it would be at most two more hours, and the midwife asked whether anyone should be informed. I said she should call my mother.

But as it turned out, I was in labor all night. It's true that it hurts, but I felt proud and strong and in complete control of myself. I'd asked the midwife to turn out the light, and she'd done that, so I lay there all alone in the darkened labor room, with only a glimmer of light coming in from the corridor. Everything was still. The doctor and the midwife had lain down to catch some sleep, and it wasn't until later, toward morning, that another woman was put in the room with me. Between contractions I exchanged a few words with her. We were perfectly calm, and I found myself thinking of Kleist's letter: "Serene, as near the hour of death." Then I saw that it was getting light outside. As long as it had been dark, it had seemed to me as though I could still change my mind. But when daylight came, I knew there was no going back, because everything was starting up again: people came in, people went out, they talked and made a lot of noise, a new time was about to start, the pace was picking up.

Outside the window I saw a tree; it seemed to me it had turned yellow overnight.

Then it was time for the child to be brought into the world. And suddenly everything was upside down, and I felt as if I were racing through all the elements at once, fire, water, and a hail of stones, and I could no longer tell whether I was giving birth or being born myself. And when the midwife said, Hold your breath, I didn't know how, I didn't know what she meant, for I couldn't tell my various limbs and organs apart—they were all fused into one. It got louder and louder and more and more hectic. The midwife was barking orders like a captain in a storm at sea. Finally I kicked her and the doctor and spewed out the child. And a moment later perfect calm reigned. Not a trace of pain in my body, nothing but peace.

When I left the hospital a week later, everything in my apartment had become completely strange to me. Bed and chairs, books and pictures. Everything that wasn't the child and belonged to an earlier period in my life now seemed "outside." But the child seemed utterly natural to me and as close as I am to myself, and it seemed ludicrous to say, "I've had a child." There was simply more of me now.

Other than my mother and my women friends, no one was waiting for the child. On all the forms I had to fill out, wherever I saw the word "Father" I simply drew a long line. And make no mistake, that's not easy to do. Not because a specific father is missing, but because it's like placing the final stroke on the certificate of abandonment.

And then I hung around home and watched over my son and nurtured him like a little plant, starting from almost nothing. Every evening I sat by his little bed and just stared at him and wondered at him, the way he lay there so still and was asleep and yet alive. And every morning I would pack my child up like a little bundle and carry him down the three flights of stairs and put him in the carriage and take him for a walk in the park. Soon the long winter came, and there wasn't really anything beautiful in the park, but I always had the sense I was leading a wonderful life now, and I was perfectly calm and focused during this period. I would sit down on a cold park bench and read my book and glance into the carriage again and again, unable to grasp that it was my child lying there, not just a child, not just any child, no, mine, my child.

I'd never felt happiness in my entire body before, like warm, soft, rolling waves. Suddenly it had become impossible for me to imagine that I'd been alive for any length of time before this. Every remnant of my former life filled me with amazement, all the things that had been there before— the nail polish on my toes, for instance; why was it still there? I found myself thinking of ruins, with walls still standing and scraps of wallpaper clinging to them; sometimes you can tell where a picture used to hang. It was as if I had to reacquaint myself with everything from scratch; and when company came it bothered me, because I much preferred being alone with my child. I have no idea where such a powerful love and sense of being tethered can come from all of a sudden. "Feeling tethered amidst a gale of feelings of freedom: that is revelation." Someone told me Nietzsche was supposed to have said that.

I began to sleep differently, too; I was no longer lost to the world as before; it was a sort of half-sleep, in which I kept a sense of how I was lying and the position of all my limbs, a dimness in which the boundaries between my body and that of my child melted, and I often felt as though I were lying in the bassinet myself, and didn't know whether I was the mother or the infant.

This continued for a long time. When my son got his first tooth, I often caught myself standing in front of the mirror with my mouth open, looking for his tooth in my mouth. And one time my son and I were kissing each other on the mouth, and we were holding onto each other tightly and pulling each other close, more and more tightly, until the child was so firmly attached to me by suction that neither of us could breathe. Everything went black before my eyes, and I felt dizzy, as if just before death, and I pulled him away from me with all my strength. I had saved both our lives.

But that didn't really happen; it was a dream.

You want to do nothing but loving things for your child, yet somehow you do exactly the wrong things. That's how it is with other people, too; when you really love someone, it's always an imposition on that person. I'm convinced that parents always remain in their children's debt, not the other way around.

But I couldn't get over my amazement at the way one immediately becomes so terribly fond of this little child, whom one didn't even know before and who for a long time isn't even a proper human being, but more like a little animal. It's nice that at first the two of you live with each other in silence for so long and only gradually find one word after another and learn to spell out all of life.

Before this, I'd thought that when you had a child you were more protected and buffered against the outside world and against everything. But that's not true at all—everything is a source of so much fear and worry, and you get even more sensitive than before. Before I had the child, I was never scared to walk at night through the park, and I was never afraid in an airplane or a car, and never locked my door. But now everything's different—I'm afraid in a car, I'm afraid of flying, at night I lock the door from the inside and am fearful of hundreds of things that could happen to me or my child.

Just after Johannes' birth, on the long evenings when it was always so quiet in my apartment, I read *Wilhelm Meister* and then *Green Henry*. Actually I have no idea why I would feel close to these two protagonists. To Green Henry, perhaps, because of his boundless expectations and his failure in the end, and with Wilhelm Meister I'm sure it was because of this passage in the *Apprenticeship* where Wilhelm is watching his son Felix sleep:

> "Oh!" he cried out, "who knows what trials still await me, who knows how much past mistakes will continue to torment me, how often good and reasonable plans for the future will go awry; but let me keep this treasure, now that I possess it, merciful or unmerciful Fate! If it were possible that this best part of myself could perish before me, that this heart could be ripped from my heart, then farewell to understanding and reason, farewell to all care and caution, begone, O instinct for self-preservation! May all that distinguishes us from the animals vanish! And if it is not permitted to put an end to one's sorrowful days voluntarily, may early madness obliterate consciousness, before death, which destroys it forever, brings on the long night."

Once, a year or two later, we had an unusual day. I was staying with my friend in her little house on the island of Usedom, and it was already very warm, though it was only May. I was sitting naked in a lawnchair reading an illustrated paper we had just picked up at the grocery store in the village. Johannes, my son, was playing with the garden hose and had got himself all wet. Under a shade tree my friend's baby was sitting in his little chair. I wasn't really reading the paper, just paging through it and looking at the pictures. On one page there was a very small photo, a photo from the war, and I didn't pay any attention to it, but when I had already folded up the paper, I suddenly wanted to go back and look at the picture. It showed a German soldier aiming his gun at a woman. The woman had a child in her arms. The woman with the child in her arms was running away from the soldier. The child was already a big boy of five or six, and for some inexplicable reason his pants had slid all the way down to his feet. The soldier was shooting, and the woman was running. The soldier was pursuing the woman; he was not only shooting her, he was also pursuing her.

My friend came out of the house and I don't know why, but I quickly folded up the newspaper. Later I actually hid it from her; I didn't want her to see that picture. Maybe because I wanted to spare her, or because looking at it together would have made us feel helpless and would have driven a wedge between us, I don't know.

Later we went for a walk with the children, all the way to the next village. It has a Baroque castle by a pond covered with water lilies. It once formed part of an estate and is crumbling away, the interior almost ruined with layers and layers of oil paint, but at least it's there. It was a lovely, mild afternoon, and all the people seemed so friendly, and I myself had a great desire to be friendly to everyone, and somehow grateful. We felt fond of our children and fond of each other, my friend and I, and suddenly everything seemed to be pressing in on my heart, for it was still soft and vulnerable from the sight of that picture, as though I myself had just survived something terrible and oppressive.

On the way back to the cottage we picked an armful of white hawthorn, in homage to Proust, and talked about the beginning of *Remembrance of Things Past*, about the role of sleep and night, and how ultimately the whole book becomes a surfeit of wakefulness, in which nothing remains unseen, unheard, untouched, unsmelled, or untasted. At some point I'd opened the first volume of Proust, out of pure curiosity, and begun to read, but then, after the passage with the madeleine, I'd gone on to read all seven volumes, almost without stopping. I revere certain writers, but none as much as Proust, for Proust speaks so clearly that it's as if he were reading my own thoughts to me, thoughts I didn't even know I had.

And when evening came and I was alone again, and Johannes was asleep next to me in his little bed, that picture came back to me: the woman running with her boy, and the soldier taking aim at her, and the way the boy's pants had slipped down. Somehow that was the worst part: those pants.

And then I thought: strange, today was a day entirely different from all the others, no trace of my usual absentmindedness; no, I was alert, I could see, I could hear.

And then I thought:

They can't kill all the children, can they, so that none of them have a chance to grow up? Who is it who murders them so that none of them can grow up and become adults? It's them. Them: who are they?

Children, now we're going to play the very last game.

Count off.

Run and hide.

When they come, they mustn't be able to find us.   ·

They want to finger us, but we won't be anywhere to be seen.

Get out of here, quick, pack your stuff, quick, they're coming, run, and if one of you falls down, get up immediately.

Quick.

But they'll get you.

Hide.

But they find everyone.

Not us.

One day I went to look for the little synagogue, the only one in Berlin, and found it in a rear courtyard in the middle of the city, where the city is at its most crowded and most terrible. The synagogue was decked out, for it was the evening of the Seder, the first evening of Passover, and many people were expected. But we sat in a very small room, like a classroom, I thought, and the few people who were there huddled together, like school-children in a classroom when most of their classmates haven't returned yet from summer vacation. I felt like a stranger and at the same time welcome.

I sat in the back with the women. We sat close together, and I took a book like the others, opened it to the back, and leafed backwards, returning with the others to ancient times in Egypt. The ark of the Torah was draped with a white cloth on which a gold Star of David gleamed, decorated with jewels that formed bright ornaments. Because the room was so small, even those of us in the last row were so close to it that we could see the jewels were only glass. The prayers were rapid and almost hasty, yet strong and masculine, not pleading but demanding. The service very short, everything soon over, and then all those present stood up and wished one another a happy holiday, and those who knew each other better kissed.

Then those with families went home, and those who were alone, and I with them, went to the community center, for a Seder had been set up for them there. The community center is on a different street from the synagogue, so the tiny group piled into a couple of cars, and as they drove off in the battered little cars, I was really seeing the most dispersed of the Diaspora, the Jews of the Jews. We drove by way of Prenzlauer Allee and Alexanderplatz. Alexanderplatz always used to be such a challenge to me, presenting an obstacle through which I had to fight my way, and then the whole trip was usually in vain: from all the running and waiting and moving on and up and down steps my strength was exhausted. But curiously enough, on this day, when I rattled across the square in the midst of this random little group, the square became so easy for me, even laughable, for we didn't have to force our way across it; it opened up for us, like the Red Sea, and the eternal, gray, lowering column of clouds shook out its rain, and when we looked around, it was storming and raging, and Alexanderplatz was behind us and couldn't catch us anymore and had vanished into the rain and mist like Pharaoh's army.

When we reached Oranienburger Strasse, the tables were already set. Each person looked for a place to sit, but I didn't bother to look; I simply sat down at the first table I came to. A few old ladies were already sitting there, and I talked with them. Then someone joined us; at first I was so caught up in the conversation that I barely noticed, but I sensed a presence, glowing, big, beautiful, dark, and erect, and I had to stop talking and look, for it might be the Queen Sabbath. And the Queen Sabbath addressed me and said, "Hello, Babu." She knew me, and I knew her, too. It was Daisy. I'd gone to school with her, a few grades behind her. I'd always admired her, because she was so beautiful, but in all our years at school there'd been just a few times when we'd stood together in the schoolyard, and since then I hadn't seen her, only sometimes heard something about her. Now she was here, and she sat down beside me and stayed with me the entire evening, and we chattered incessantly, and no one scolded us. There we were, in a ground-floor room off a rear courtyard, in the "Cultural Room" of a Jewish community center, and the prescribed question was asked: What makes this night different from all other nights? And then the narrative began, the long Haggadah; the cantor sang the long song of servitude in Egypt, and we read the text in a brightly illustrated book that we'd found at our places. Four hundred and thirty wretched years of servitude. With the others I dipped a hard-boiled egg in salt water and ate bitter herbs and unleavened bread and drank wine, four goblets full, no more and no less. The wine came from Israel, and the matzoh from Budapest, and the books in our hands from Basel, and the cantor who sang for us from West Berlin. And where would Elijah, for whom we'd left the door open, come from? And would he come? But somehow I knew already that he wouldn't come. I'd thought about it so often before, Elijah or the Messiah or God: none of them can risk making an appearance here anymore.

Then, at some point in the middle of the long tale, the food came. A large, lavish meal, as if before this we'd really had only sand in our mouths. The meal came from the kitchen in the next room, and was passed through a little window. We had to stand in line, like in a company cafeteria, and people shoved and pushed in the line.

The first to receive his meal was the cantor, and I looked at him and saw that the strain of such long, dignified singing must have been very hard on him. What else would make him gulp down his food so ravenously, as if hunted, with his head almost in his plate as he glanced furtively to left and right. He was sitting all alone at the long table, which in the meantime looked somewhat the worse for wear, little old Polish Abraham Süss, whose name, after all he had gone through, should perhaps have meant Bitter instead of Sweet. I had to look away.

Then we all ate, and the food warmed us through and through, and all the people were talking and having a good time; most were talking about the way things used to be, and after a while they were overcome with sadness. The old women at my table wanted to see a picture of my son, and I showed them one, and they admired him and became quite merry. And then sad again. Then they were all full from the large meal and drowsy from the heavy wine, and it was late already, and through the window you could see out into the dark courtyard, and you could see a little light glowing on the fire escape, a pale Star of David on a rusty Jacob's ladder.

Abraham Süss began to sing again. The second part contains the great prayers and quite a few songs, and the tale was still long, but gradually it was nearing the end, and then came the part where in large letters is written:

NEXT YEAR IN JERUSALEM!

That's where it stopped, and the evening was over. We stood up and said good-bye to each other, and one of the old women drove me in her old car through the dark city to my place.

Once I had a dream. I was with all the others in Auschwitz, and in the dream I thought: finally I've found my place in life.

But then I thought of the pale star and the Jacob's ladder.

Dear Josef,

Now I've actually started this letter. Of course I could never tell you everything the way I've written it down. In a letter one can write things much more easily; in a letter one feels safer.

Downstairs, outside my house, is the mailbox. In the morning I drop all my letters in and bang three times to make sure they get to their destination; that's something my girlfriend showed me. But sometimes in the evening I'm afraid, and I find myself wondering whether it's a real mailbox, and whether some day, when I look more closely, I'll discover that it's actually an old cardboard box, with nothing inside but dead leaves. What if we never see each other again? Sometimes I feel so mournful about everything; out of sheer mournfulness I wake up at night, and during the day I'm so sad I sometimes burst into tears.

Sometimes I have such a yearning. A yearning to have you near, so we could sit together and talk, not because I have anything in particular to say or because I want to hear an answer; no, just the warmth of sitting close to each other would be enough. In such a conversation a moment sometimes comes when you feel really close to the other person and everything seems so cozy that you'd like to stretch out on all the words and lie down in the sentences as in a comfortable old easy chair. In my mother's apartment there was a big chair like that, and I would lie in it and read a book when I was all alone in the apartment, and, at least as I remember it, I was almost always alone in the apartment. When you're stretched out in such a chair or in a familiar conversation, sometimes you're filled with courage, from where I don't know, not a big courage, just a small one, just big enough to let you think: ah, maybe I'll manage after all.

And what is it you want to manage, you ask me. What I mean is life as a whole. You see, usually I think I won't manage, that I can't manage at all. A day comes when I go into the bathroom and there's a puddle on the floor, and I see that it comes from the toilet, and I feel sick to my stomach because I realize that the toilet is stopped up, and all my courage ebbs—how am I supposed to get it fixed? But then I pull myself together and lift the cover and bravely begin to bail out the toilet, and I feel like throwing up, but I reach far in and pull out laundry, laundry, yards and yards of dirty laundry. And then I finally call my boyfriend, who's been sitting in the next room all along and must realize what's happened, but doesn't stir to check up on me and offer help. Then he finally comes, but he immediately sits down on a bucket and leans his head against the wall and turns pale and faints.

And I stand there, between the clogged toilet, the dirty laundry, and this man who's passed out.

That wasn't real, that was a dream, but then it really is that way. It's so hard for me to live in so many worlds at once, because things don't fit together. I often wonder whether it's the same for you. But for you things are surely different; you seem to live more straightforwardly, without all this vacillation.

Even in his shape a man is straighter, with sharper lines and even some sharp edges. The last two winters I often went to an evening class in life drawing. We had men and women as models, and for the first time I really noticed how straight everything is in men, whereas in women everything is so curved. And I often thought that men can probably stick to such a straight path simply because of the way they're shaped.

Sometimes I have a waking dream that a path comes to me and lies down before me and speaks with me and says, Come, follow me, I will lead you.

But now I want to write to you about something else, something where I was very weak and very vacillating, and which I'm afraid you won't understand.

You see, I almost got married, and now I don't know how I ever came to want that.

I had a lover, and he asked me once. He asked if I wanted to marry him. I couldn't say anything or give any reply, and just said Hm, hm, and that didn't mean anything. I was touched, because no one had ever proposed to me, and then I said I had to ask my mother. It was my first thought, that my mother should tell me, that she should decide, since I couldn't. I was shocked to realize much at a loss I was. I talked it over with my mother, and she encouraged me to say yes. But to him I didn't say anything for a long time, either yes nor no.

Something strange came over me. I was overcome with a boundless desire simply to give in. I can't begin to describe how I longed to give in and not always be saying no, but rather yes for a change. I wanted to be a good girl, I wanted to give in. It's so nice to give in.

But it was all so difficult. I had to go to the authorities and get permission. My lover was a foreigner, and for that you had to have official permission. You had to submit an application and then wait several months, sometimes up to a year. It was all utterly absurd, and I had to go again and again to that huge red building, which was once Berlin's poorhouse, along hundreds of corridors and up hundreds of steps, and then wait for hours in a lobby with many identical doors, and then be called in by female officials who were all so much alike that I never could tell whether it was the same one again and again, or a different one each time, and ask questions, and explain, and answer, and fill out forms, and plead, and the answer was always No, no.

Nevertheless it seemed to me as though it was already Yes, and as though everything had been decided from the first moment, and I had only a little time left and should already be packing my bags. I went into a panic, and while everything was taking its course, it suddenly seemed to me as though I didn't want this myself; it was the others who wanted it.

I wanted it and didn't want it and was torn. For a while I was euphoric and blissful, thinking I would win out, but then I was filled with fear that I would lose everything. From the beginning everything was so vacillating and changed so often that it sometimes took my breath away. I was really fond of the man in many different ways, but at the same time I often felt he was a stranger, and very far away, and then there were times when suddenly he didn't matter to me at all, and sometimes it even seemed that he wasn't my friend at all, but my enemy, and that we didn't really want to live together but to fight each other.

Because of all these shifting emotions, I kept feeling guilty; it was like chills and fevers. Yet I thought that if people loved each other they would feel very calm, and very close, never strange and distant. But that wasn't the case, and that made me very sad and even disheartened. But he didn't understand this, and I couldn't explain it to him either, though I tried; he just got angry at me.

And then something like a magic door sprang up between us; it was always there and I could never get through it to him again. I felt as though there were too many demands on me, and at the same time too few demands; everything was at once too much and too little. I constantly felt the man was making demands on me, and that drove me crazy.

At first it was good, but then everything got worse and worse. We often quarreled, and then we made up again, but in reality such reconciliations have no validity. After every quarrel something ugly, something hurtful remains, a rift that doesn't heal. And all this made me so weary, so weary.

And I so longed for peace. A peace like on our vacations. But this peace didn't come from us, it was there on the Hartstocks' farm—they were our neighbors in the village where I spent our vacation with the man and my girlfriend and her son. For us, everything was difficult and stressful and so much commotion, and the children screamed and bickered constantly, and there was so much discontent in all of us. But on the Hartstock farm everything is entirely different. Herr and Frau Hartstock are stepbrother and stepsister; they grew up together from when they were very small, and later they married and now live with their three children and various grandchildren on this farm, next to the one where we stayed. Everyone in that family is so warm-hearted, so kind, jolly, and generous, even the animals. Their dog doesn't bark when a stranger comes into the farmyard, but greets the person amiably and lies down on his back and lets himself be petted. Once a three-year-old boy bit the dog on the nose, but the dog stayed amiable, the dog of amiable people. Every visitor is welcome at the Hartstock farm, no matter how often he comes and how long he stays. And when I was there with Johannes, he was allowed to look at everything, the yard and the barns with all the livestock and the machinery, and they let him climb up on the tractor and press all the buttons and turn the steering wheel as much as he wanted. Herr Hartstock sometimes took him on his lap for a ride on the tractor.

Frau Hartstock often invited us over for a meal, and when we happened to have guests of our own, they were included. On the last day of our vacation she baked a large cake for us, and we all sat together on their porch, with a view of the nearby ocean, and ate Frau Hartstock's cake with whipped cream. As we were sitting there, Herr Hartstock remarked, "Nowadays we don't give any thought to how many people the sea has swallowed up. At the end of the war the farmers went into the water and drowned themselves. They were afraid their Polish forced laborers would take revenge, and the Polish border was nearby and the war lost. How much they must have had on their conscience to be so afraid." And then Herr Hartstock said, "This is what I think about peace: first you achieve peace between man and wife and the children, then peace with your neighbors, and if this continues to spread, very gradually, eventually, there may be peace among all human beings."

Then I was ashamed, because I did want to live with my man in peace, but I couldn't. I wanted to, but I couldn't. It was like in the dream when I was supposed to appear in a big concert with Mauricio Pollini, playing four-handed piano, but I didn't know how to play the piano; I couldn't even read music. But Mauricio Pollini began to explain it to me, and I wanted to pick it up very quickly. I really believed I could learn it during the concert. I hoped I could do it if I made the effort. But I couldn't do it, even though I tried.

It was not peace when the man arrived on Sunday and Johannes and I were cuddled up in bed together, and he undressed and got into bed with us and wanted Johannes to get out so he could be alone with me. And I was cowardly and tried to persuade Johannes to go to his room, but of course Johannes didn't want that at all, he wanted to stay in bed with us. So we all quarreled, Johannes began to cry and hit the man, and he got terribly angry and carried him off to his room and threw him down on his bed, and Johannes bawled, and the man slammed the door of his room shut, "to punish him," and then began to make breakfast. And I lay in bed feeling absolutely wretched and had to smooth everything over, comfort the crying child and placate the man, who was aggrieved, though I would have much preferred to be the aggrieved one.

Then I wanted to run away and not have to put up with this sort of thing anymore. Sometimes I thought being married might be nothing more than a new kind of solitude that I wasn't familiar with yet, for I was familiar with other kinds and was used to them and felt at home with them, and perhaps I was supposed to dispense with this last remnant of comfort. But no, I thought, it can't be that kind of double life.

Eventually all my love disappeared, and I was left with the feeling that I had to choose between two evils. I didn't want to get married anymore, and I didn't want to live alone anymore; I didn't want to stay here, but I didn't want to move away. For a long time I was absolutely rigid with fright and just kept very still and thought: if I don't move, maybe everything will just go away by itself. But soon keeping still also frightened me, and then I wanted to decide, and just as at the beginning I'd had a great desire to give in, now I didn't want to give in at all, and wanted to say no and not smooth things over, and not be accepting. I wanted to say no, once and for all, I wanted to say, No, I don't want you anymore, and I don't want to marry you;

I find you awful now, I find you and the two of us, and this whole business ridiculous. I don't love you anymore, I don't even like you anymore.

Why did I suddenly get so angry? At first, when it all started, I was so eager to give in, but then, at the end, I wanted to be angry.

When it began, it was October, and Johannes had just turned three. And now it was October again, and we had celebrated Johannes' fourth birthday. There came a day when I took a postcard and wrote on the back, "I don't want to see you anymore." I sent it to the man.

And then I had to go to everyone, even to the authorities again, and inform them of my decision and tell it all and explain it all. After that I was utterly exhausted and got sick again and spent three weeks in bed. That's how it was. And to this day I don't know whether it was courage or cowardice that made me call everything off. And when I was lying in bed, I felt weak as a sick child, and I wished so much that my mother would come and ask me if she could get anything for me when she went shopping, and that she would tell me in the evening that I didn't have to go to school and that I could stay home for a few more days. That's how it all was.

But of course, this vacillation is really a much bigger vacillation; it's the vacillation between always staying home and in bed, and leaving home and taking a long journey and never coming back, but staying in a foreign country and speaking another language and carrying one's mother tongue around with one in secret and not squandering it every day like some trifle.

I can't say how much I long for foreign cities and foreign countries. I can't tell you how much. Sometimes, when I'm sick in bed, I think it's often because of the pain of being cut off from all that.

Then I lie in my bed and yearn for broad, sunny landscapes with gentle hills and vineyards and old trees and old cities with bridges and steps and squares and windows that swing open, and rich palaces, and for foreign, friendly people, and for foreign smells and tastes. I yearn for Rembrandt's Amsterdam and Proust's Paris, I yearn for France, I wish I were in Italy, in Tuscany or Umbria, Rome, Florence, Venice, and I yearn for Greece, for Athens and all the islands, and the shores of the Mediterranean. I yearn for Jerusalem.

You know, Josef, I dreamed not long ago that I was in a southern country. It was already evening, and the evening was all blue and mild and warm, and I had on a thin summer dress but wasn't cold in the slightest, as I usually am. I was sitting there in an outdoor restaurant, and yellow and gold paper lanterns were swaying and giving a faint, peaceful light. I was sitting there with an old woman, a delicate, slight old woman, and she took me by the hand and led me to a broad, elegant flight of stone steps, and we stood there and looked down the steps. They led all the way down to the sea, which lay there calm and black. And then the old woman took my hand and ran down the steps with me. There were so many steps, and more, and more, as though they would never end; we ran and ran, the old woman and I, down and down. Like Jacob's ladder in reverse.

Dear Josef,

Sometimes I think that you think that I never think of you anymore. But that isn't true. Do you remember Moscow, how the snow was so deep, and every evening we went to the theater and then every night we took a long walk through the snow? The whole city was so bright from the snow, and we didn't walk along the streets, but through the courtyards; everything was so white, and there were no paths and no streets anymore. And we talked about the theater so much, every day, every evening, never about anything else, only about the theater. But now, after all this time, it seems to me as though we also discussed everything else.

And one time we ended up in this dive; it was an old hotel, and was supposed to be fancy, and it still had plush and old elegance, but otherwise it had gone downhill and become a sleazy tavern. But it had a band, which made a murderous racket, and it was crowded, and one could hardly breathe for the cigarette smoke. On the tables were piles of food and dishes, which were apparently never cleared away, and between the tables they were dancing in the narrow aisles. And we had landed in the middle of this and sat there for an eternity and didn't want to leave, and it was very nice after all.

Dear Josef,

Actually I wanted to tell you only one thing in this long letter: every day I lose all my courage, and every day I somehow find it anew.

Can you see me, Josef? I'm waving to you!

ROBERT SCHINDEL

Memories of Prometheus

a)

What we consist of
Of a skeleton
    And flesh
        And senses and
Overload.

b)

What we consist in
Where the moons
    Float pale
        And old and
Waxing.

c)

What we insist on
Where heaven and
    Earth touch
        One another. The morning-like
Caress.

a)

In any case, I was whelped in the middle of the Eastmark
In the village of Bad Hall, today a major mineral spa
As the changeling of racially inferior parents
Who claimed to be forced laborers from Alsatia
In defiance of Hitler
In their own homeland to save
Their own skin

Which on my mother's part was thirty-one and
Which on my father's part, one year before the liquidation
Was thirty-three years old.

I am told that before their arrest an almost
Good relationship between parents and child
Existed.

Around my first birthday, in early April forty-five,
My mother was knocking about between Berlin and Hamburg
In cattle cars, the devil knows why

In these cattle cars, I am told, Mother was not alone
Though the temperatures in early April were low
The people could warm each other. They stood close together
Some of the people are said to have died, others lacked
All inhibitions from hunger. They dug their fingers into the
        flesh
That was standing around.
That flesh also consisted of my mother, three
Weeks in transit, why, God only knows. Five hundred and four
Hours standing between Berlin and Hamburg. Mother
Still consisted of an almost intact skeleton
A glimmer of flesh and overalert senses.

Around my first birthday in the spring of forty-five
My father had already arrived from Auschwitz
At the periphery of Dachau. There
They buried him. My father, I am told,
Loved music and gymnastics and also
Had a wonderfully analytical mind in his day
He too consisted of that bony shield and his skin
But around my first birthday in the spring of forty-five
Was already sense-less.

So I learned a myth and knew nothing.
Fairy tales are extracts of life
Extended into the wondrous, with a happy ending: I was alive.

It is not impossible that the changeling of those days
And the writer of these lines are one and the same
Person, not impossible that they have one and the same *I*
Certainly possible, but not all that likely.

Rather the infant of those days—who also
Did not have exactly the same name as I, who am
Called Schindel—lent this Schindel
His fears and his raw dreams
Of galloping pianos and the dark
Song of the insect-nightingale. Lent this Schindel
His gestures, glued
His old being with great silent eyes onto me.

What results from this
The devil doesn't know, and God seems at a loss
In the face of this shared past.

b)

In any case, I can see the moons floating there:
Here the concrete, to the right and left of me crumbling
There these many swollen tongues angry
The eyes dull and inward. A bit venomous
The inhabitants of the city teeter on the yesterday beam
And puzzle over me, because I am here, did not float away
With the moons

Cry in the night their innocence
They howl silently without being told to. That is the instinct
Of all jackals, to howl.
With eyes squeezed shut they bit into the earth but
No buried human beings got between their teeth.
People speak in other words today

And ask me to fetch back from the Black Sea
The Danube water that's flowed into it, so that
It can flow again as distilled water
And the blond sun can sparkle peacefully in it.

I can do it only as a backward flip

Ach, they forgot me. I run
Around and unintentionally give them
Upset stomachs.

Many are angry because of the floating moons
Of the flowed-away Danube, and the rest.

Instead of speaking, speaking, greeting, noticing such
Yids politely, all fuzzy with tact, from yesterday one could
Regard them as what they are: buried and burned, that
                is what
We consist in. To the goyim we owe and to ourselves
A laughable deadness, unscrutinized.

c)

In any case I insist
Where heaven and earth touch one another
On touch

In a speakable sense
On a morning-like caress
Where heaven and earth go together.

Since light was already stolen from Helios
By the infamous P. and senselessly given away
To certain races

MAXIM BILLER

See Auschwitz and Die

MAMA HAD A DREAM ABOUT SS-MEN. She, a Russian Jew
who as a child during the war had never seen a single damned
Nazi face to face, suddenly, at twenty, developed elaborate
visions of persecution. Every two months she would wake up,
limbs aching and head spinning, and ask herself what it could
mean: dozens of black-uniformed soldiers armed with whips and
submachine guns chasing her over hill and dale, intent on taking
her worthless Jewish life.

This idiotic dream came to my mother in Moscow, and again
in Prague, but in Germany, where our family finally settled, she
never dreamed it again. Cured? Cured of what? And why here,
of all places?

I also had a dream: in April, in Poland. Frau Jakubowicz was
singing Yiddish songs in a reedy voice. Behind enormous far-
sighted spectacles that magnified her eyes into monitors, the old
woman looked like a terribly clever child. And she must have
been clever, for she had survived the ghetto and the camps, and
now, as head of the Jewish community of Cracow, she was
forever wrangling with the Polish authorities, bullying these
anti-Semitic Pollacks into showing the modicum of tolerance and
forbearance that was necessary to preserve, organizationally and
ideologically, the last remnants of Jewishness in this splendid
former royal seat.

Frau Jakubowicz had invited us to dinner at the community
center, in the bright dining room with its simple wooden
tables—but the most important part, the food, she could not

provide. So we had to bring ready-to-serve kosher meals in cans all the way from Germany, where for the last forty years the food supply had once again been first-rate, and where rabbis had been permitted to renew their supervision of our rigorous dietary laws.

There we sat, fifty young Jews whose parents had been so crazy even after the whole Holocaust shit as to leave Russia, Poland, Romania, Israel, Latin America, or France, and go to Germany, of all places, to beget us and raise us. There we sat, some of us the offspring of people who had survived the war outside the greater German sphere of influence, others of us the offspring of people who had survived it right in the eye of the storm: in hiding places, in attics and closets, and some in concentration camps.

The meal was over, we felt full and tired and contented, and then one of us asked Frau Jakubowicz to sing, in Yiddish, so Frau Jakubowicz sang, and she sang sadly, heartbreakingly. This made most of us sad, it broke our hearts. It reminded us that there had once been a Jewish world here and that the Nazi assholes had destroyed it forever. On the one hand this is indubitably true, but on the other hand it is by no means an original, energizing insight, which just goes to show that sentimentality about genocide can become stereotyped—and hence somehow a little untrue. But not false. No, really not false—we were about to see that all too clearly in Auschwitz, Birkenau, and Maidanek.

Not everyone will understand why I fell asleep while Frau Jakubowicz was singing. But I did not simply sleep, just like that, relaxed and uninvolved. I dreamed that I was an emaciated camp inmate trying to cut through the barbed-wire fence, in order to escape. My first concentration camp dream! Dreamed in Poland, not in Germany. Would it come back in Frankfurt? Mama says: Certainly not. Mama knows: Germany is the place of forgetting, in Germany they clog your brain with their false remorse and sympathy, with their pathological philo-Semitism and their fucking "grieving process." In eighteen years, Mama hasn't seen a single SS-man in her dreams—she's delighted about my trip to Poland.

What kind of tour group are we? The stench of our forebears' corpses clings to us, we're children spoiled by the prosperity that our parents built up in tandem with the murderers, we understand black humor, the finality of history, and our non-Jewish friends. Now we find ourselves in Poland, the country where the Hitler–Himmler–Eichmann trio exterminated almost half our people. We've come here to get a handle on what happened; we want to learn something about ourselves and about anti-Semitism. We are struggling, without realizing it, to achieve a crystal-clear Jewish self-definition. So we are visiting, between Breslau and Lublin, the sites in this part of the world where Jews lived and bit the dust. Concentration camps and cemeteries, ghettos and shtetls.

Back to Frau Jakubowicz: she sang only at the very end. Before that she guided us through the former Jewish quarter of Cracow, showing us two synagogues, two museums, and the ghetto where the Germans had kept the Jews cooped up for a while in the smallest possible space with hunger, typhus, and self-hatred, later shipping them off little by little to the extermination camps. With small, pattering steps Frau Jakubowicz led our historical self-discovery squad, explaining in Yiddish where she had lived and where friends and relatives had been shot, beaten to death, or starved. As a finale to the tour, she directed the Yugoslav driver of our double-decker bus to the Plashov labor and death camp outside the gates of Cracow. It had once been ruled, with an iron and deft hand, by a certain Amnon Goeth. I had just seen a photo of this German man in a display case at the ghetto museum: gazing out at me was an intelligent and handsome man with an 80s-style haircut, almost an artist's face, and for a few minutes I couldn't tear my eyes away, fascinated by the idea that Amnon Goeth—with a little help from a time-machine—could easily have been one of my painter or photographer friends, or even my editor at *Tempo*: not a killer, just a crony.

The Yugoslav driver opened the doors of the bus, and just as we were getting out to make our way to the Plashov memorial, it began to pour. Huge drops pounded down on our heads, and by the time we reached the commemorative stone atop Plashov Hill, to think of the murdered and to say the Kaddish for them, we were all soaked and freezing cold. After the Kaddish, Frau Jakubowicz pointed to the stone and said, weeping, that it was all that was left of the Jews here, and I thought again for a moment of that terribly interchangeable Amnon Goeth, but my thoughts quickly took a new turn, for Frau Jakubowicz now remarked that raindrops were the tears of the dead, and although I am ordinarily not susceptible to this kind of emotional sappiness, I made up my mind, quietly and sadly, to remember always the picture Frau Jakubowicz had sketched for us.

From Plashov we drove back to the city. There we ate, as I have already described, at the community center. Yes—and after the meal came the famous Jakubowicz songs, and then—we had just said goodbye to Frau Jakubowicz—came our epoch-making *faux pas*: instead of taking the back stairs of the large, turn-of-the-century building, as we had when we entered, we decided on the spur of the moment to go out by way of the front door. We would certainly never have thought that we would be blocked by the taciturn doorman in a gray smock. He bolted the heavy door before our noses, draped his small body protectively over the handle, and refused to budge. First we were amazed, then amused, then irritated. After extended negotiations, which we were not happy to have to conduct with this fellow, it turned out that Jews were not allowed to pass through here. For them— and therefore for anyone connected with the Jewish community center housed on the third floor—the back door was reserved. "So the front for Aryans and the back for Jews?" one of us exclaimed in Polish, jokingly. "Yes, exactly, exactly," the doorman replied in total seriousness, upon which our jaws dropped in unison. We had just had our first authentic anti-Semitic experience, an experience which would have been absolutely unthinkable in guilt-ridden post-Holocaust Germany. As a result,

one image of the enemy was altered for a couple of days: now
it was the Poles at whom we directed our Old Testament wrath,
and from now on we missed no opportunity to inveigh against
them.

But actually we should not have been surprised at all. In
most Polish hotels we, a group of tourists from Germany, were
put down in the guest registry as Israelis. Almost daily, Polish
passersby, feeling secure in their Slavic idiom, reviled us as
"Jewish filth," "Jewish swine," and "little Yids," and that happened to us not just in Warsaw and Lodz, but also twice at
Auschwitz I. And the people who titled us thus were school-
children, which not only said something about their generation,
but also about the ontological factors in the phenomenon of
"anti-Semitism," because one had to assume that these eleven-
and twelve-year-old hep-hep Pollacks had not seen a single Jew
in their young lives. For there are hardly any Jews left in
Poland—the Germans had been the first to take them on, but not
the last, for indignant Poles picked up where the Nazis left off,
doing in quite a number of Jews in a few juicy postwar pogroms,
which caused the resulting double-survivors to leave this
country for good in the years between 1946 and 1948. Some went
to America and Israel, but some to Germany, and many of us
who traveled to Poland this particular April were their children.

The last great wave of hatred followed in the late 1960s, when
the Party, supported by the Polish people, instigated a major
anti-Semitic campaign in order to distract attention from its own
mistakes. In this period, over thirty thousand Jews emigrated
from Poland. Today, hardly more than five thousand live there.
This is the place, naturally, to mention the "Schmalzovniks,"
Poles who put lard on their bread during the Nazi occupation
by leading the Germans to Jews and turning them in for "special
treatment." I must also quote what a Polish newspaper wrote at
the height of the Holocaust butchery: "The Nazis are solving the
Jewish problem in our favor as we would never have been able
to solve it ourselves." And finally it must be stated, categorically
and without ifs, ands, or buts, why the Germans chose to do the

lion's share of their dirty work in Poland: it was because here they could count on the assent, cooperation, and silence of the natives. Let us put aside the fact that these natives were slated to have their turn after the Jews, an un-consummated historical irony in which we cannot really take satisfaction.

What does all this teach us? Nothing, actually—because who can still be surprised by virulent anti-Semitism? It teaches us nothing, except, perhaps, that the explosive combination of active hatred of Jews (as demonstrated to us by the Poles of today) and the mummified apocalypse of the concentration camps (which we observed several times during our little sado-masochistic excursion) was calculated to bring home to us in an educational and consciousness-raising fashion that we are Jews, nothing but filthy Jews, fucked-up Jews, fucked-over Jews, the real thing. We did not give a damn how the Polish school-children who harassed us at Auschwitz I had recognized us, but after we saw the Cyclon-B canisters on exhibit there, our stigma filled us with pride, and we laughed, arrogantly and calmly, at every damned little Adolf within every damned Jew-devouring goy. We grasped how important and splendid and reassuring and empowering it is to have our own country in the Middle East; our hearts took on the negotiated and reduced contours of peace-time Israel, and at that moment we were thinking about many things, but certainly not about the PLO and its Palestinians. We were thinking, for instance, about gas chambers.

A timely transition, for many will have been wondering for quite a while now: How did the young Jews like the concentration camps? We didn't like Auschwitz I very much, because the only significant and bellicose Nazi fetish we encountered the first time we were there was the *Arbeit macht frei* ["Work Liberates"] inscription above the gate. Aside from that, all we saw was a couple of nondescript brick buildings in which the Polish authorities had installed a couple of nondescript exhibitions: behind glass were heaps of clothing, piles of shoes, and thousands of eyeglass frames that the SS, after killing their owners, had presumably stockpiled for eternity. This collection of personal belongings did not have any particular impact on us; we were already familiar with it from photographs. Besides, most of Auschwitz I's victims were not Jews, and we had come looking for Jewish death, which was only right and proper. That probably explains why at this camp we whiled away the time with unintentional super-ego conversations and indulged in perverse skits, which resulted, among other things, in an exchange between Yael and me in which she pictured her arrival at the "selection" platform. Would Dr. Mengele have sent her to work or to the gas chambers? "To work!" In the brothel or the vegetable gardens? "The brothel!" Would she have preferred to be screwed or shot by the Nazi swine? "Screwed!" And if an SS-man had made a baby with her? "I would have hated it," Yael shouted, "absolutely hated it!"

Shortly before that, Micky and Ari had improvised a Holocaust-rap à la Mel Brooks, parts of which were quite blasphemous, but no one was much taken with the rap except them. Gaby and Michal were planning to go out the next day and buy caviar in bulk—a one-kilo can went for two hundred marks at the black-market rate. Meanwhile, Gil kept following Susy everywhere and putting his hand on her hip, which she patiently removed each time, and Harry was telling for the fifth time the story of his friend Yoram, who had been to Auschwitz four years ago and whose overprotective parents had forbidden him to come back, because they felt that seeing Auschwitz *once* was enough. Leo responded to Harry's story with the witty remark, "See Auschwitz and die," but by then we had all had enough of our own outrageousness and blasphemy, which in any case was merely a defense mechanism, so we decided to shut up for a while.

No, our first tour of Auschwitz I had not really been a smashing success. But we returned a few days later to take part, along with two thousand Jewish young people from all over the world, in the March of the Living organized for Holocaust Memorial Day, Yom Ha-Sho'ah. Only then did we, Yael and I, stumble upon the gas chamber and adjacent crematorium, well hidden on the periphery of the camp, which our Polish tour guide had withheld from us three days earlier. Here tears came to Yael's eyes, but I caught the first glimmer of an insight whose full contours became visible to me only at Maidanek, a similar place.

But before Maidanek came Birkenau, also known as Ausch-witz II, the camp where the Germans accomplished most of the work that resulted in over two million slaughtered Jews being credited to their Faustian bank account in hell. Birkenau presented us with a concentration camp as we had imagined it, with barbed wire, wooden barracks, watch towers, instruments of destruction, and the famous selection platform, where in the busiest annihilation period— between 1942 and the begin-ning of 1945—several trains arrived almost every day from vari-ous parts of Europe. Here the Jews had to get out, surrender their money, their clothes, their provisions, and then be "selected." For most of them the destination was death. That was the case with the father of André, with whom I suddenly found myself alone by the deportation tracks that ended in this no-man's land. While the others had gone on ahead to see the barracks, we remained behind, sitting on the grass that grew everywhere here, quietly and peacefully, lending a grotesquely natural and normal air to the camp's grounds, especially if one thought of what had been here before: no grass, just muck and blood.

André told me how his parents and grandmother had arrived in Birkenau at this very spot, how the two women had been selected for the work camps, but his father for the waiting arms of Cyclon-B, and how his grandmother had, at the very last, absolutely impossible moment, managed to bribe a watchman with a diamond, whereupon this man pushed André's father in the direction of life. I looked at André, then I looked around. I surveyed the whole symmetrically laid-out camp like a king of survival. Suddenly I was a survivor myself, like André, like his family, who were eventually sprung from Birkenau by the leg-endary munitions manufacturer Oskar Schindler, a man who saved the lives of several thousand Jews during the war, proving that it could be done if the will was there. André, I thought, you are alive—you live in Frankfurt, you work there, go to restaurants and discotheques, play soccer in the park on Sunday with your friends, and now and then steal somebody's girlfriend. Death, or life, or never even being born—chance decides, chance that was never so random as for Jews in the Thousand-Year Reich.

In Birkenau pathos was difficult to ward off, but then why should we have tried? In Birkenau there was a pond they called the Sea of Ashes, because the Germans had dumped the ashes of the dead into and around it. When we got very close to its banks, we actually noticed that the water was cloudy and mealy, and the few stones we could see in the shallow parts were covered with a thick, milky-brown film. The pond was full of fat little frogs. Hundreds of frogs were jumping about or lying motionless in the sun, and while Gaby was musing out loud whether these frogs could be reincarnations of the dead, Esti yelled, "Watch out!" and I leaped to one side, only to discover that I had almost crushed one of the Holocaust frogs. Frogs are tears are the dead are drops of rain, Frau Jakubowicz, we will never forget Birkenau . . .

This is not the place once again to unfurl before the eyes of the ignorant, whether well-intentioned or ill-, the horrors of the extermination of the Jews. I could talk about mountains of corpses and shattered skulls, about Jews who first had to dig the graves into which they shortly afterward tumbled, their bodies riddled with bullets. I could tell the story of an SS-man in Treblinka who in a rage pinned a fleeing child to the plank wall of the barracks with his bayonet, like a rare specimen of beetle. And I could quote figures, astronomical figures of the dead, allegedly so terribly incomprehensible, although six million corpses seem like exactly six million corpses to me, no more and no less, and anyone who is intimidated by this number is in my eyes not a sympathetic sympathizer but a morally deficient shirker, like those who turn away when they see the crippled and retarded on the street.

There are many things I could do to present the horror of the Shoah in graphic form and thus convey some of the feelings that stirred us that April in Poland. But I have something else in mind, I want to move on, I want to get at the rationality and the arbitrariness and the metaphysics *behind* the feelings, and the road to that leads me, by way of two quotations, directly to Maidanek.

At the end of March 1942, a good two months, that is, after the Wannsee Conference, at which the Nazis had commited themselves to the total extermination of the Jews, Goebbels wrote in his diary, "Starting with Lublin, the Jews are now being deported to the east from the Government General [the main portion of occupied Poland]. A fairly barbarous process, not to be described further, is being employed, and of the Jews them-selves not much is left . . . In these matters one must not permit any sentimentality . . . Here, too, the Führer is the unswerving pioneer and proponent of a radical solution . . . " And on October 6, 1943, SS Reichsführer Heinrich Himmler declared in Posen to the assembled Reichsleiters and Gauleiters of the NSDAP, "The Jewish question in the territories we have occu-pied will be taken care of by the end of this year. There will remain only a residue of individual Jews who have gone into hiding. I would ask you to listen to what I am telling you in this closed circle and not to speak of it in public. The question came up: What about the women and children? I have decided to adopt an absolutely clean solution in this respect, too. You see, I did not feel justified in exterminating the men—that is to say, killing them or having them killed—and allowing their children, those who would avenge them on our sons and grand-sons, to reach maturity. The difficult decision had to be taken to make this people disappear from the face of the earth."

So—and now to Maidanek, the concentration camp of Maidanek, at that time a suburb of Lublin, today a part of the city, which has grown in the meantime. It began with the Polish taxicab driver. Our bus driver had asked him to pilot us to the concentration camp, and he let loose a flood of invective directed against us Jews that would be hard to equal for its passion and obscene inventiveness. It climaxed in the words "Jewish filth! Jewish filth!" The second taxi driver, an older man, represented what one might characterize as the other extreme. Not only did he lead us to Maidanek for a dollar; he also spoke frankly with André, who had chosen to ride with him, about Lublin during the war. All the city's inhabitants knew what went on in Maidanek, he said. The trainloads of Jews arrived at the Lublin station. From there they had to march across the entire city to the camp. They were emaciated, half naked, ill. Any who tore leaves from the trees and greedily stuffed them into their mouths were shot. Any who fell down and remained lying on the ground in exhaustion were shot. Any who tried to escape were shot. Lublin saw the Jews making their way to the gas chambers. And the following day Lublin smelled Jews burning. Those who wanted to avoid the sweetish smell of burning flesh stayed indoors and kept the windows closed.

André of course regaled us with the taxi driver's stories as we began our tour through Maidanek. Yet no one was horrified, no one was surprised; that was how it was, everybody knew— the Pope, the Poles, the Lithuanians, the Ukrainians, the Allies, the Red Cross, every German. But our calm response to this insight had nothing to do with our having learned too much about death and hate and destruction on this trip and, therefore, being somewhat numbed. Our Jewish consciousness had been extraordinarily raised in the last few days through exposure to all the memorabilia of genocide, and it was only logical that the anti-Semites, together with their filthy ideology, had come to occupy a central position in that consciousness. We had grasped the equation: No anti-Semites without Jews, and vice versa. At the same time, our occasionally heretical Holocaust jokes were spawned not by disinterest or disrespect; they were an expression of a peculiar hysteria that usually came over us just before or just after a visit to a concentration camp. Suddenly we would all be in a terribly good mood; one explanation might be that we were somehow happy to be alive.

So we quickly and proudly filed the Lubliners' complicity in the drawer labeled "Collective Guilt" and greedily fell upon Maidanek, for we had heard that it would pack a particular emotional wallop for us. At the entrance stood a huge, ghastly monument in 60s-style cast concrete. We did not linger there, and after only a few minutes we reached the first gas chamber, directly adjacent to the little open square where the new arrivals were selected. We looked around once, twice, inspected the openings in the ceiling from which the gas had come, saw the marks where asphyxiating Jews had clawed the dark concrete walls. We looked at the floor, once trodden by hundreds of thousands of bare feet, and we sensed that more was still to come. True enough: at the very end of the sprawling camp stood something that looked like a giant stockpot, with a large lid. A stairway led up its side, and we climbed to the top. Once there, some of us turned pale and our faces froze: this pot, which was ten or fifteen meters in diameter, was full to the rim with ashes, human ashes that the Russian soldiers who liberated the camp in July 1944 had found scattered all over the landscape.

As we were standing there motionless, we suddenly heard screams and loud, terrible groans coming from an L-shaped barracks with a tall chimney. Again it was Yael who took me in tow, and we set out for the barracks while the others stayed behind at the ashes to hear out the Polish guide. The screams came from young American Jews who were coming out of the barracks in groups of two and three, their arms around each other. They were weeping, dragging themselves along, their faces distorted with horror. So we went inside. First we came to a room with a large dissecting table and an opening in the floor where an X-ray machine had stood. It had been used by the Germans to search for hidden valuables in the corpses, which would be slit open if necessary. The second room was a gas chamber: a nice big gas chamber. Against one wall stood a pedestal, around the pedestal lay flowers, wreaths, and on the pedestal was a round, transparent glass container. It was full of human bones and skulls. Yael cried. I thought for a moment I was going to collapse, but then I told myself I had to stay rational and look at all these bones until I had impressed every single one of them on my memory for all time. So I stood there and stared for five minutes, and then I'd had enough, and we entered the third and final room. It was here, in the crematorium, facing a bank of ovens where they had shoved in the motionless bodies and turned them to dust, that I finally grasped what made the Nazi crime unique, and in so doing I made my own private contribution to the despicable Historians' Debate. I grasped that the Nazis had not merely murdered cold-bloodedly and according to a plan, which is what most people consider exceptional about their misdeeds. No, the Nazis had turned the murder of the Jews into a quasi-religious act; they were carrying out a human sacrifice for themselves and their ideal. They were the Aztecs of the twentieth century, with a ritual of execution and death, fructifying an epoch that in spite of war and criminality was a product of the Enlightenment and humanism. They fructified this epoch of reason with an atavistic blood-worship that had apparently been long since forgotten; this should arouse less anger in us than the recognition that the human being is, as Hobbes put it, no human being but a thinking animal. The Nazis' technocratic cold-bloodedness and fanatical perfectionism was their tribute to modernity, to the technical, industrial, and cultural revolution. But the deed itself was the deed itself, that is to say, a ritual crime, which is possible *in any era*. To be sure, this insight offers no comfort, but it paradoxically deprives the Holocaust of the aura of inexplicability. Long live rationality! To hell with legends!

Our ten-day excursion into the past, intended to teach us something about the present and presumably also about the future, was drawing to a close. We had been in Maidanek and Auschwitz and Birkenau, but we had skipped Treblinka because at some point we simply ran out of the stamina needed to endure these psychological maelstroms. We had visited the Jewish cemeteries in Breslau, Lodz, Lublin, and Cracow, likewise the local community organizations. But these last sites of Jewish life in Poland resembled bleak satellites, aimlessly orbiting the sad remains of former Polish-Yiddish glory, inhabited by a small cluster of elderly, ailing people à la Frau Jakubowicz, whose death would mark the end of the Nazis' program of annihilation. For after them comes nothing more, no Bar Mitzvahs, no weddings, no Seders—only museums, empty synagogues, and vandalized gravestones, of which we had in fact seen a multitude on our trip.

Some in the group had set out on their own to see the towns from which their parents and grandparents had come. They were in search of something, a missing piece of their fractured Jewish identity. But they had found nothing, only Poles with pale, high-cheekboned faces who were living in formerly Jewish houses, and reluctantly rummaged through their hostile memories. "Yes, there were Jews here," they said in unison, but they said no more than that, and then they slammed the doors in our faces, further exacerbating my traveling companions' spiritual deracination by slyly imparting information in this manner, at once specific and non-specific. Rina was the only one who did not take no for an answer. In her forebears' village she peppered the inhabitants with questions until a farmer finally went to his barn and fetched a Jewish gravestone on which Rina found her family's name. She bought the stone from him for a few hundred zlotys, later stuffed it into a suitcase and smuggled it in our bus over the border into Germany. Rina had got her hands on a piece of the past . . .

Our final stop was Warsaw, for it was the forty-fifth anniversary of the uprising in the Warsaw ghetto, which we, together with several thousand other Jews from all over the world, wanted to commemorate. We did this in private, however; we did not participate in the official Polish ceremonies, for we did not want to be coopted for the purposes of their pseudo-communist propaganda. But we also avoided the ceremony conducted the previous day at the Jewish cemetery by Marek Edelman, a survivor of the uprising and a member of Solidarity; for the Polish authorities had warned that if we took part in the illegal Edelman demonstration they could not guarantee our safety: a potent threat. That was on Sunday. On Saturday night our bus was demolished and, shortly before that, members of the French Jewish delegation were beaten up on the street by persons unknown. That happened a few hours after it had been reported that an Israeli commando had shot down the PLO's Abu Jihad in Tunis. At the same time, our hotel, occupied mainly by Jews from the West, was surrounded by Polish security forces "for our protection." Protection from whom?

Out on the streets of Warsaw every third person was suddenly a police officer in plainclothes or uniform—or at least so it seemed to us. Inside, in the hotel lobby, we huddled together. One could hear Yiddish spoken, and Hebrew. Everywhere were men and boys in yarmulkes, and to the right of the entrance a few orthodox Jews had gathered for prayer. We decided not to leave the hotel alone, but only in groups, and then, when we heard the next morning that during the night the Jewish community center in Frankfurt, fifteen hundred kilometers away, had been firebombed, our Polish Masada-mood was complete. There we sat, like the Jews who had fled two thousand years ago to the fortress of Masada on the Dead Sea to escape the Romans. There, after a futile battle, they had committed mass suicide. Perhaps we were not really threatened, but we were certainly cut off, sensitized to persecution and persecution mania by our recent visits to concentration camps. We sat in Warsaw's elegant Forum Hotel feeling a general sense of oppression. But of course we did not contemplate suicide; instead, we set out for Germany at noon on Monday.

The trip lasted almost twenty hours, and it was somewhere between Breslau and Görlitz that some of us became involved in the long-overdue discussion of whether it had been right to direct all our invective at the Polish swine, who had indeed showered us with fresh, authentic anti-Semitism; had we forgotten who had invented the concentration camps and launched the Holocaust? Now, after a bit of polemical back-and-forth, we recalled, in a comradely consensus, that it had been the Germans, the Germans alone. And now we also realized why we had done such a good job of repressing their guilt during the ten days just past: we were living in their country—again—and it did not matter whether our parents were responsible for this absurd fact or we ourselves. The whole business had always made us feel lousy, even in the presence of Poles, yet now, at the end of our trip, it began to loom large, for we had seen the bones of Maidanek. All this we faced up to between Breslau and Görlitz, without self-pity or arrogance, and we were sufficiently smart and pragmatic not to draw any hasty conclusions from this sudden rush of feeling, certainly not to make premature plans to emigrate. At some point life settles down at bit, even for nomads.

Then, toward midnight, we crossed the border between Poland and East Germany. It was already getting light when we reached West German territory. In the gray light of dawn we glided along the Autobahn. The sun rose, wisps of fog hovered over the fields, and it was going to be a nice, mild spring day. In the distance we could make out the silvery gleaming sky-scrapers of Frankfurt.

We were home again.

MATTHIAS HERMANN

Six Poems

Autumn Fire

1938.
From Alpine peaks to ocean
Smoke storms over the Reich,
An army of sparks in motion.

Strangely on that night-day,
The crackle of a German fall
Resounded and burning in the foliage
Scrolls, straps, shawl.

Fiery chasms engulfed
A strange structural jumble:
Baths, libraries, schools
All aglow in their tumble.

The houses turned to ash
And many therein roofed;
In the smoke assembled there,
Only smoke moved.

For Kurt Tackmann

Translated by Robert Wechsler

4 Green Tin Canisters

From the Red Cross truck
Climbs the driver, pushes back
With great precision the canvas flaps
And takes 4 of the canisters, gently

Cradling these in his hands,
He walks slowly, step by step
Across the lawn to the concrete pad,
There he stops.

From his beltpouch he pulls
His mask over his face,
Props open the hatch,
Looks down, and breaks

The seals on the 4 canisters.
Violet-hued crumbly material
He pours with German meticulousness
Lest any crumb be wasted

Into the hole, and from deep below
Comes a gasping as if for air
He lets fall the iron plate,
Pulls the mask from his face.

From his pack of cigarettes
He pulls one, lights it,
And the smoke rises into the greater
Smoke

Former Synagogue in Biebesheim

Where once
Torah hands
Unrolled the time of the LOrd,
Today clocks for sale
Point to the hour
That has struck.

Not Jews,
Hands point
To Zion,
Where one day
The hour shall strike,
The end of time.

Then the clockmaker
Will be unemployed
As here and now
The LOrd.

Jewish Cemetery in Mainz

Dog cemetery is what
Old residents call it, and swear
Howls issue from the graves,
Disturbing their sleep.

From the scratching of paws
There remained on the tombstones
Legible scars: a
Hebrew SOS of undying
Grief, perhaps.

They say these laments
Could melt stones,
But that death chases
No one back to the gates of life,
Which never wanted
The likes of these people
Not in Mainz,
Not anywhere.

Jewish Cemetery in Worms

I drift
In the leak-beaten boat
Of my days
Past tombstone planks
From which dangle,
In profusion,
Relatives,
Drowned in life.

In the earth's tides,
All entangled like algae
They come dancing
Toward me.

The Shower Rooms in Prison

I wince
Beneath the droplet blows
Tiled into the steambath
Of a hereditary memory
That robs me of
My breath.

PETER STEPHAN JUNGK

from

Shabbat
A Rite of Passage in Jerusalem

*Translated by Arthur S. Wensinger
& Richard H. Wood*

*. . . IT'S CIRCLING IN MY HEAD, in my chest, in my belly—the
ballast of myself, lodged deep in my center, so clearly measured off and
defined on the outside. I sit and lie deep inside myself. And to my
surprise, I swing myself up on that very feeling, as onto the back of a
beast of burden, and break it, as if it had a thin carapace, like a shell-
fish. And subdue it. Today I manage that for the first time, thank God.
Thank whom? How quickly I speak of Him, without thinking of Him,
without being with Him, before I pronounce the word that is supposed
to designate HaShem. There, where I grew up, everyone says "Grüss
Gott!" when they greet each other. I share the woods, cities, tavern
tables, I share the language of the inhabitants of that country and am
obliged to forget, forget each day anew, what took place there, forty
years ago. I must speak with You in their language, the only one whose
subtleties I really know. I beg You, forgive me.*

*On this second day of the Feast of the New Year a stony path leads
me uphill. In my hand a light walking stick. I reach the edge of a wood;
the wonderful, fragrant fir trees were planted no more than thirty years
ago, yet they stand firmly rooted in the earth, as if there had always
been woods here, in this place, on the barren soil of this land. Next to
me, a bush in white blossom, its smell intensely familiar, though I have
never smelled it before; it exudes that same feeling of certainty that*

HaShem was calling for me as when I was standing restlessly beside the gaping suitcases—did You call me? You want to give me a message? HaShem wanted me to hike a short distance out of my neighborhood and make a climb, up one of the hills? Did You call me?

I follow a marked path, the forest floor covered with brown fir needles. A family walks toward me, the three children gathering mushrooms. A tormenting idea: to have to exist at all times for the sake of one's own children—compelled to remain with their mother, so as to be there for one's children. HaShem, I must become a father, like this man? I hear him say the word leilah; *the night steers a course for the day, I think, it unites; and the day sunders? I am guided by sleep and dream without remembering their navigation when I am awake? What happened to me before I came into this world? What happens to me when I am asleep? Is that which is written true, that dream is one-sixtieth part prophecy? Is that which is written true, that sleep is one-sixtieth part death? I cling to life, day person that I am. I never want to have to miss anything while on this earth. HaShem lets a stone live longer than a tree, a tree longer than a turtle, a turtle longer than a human. And toy cars made of iron, and this silver ballpoint that I carry around, HaShem lets them live longer than the stones. I stop and write in a notebook: "Sleep would not exist if life were followed by nothing. Otherwise we would come into the world and remain awake at all times, until death came. Sleep is preparation." I am forbidden to write today, but go on nevertheless and add: "Because there is a soul in me, I need sleep." Writing is one of the basic activities that are forbidden on a holy day. HaShem will exterminate me from the midst of my people? He will infect me, or someone close to me, with a sickness, because I have written a note for myself today? A girl on a park bench, looking at the view—You want me to speak to her? You have placed her on my path? Her name is Leilah? She has lifted her arm a little and is waving her hand in the air. "Are you speaking to yourself?" she asks. "I've been looking at you for a while; you speak to yourself, don't you?" She looks familiar to me, and I remember, she works in a supermarket, helped me recently find radio batteries in the maze of aisles and shelves. And now she acts as if we had been destined for each other from the beginning. "Come over, sit down," she calls*

out, and I feel hot in my head and shoulders. I look out toward the
desert, over to stony hills, yellow light on their bald, rounded tops. The
city, high over the surrounding land—it dominates the Desert of Judea
like a mighty fortress. The girl asks for a light; sorry, I tell her, don't
have a match on me. I stand up close to her, she smells of light and
woods and desert, her black hair is spread out wide. I choose my words
awkwardly, wish her a good New Year, promise her, too, that I'll come
to visit her at work, and wander off quickly, on a stony pathway, away
from her. Underfoot the fir needles . . .

I would often sit in the great lobby of the King David Hotel,
read the newspapers and magazines, make appointments to meet
people there, study the kinsmen who were strangers to me, who
had arrived here from the lands of their birth. Between revolving
door and broad terrace, between restaurant and coffee shop—
there was a place to feel at home; porters and errand boys,
elevator operators and waitresses, my homemates; the transients
our guests, visitors to my city. In a park behind the wide brick
building, I walked among palm trees, plane trees and cactus in
bloom, past the swimming pool where children played and
young women lay in the sun, their eyelids closed.

On a Friday afternoon in the month of Elul, a few weeks
before the New Year's Feast of Rosh Hashanah, I entered the
lobby after a walk in the park, bought the Sabbath edition of a
great daily paper, watched my guests telephoning, telegraphing,
departing, arriving. It was like the belly of an old ocean liner
minutes after the anchors had been lowered and she had docked.
I saw relatives greeting each other after a long separation,
embraces so impassioned, as if life lasted only half the short time
it does. I walked back and forth in this busy foyer, close to the
groups of travelers. ". . . everything so dark, so brown in the
streetcar compartment; tried to keep from crying; had to," said
a woman's voice. And a second voice: "Yes, the things that could
never happen, have happened, in this century." "Is that paper?"
"Is that your handwriting?" "Every people has its guardian

angel—except for us; because the Almighty Himself watches over us—or so I once believed." "Us? At home? Television? Never! My husband always says, that's as if you had a goy twenty-four hours a day with you in your house." "I was just about to have Chaim, and somebody comes into the store; he wants to weigh this huge carp he just caught, puts it on the scales, and I had to hold on to the tail for him, and all at once it gives a flip, still a little life in the thing, what a scare that gave me, terrible. And Chaim—day after tomorrow he's thirty years old; never would he eat a fish I fixed for him, never even touched fish."

Two ladies in gossamer silk dresses, covered with massive jewelry, holding on to each other, their fingers intertwined; one of them asked if she might have a look at my newspaper. "Only the headlines," she said. I handed her the thick evening paper. They were reading the headlines to each other—one minute, two minutes—when suddenly a figure attacked me from behind, calling out the name "Pinkas!" as he leapt. I was startled; the ladies let out little shrieks of alarm. I found myself looking into a pair of wide-open, alert eyes: a slender boy was standing before me. Tousled, a bit flushed, but without a particle of fear, he looked up at me. A girl in a yellow uniform asked him, "Are you a guest of the hotel? Where do you live, my funny little friend?" and his great eyes grew calm, became part of an astonished smile; his skin translucent, blue veins shown through his delicately chiseled cheeks. "You're not Pinkas at all," he said with a raspy adolescent voice. "I thought you were my cousin, because maybe he's coming to see us soon—please forgive me." And he laughed gently, straightened his kipah—it was a transformation like a cloudless sky, pure, cool air, after a sudden summer storm. I felt as if I knew him intimately—I looked almost exactly like him once, or so I imagined. Softly he said, "I watch people watching other people, I study them when they are studying each other. Sometimes I speak to them, ask them questions; you do the same thing, don't you?" I nodded; I was calm again; the boy simply stood there beside me; an amorphous sense of security. The features of his face were like filigree work; brown eyes, fragile body, he only came up to my shoulder. He wore a white shirt and black trousers, wore the fringes at his waist. "These lost souls are only here on a visit—I tell them they ought to stay here," he continued, "because they belong here, the way my parents came, and now we have made a home here—*Baruch HaShem.*" I wanted to keep him with me. Embarrassed, I asked him what his name was. I felt slightly feverish. "Wanting to do everything at the same time is doing nothing at all, it robs you of your strength," he said. "I observe the Law, and I do it not only because it is pleasing to HaShem, but to keep my soul from cracking; every little slip puts a scratch on the crystal. Are you going to come with me? Will you tell me what it is you tremble for in life and why you do what you do?" As he spoke his whole body was in motion, and his voice seemed to produce little round volleys like the concentric ripples when a stone falls into the water. I wanted him to guide me. The ladies went on reading my newspaper. "Are you always so quiet?" he asked. "You're much too thin for someone your age, and those sunken eyes, and so pale. You've got to get some strength back. You never wear a kipah? Or don't you want to be recognized? It's to stop you from becoming arrogant—that's what it's for. I have to go now, the light is fading. Sabbath will begin very soon."

Shortly after sunset—automobiles were blowing their horns at us, the waxing moon was high in the sky. We walked through a street named Abraham Lincoln; nearby was a soccer stadium, and the cool smells of shrubbery and stone. "You don't have brothers or sisters, right?"

"How can you know that?"

"From looking at you," he said. "I'm an only child, too, but my parents aren't worried, they know I'll be home in time for supper."

"Where are we going, anyhow?" I asked.

"You wanted to know what my name is? It's easy to remember because Ilan Baum is nothing but two times 'tree', Ilan means tree and Baum means tree—and what about you? Are you really Pinkas?"

And so, going way back to my beginnings, I told him about myself, the words flowed from me, as my companion floated along beside. Incorporeal, unknown kinsman, central knot in the invisible net—I shall follow you, I shall follow you. I felt as if a portable tent had been constructed around and over me. Ilan told me that his forebears had also come from the Imperial and Royal Austro-Hungarian Monarchy, that his father was a book-binder by profession, as his father had been before him. "You can live with us," he said. "I'll give you my room, you must not leave here, there is so much you have to learn. We shall learn together. Hey, how old do you think I am?" Ten, fifteen? One of those astonishing beings that seem ageless. "Sixteen?" I ventured. He laughed. "Thirteen and a half, less than half your age. Yet for HaShem, a hundred thousand years are but the blinking of an eye. And as for dying—it's as if you were a twin in your mother's womb. One morning your brother is born into the world, and you are left alone, you think, oy veh! my dear brother is dead, he is gone from my world. Up until the moment that you, too, are born, you will think: I have lost my dear brother."

We had arrived at the intersection of Gershon Agron and King George streets. An old woman, bent with age, was waving her cane at a bus driver only a few yards beyond where he had made his last stop. She banged on the windows and door; and when the driver still wouldn't open, she screamed like someone being tortured. At that point, Ilan ran up to the red-and-white bus, stood in the street directly in front of it, and grabbed hold of its old-fashioned radiator grille. Horns blew, pedestrians gathered. "Forget it," someone said, and pointed at the driver, "that's not a human being"; others tried in vain to persuade him to open up, wringing their hands, beating wildly—the door remained closed. I ran to Ilan's side; we braced our feet and leaned against the grille. Angry gestures from the passengers; we nodded and smiled; the bus driver sat on his horn; twenty passersby encircled us. I was surprised at how cool I stayed. We did not relent until three drivers of a truck carrying oxygen tanks got trapped in the traffic jam, climbed out, spat on Ilan, and seized hold of me like a pack of rabid dogs. The bus roared ahead; the old woman stood there, helpless and lost; the line of backed-up cars drove past. A pair of guttersnipes is what we are, I thought; but Ilan still wasn't finished. He hailed a taxi, helped the bent-over woman get in the back, gave the driver some money, and the taxi drove off with a jerk, the rear door still half open. At that moment the howl of a siren cut through the air like an alarm in wartime: it was the shrill Friday-evening signal announcing the start of the Sabbath.

On the main floor of an apartment house in a part of the city called Rehaviah, we entered a little synagogue. Ilan told me I had to empty my pockets and deposit everything in a little niche in the wall behind the door. "Today you are not allowed to carry anything with you; you must be in HaShem's hands without any symbols of security, otherwise you will not feel the Sabbath—no money, no papers, no nothing, you must not even think about them." Evening prayer had already begun—loud lamentation and chanting, a proclamation of sorrow. I wanted to get out of that room, but instead hesitantly handed Ilan my wallet, comb, note pad, ballpoint. "You don't want to stay here," he said, "I can tell that, but please try, Pinkas, please."

My passport! Where was my passport? Hotel lobby? Shirt pocket? When Ilan jumped and hugged me? "You'll just have to go back tomorrow evening; no problem, they'll keep it for you at the hotel; forget it now; it's your duty to act like a king today— forget your little worries."

The men studied us curiously. I stared at the floor, felt drops of sweat coming from my pores. A narrow room, rough floor-boards, yellowish walls, network of cracks on them, neon light pouring down from the low ceiling. Hemmed in by these supplicants dressed in black; old wooden desks in front of me, behind me. I was grieved by my ignorance; it seemed to make my whole body glow with shame. I pretended to Ilan that I had no trouble reading along with the others. I turned the pages of a faded, moldy-smelling book whenever I saw my neighbor turning his. When they sat down, I sat down. If they stood up, I stood up. It was like Sunday Mass when my nursemaid Erna used to take me along: rise and kneel whenever the others rose and knelt. A side-glance from Ilan made me giddy—it brought back a dream I had had the night before: In the nave of a church, my relatives and an unrelated group were at prayer, both under the same roof but on opposite sides of the aisle. When a woman knelt and made the sign of the cross, someone who looked very like Ilan suddenly laughed aloud. The woman went to a more remote spot, crossed herself again; we studied her as if she were performing some jungle ritual. We were eating and drinking, that was an important part of our holiday; I was embarrassed in the presence of these strangers for the fact that we didn't want to take our meal in front of the cathedral.

"Mother and I will take good care of you," whispered Ilan; he went back to his prayer, recited loudly, swayed back and forth, more driven even than the men. "He rolls back the light before the darkness," I was reading the text in translation, "and the darkness before the light, and He divided day and night. Praise be to You, Almighty, Who causes twilight to descend." The men turned to face the rear wall: "You spread yourself out in all directions," they exclaimed. "Welcome, Bride, welcome, Bride!" Thus they received the Sabbath. I was a visitor to another planet, Ilan an alien. It was all a swaying and trembling, peril on the high seas, not an atom of quiet contemplation. The absence of any sense of deliverance in these prayers suffocated me. I remained in the synagogue only for Ilan's sake, only because I was in awe of him. The silence of prayer in churches— how good it used to be in those lofty spaces, within their cool stone walls, alone, kneeling on a low wooden bench, praying my unwritten prayers. How blissful I could feel in a cathedral, in a great church, in a chapel. Here: assaulted by the noise of this synagogue, this tumultuous atmosphere of people being forced to wait for something, this having-to-be-on-earth-without-the-

Messiah. And yet, in the church, salvation is only something dangled before the eyes: it is total theater, an illusion to be seen through. Here: noise and restlessness, prayer as though earth were nothing more than a world made of war, suffering, and vileness.

Keys rattled; the men were locking their prayer books in their desks. Near the prayer leader someone raised a goblet of red wine. "Kiddush!" they whispered to each other, "Amen!" they spoke, and gathered together in the narrow corridor. They all shook hands with one another; "Git Shabbes!" they called out. I shook hands, too, stranger in their midst, one question after another was directed at me. I answered each time, "Sholem Aleihem!" "Git Shabbes!" Nothing else; I heard Ilan's voice in the midst of the confusion; he was speaking with a group of elders: ". . . and he tells me he's here for the first time, in Eretz Israel, never had a feeling for his roots before." Ilan was giving away everything I had told him on our walk. "When he was twelve he suddenly made up his mind to learn how to read the Torah. Wait, Pinkas. Don't go away. After the Bar Mitzvah, he decided never to go to shul again, isn't that right, Pinkas?" Someone from the group came up to me. Ilan exclaimed, "Pinkas, this is my father." A powerful man, full beard, head like a living mountain—I saw his great projecting nose, full lips beneath it; he pressed me to his body, stroked the back of my head. "Be welcome. Very good that you have returned, to Eretz Israel, your homeland. I know that place where you grew up, two years ago I visited my nephew there at Yom Kippur."

He began to tell his story, simultaneously taking leave of the other men. We left the synagogue; he had one of his massive arms around Ilan. "He's not living where he belongs, my nephew, but where he became a rich man, and on top of that, in the country where it all happened. He's playing a game of chess with the guilty conscience of the people whose country it is. We go one time to Kol Nidre, never heard such a loud racket in all my life. The rabbi began to speak, a few people kept going shhh! or rapped on the benches, didn't help in the slightest. But

the people next to me, I could make out every word they were
saying: the horse races, price of gold, of crocodile skins, special
sale on coats, not for one second the slightest feeling of being in
HaShem's presence, nothing but a fashion show, what a curse I
let out against those assimilated people," said Lavan Baum. We
were walking down Balfour Street in the gathering darkness.
"Enough of cursing now, preserve my tongue from evil, and my
lips, that they not utter falsehood. For you should not do unto
your neighbor what you would not have them do unto you. The
tongue of a man is mightier than his sword, my father always
said—a sword can only kill a man who is standing right there,
but evil talk can kill a man at the other end of the world. But
now *this* year when Yom Kippur comes, one more month—then
you'll see what kind of a day that *really* is."

Ilan's mother welcomed us in the entrance hall of a small
apartment, she received me as if I were an old acquaintance, her
features were very similar to Ilan's. Her dark eyes—they seemed
so familiar to me. "We're so used to his bringing people home
like this," she said, "mostly from the King David, that's his hunting ground—sometimes even older people, then he makes them
spend the night with us." Ilan, rightful teacher of his own
parents, gentle king of this little space, showed me his room. No
pictures on the walls, no record player, no television set, no toy
cars or plastic Indians. Nothing but piles of books, heaps of
magazines, black clothes, writing paper, and ballpoint pens. On
one table, a cardboard model of the Second Temple. I thought
to myself: if my parents had moved to this land after the
Unspeakable happened, would I have become someone like Ilan?
"I know what you're thinking. I know what you're thinking," he
said, without looking me in the eyes—and I believed him, without asking. He showed me his father's workshop. Tall wooden
frames and the tools of his trade, strips of linen and pieces of
leather strewn everywhere. On the worktable, mountains of
books. Smell of glue and leather.

Gleam of eighteen flames, their fire fed by pure olive oil.
"You have chosen us and blessed us among all peoples and

granted us your Sabbath in love and affection. Praise be to You, Everlasting, Who sanctifies the Sabbath." Lavan had spoken the blessing over the wine; gave us to drink. (Us *alone* have You chosen, HaShem? I pushed the thought aside.) Lavan blessed the bread, dipped it in the salt, broke off a piece for each of us, passed it along. Ilan in silent jubilation looked at me as his guest at this table. Rivkah told me about her and Lavan's land of birth, recalled the hilly landscape, the deep and fertile soil, which she had lovingly preserved like colored snapshots in her memory for thirty years—since her childhood—without ever wanting to return there. "Do you know why they hate us so much?" Lavan asked; I couldn't be sure whom he meant, but shook my head anyhow. "Because they know for a fact that we have made a covenant with HaShem, and they haven't. We, before all other people, are His possession; we have a compact with Him. And they have none. The goyim will come running to us one day, begging for permission to learn the Torah." An anxious look out of the corner of Ilan's eye. I disapproved of that statement—he recognized it right away; he felt responsible for the words of his father. I wanted to tell them about Dana and her relatives, tried to describe the viewpoint of the outsiders, and was beginning to speak of the Armenian Quarter, when Rivkah signaled me with her eyes that I should first help myself to more red wine. I reached for the decorated carafe. Lavan's hand shot out, tore the bottle from my fingers—he filled my glass. "Forgive me," Rivkah whispered to him. And Ilan, white as chalk (did he have tears in his eyes?), stammered almost inaudibly, "If anyone has not kept the Sabbath two times in a row, he may not . . . I know, you don't understand all this—but he is not supposed to touch the wine bottle."

"He'll learn that, he'll learn all those things!" Lavan added in a loud voice. I felt ill, felt the pain of insult; I wanted to jump up from the table, leave the apartment. And I stayed there. I knew again how Dana felt in the circle of my kinsmen. I wanted to remove the fetters of this common bondage, tear myself free from such a family chain, no matter how ancient; wanted to call

up the King David Hotel, ask them if they had found my
passport—then realized, yes, naturally, all telephoning is forbidden on this day. I became flushed. An oval clock on the wall:
instead of normal numbers, little plastic roses-—all the old
furniture revoltingly ugly; how can people live like this? But:
next to the wall clock, tall bookcases, wonderful volumes, bound
in precious leathers, grouped according to size, gilt lettering on
their spines. Painful silence in the room, the Sabbath peace
ripped like a silk cloth. At moments like these I tend to look at
whatever objects are close at hand, as if every mark on them,
every color, held some enormous portent, were the key to my
ability to go on breathing. I picked up a silver fork, bent over
it, turned it slowly, examined its four tines, its handle, its shell
decoration.

"It is written, Genesis, chapter two, '*Al ken yaazov ish et aviv
ve et imo. . . .*'" Lavan was speaking with a calm voice. I interrupted him—an urge to be insolent, inflict wound for wound. I
insisted that he reformulate what he intended to say, from his
heart, without recourse to the Scriptures. "That is to say: the
man will leave his father and his mother," Lavan continued,
"and he will cleave to his wife and they will become one flesh.
Good, *Baruch HaShem;* Ilan will soon leave us; he will marry and
become the father of children. If a man wants to live in total
union with his wife, he must first cut the umbilical cord that
connects him to his parents, otherwise he can never become an
independent person." I was drinking the wine in rude gulps,
Ilan sat beside me, deflated; he looked quietly into his mother's
eyes, so like his own. I didn't leave my parents, I heard myself
think, I didn't burn my umbilicus through. We were eating
stewed pears. I bent over to look at a copper napkin ring, decorated with light-blue semiprecious stones. "You must get
married, Pinkas," said Rivkah. "You are old, could easily have
had three children by now." And Lavan, "We'll introduce him
to a girl." And Rivkah, "But *frumm,* she's got to be *frumm,* not
frei." (To be free is the Orthodox opposite of being pious! I
laughed.) Calmly I studied the swinging needle of my emotions,

read off the numbers as on a gauge inside myself. Like sand
slowly settling in water that has been stirred up, my rage sank
into more obscure regions—in deference to Ilan. My desire to
jump up from the table changed into a wary feeling of having
found an anchorage. Our supper table, a framework—I am not
driftwood; I am a passenger ship sailing out of a great harbor,
underway in any weather, bound for a new shore. With the aid
of the red wine, things emerged that I normally knew only from
dreams when the body receives messages from the soul that the
rational mind doesn't comprehend. Then blood built a bridge
between body and soul: *dam* means blood, *adom* means red,
adama: earth, soil. I am Adam, Your earth-son, HaShem. Dream
is the holy beholding of time compressed, in the dream state,
body and soul knew secrets that the waking state extinguished.
Like stars above us in the daylight (although I cannot see them),
dreams remain within our heads when we're awake, yet stay
veiled, until we close our eyes and fall asleep again.

Peaceful, rounded space in which we were sitting, behind the
blackness of the clouds is the radiance, I was saying to myself
. . . when suddenly all the electric lights in the apartment went
out. Blackout, I thought instantly. "You don't know about that?"
Rivkah asked, surprised. "You just set the thing for any time you
want and it automatically shuts off the current, and we don't
have to touch it ourselves—on the Sabbath." Only the oil lamps
now shed their light. How well I felt again. Suddenly it seemed
so self-evident: the permission to touch the Sabbath wine bottle
only after I observe the holy day with all my heart. The spines
of the books, the bars of my dungeon; in my jaws I felt reins
being tugged, they let me run, then pulled me up short, and let
me run again, in the walled-in outlet. Lavan said, "I make you
a prophecy: if you leave this place where you belong and run
back into the other world—leaving here is called *yeridah*, descent,
did you know that?—then when you are there, you will begin
to keep this day holy."

"Because you will understand that this day is our umbilical
cord to HaShem," said Rivkah, "the only day without machines,

without money, without following orders—but in exchange for that, a day for reading with awareness, for conversation, for taking walks. With everything you have in you, you can feel that HaShem is Lord of the world, not we. The Sabbath is not only a day for rest; it's there so you can feel that you're a small part of the whole and discover that during the week you'd had little time to think about that. It's like being in a capsule, quietly anticipating the age that will come with the Messiah."

"How can the goyim seriously believe—I can't get it into my head—how can they believe that the Messiah has already come?" Lavan asked. "Isn't it written as clear as day—look it up in Isaiah: 'And he shall judge between the nations'—goyim means nations—'and shall decide for many peoples; and they shall beat their swords into plowshares, and their spears into pruning hooks; nation shall not lift up sword against nation, neither shall they learn war any more.' Is that what it looks like now in the world? Tell me." And as they were saying these things, I knew: Torah is the Word which has become the People. Proclaimed not only to a caste of priests, HaShem's Revelation through Moshe Rabeinu has been passed along to every man, to every woman, an eternally new reality, transmitted for three thousand five hundred years. In Ilan, Lavan, Rivkah, it has become flesh and blood, taken up into their hearts letter for letter, every word still in its pure meaning, not patched up with the sludge of today's world. "Do you know that it is written," said Lavan, "if all of Israel were to keep holy the Sabbath only two times running, the Messiah would appear on earth at once?"

Bordered for a distance by single-story houses built of some light-colored stone, an anonymous, unpaved road climbed steadily uphill through olive groves, illuminated by the gray light of a half moon. Ilan had managed to get permission to take this evening walk with me. I envied his alertness, he seemed so much more lively, stronger than me, his stride more energetic, more rhythmic. Mud clung to the soles of our shoes, made our footsteps heavy.

"Everything is in HaShem's hands, everything—except our

fear of Him," Ilan said, interrupting our silence. By now I had learned to speak the Word-that-had-become-the-People, to carry it further. I replied, "And if you come down on the side of evil, HaShem will help you up, just as if you had come down on the side of good."

"Bravo, congratulations!" Ilan exclaimed, laughed aloud, pointed with both hands up into the endless sky above. "You've become a regular *bocher*. Soon you'll be putting on tefillin; prayer will give you strength you never knew you had. No question about it, you will observe the next Sabbath. Promise me you will!" He hugged me tight with one arm, "Promise me you will?" I gave a sort of half-nod, more like a shaking of the head than a real nod of agreement.

We had reached the summit of the Hill of Talpiot, marched along the flat, gravelly road; I scraped the mud still clinging to my shoes on the sharp edges of the little stones. Silhouettes of the city surrounded by its hills, image of the universal dream, packaged in an inky-blue, transparent membrane. I let myself fly out over the Old City, over the New City, like a falcon, and I hovered there, suspended over the most solemn city on earth. From this height its two parts flowed together, the past into its future, like music. Nothing was in the present, yet everything was, everything simultaneous—when David ruled the city, some ancestor stood on this very spot, let himself float down on the wings of his panoramic gaze. And in the coming millennium our children's children will stand on this same spot and let this mere city become again the City Everlasting as once their forebears did. "Every stone here is your possession, a building stone of your own house." Ilan spoke very softly and pointed down to the plateau where the Temple once stood and to the Hill of Moriah where Abraham was commanded to sacrifice Isaac. All the anxiety on earth emanates from this mount, the legend tells us. "Stay here, for if you do not you will seek and seek all your life long and never find another home. *Hashgahah pratit*, your own special providence, brought you here. This is where you belong." He moved a little away from me, left his words with

me as if they were beings in their own right. I felt certain then
that this was a moment I already knew, had lived through, from
another past, from another future perhaps. Foreknowledge?
Forgotten past? . . .

Suddenly a man darted at us out of the darkness, not old,
not young, neither a small man nor a big one; well dressed, in
gray, with a black hat on his head; first went up to Ilan and
then brushed very close to me, my heart beat wildly; the
stranger stopped a short distance away, and cried out to us,
"Woe! From its rising unto its setting, woe! Woe to all who are
bridegroom and bride, woe unto all the people! They beat me
for crying out this way, but I do not ask for mercy. My voice
does not grow hoarse and I cry out: Woe from its rising unto
its setting, woe to Yerushalayim!" Shivers ran from the nape of
my neck down my back. I looked around to find Ilan. The
stranger with his odd hopping gait stopped once more, shouted
1ouder than ever, "Woe from its rising, woe from its setting, woe
to Yerushalayim!" and disappeared from view. Ilan returned
calmly. "You were frightened by him? I've known him for some
time, he runs around everywhere shouting, always the same
words. He's called Joshua, no one knows where he comes from,
he never answers if you ask him something." Gradually I calmed
down, looked again out over our city, beyond the horizon of
night. Chips of stone, that is what we are, molecules in Your
sight, HaShem. "Where matter ends, what comes after that, what
lies beyond?" asked my soul-twin, as if I knew the answer. From
far away a wail resounded one final time, "Woe unto Yerushalayim!"

Downhill under tall cypress trees. Like me, Ilan seemed never
to take the same way back. The scratchy chirp of cicadas filled
the air. Smell of dust and tree bark. A frightened feeling, like a
viscous mass, was still inside me. Ilan said, "This is what we
must proclaim to the world, with a quiet but penetrating voice:
If we take man to be the measure of all things, how mean, how
dubious everything becomes. HaShem is the measure of all
things. Return to Him. As Jonah once warned the city of

Nineveh, so must we warn the world today, 'Our world will perish if we do not retrace our steps.' Flight into outer space, do you know what that is? It's nothing more than fear of the new flood of fire. Spaceships are the new arks. A New Age is coming and this city will be its fountainhead. HaShem will reveal Himself here. We must be prepared for that. This New Age can begin without catastrophe, without a second Deluge, through a great return to Him." My teacher grew silent, walked ahead without soliciting the acknowledgment of my glance. "Your monologues sound as if you were speaking to yourself sometimes, or like prepared speeches," I said, but Ilan's equanimity could not be upset. "All talk is a talking to HaShem," he replied. "Look, everything that exists is remote, buried very deep. Who will find it?"

The residential area of Abu Tor; fragrance of oranges spreading out from the circumference of a single tree. Laurel bushes. Sound of insects. A dusty street named En Rogel. The train station nearby. My amazement at my rabbi increased step by step. My silent, my inner reaction was envy and awe. Or could it have been that I was making Ilan into my mentor simply because my other half needed a teacher, that part of me that yearned to put the yoke of the Law on its shoulders? When he caught sight of the oranges there was such radiant happiness in his eyes, of a kind that I had not known myself since I was a child. Clasping his hands behind his back, he inhaled the fragrance. I wanted to offer him one of the fruits, stuck a hand in among the branches. Ilan's hand gently admonished mine, only then did I remember: picking, harvesting, too, are forbidden on this day, be it only a single ear of wheat, one leaf, one blade of grass—be it an orange. "But people, when they see the rings of Saturn, or a piece of fruit, a bee, an eye," Ilan continued as we walked along, "then they say, that came from nothing, by accident, cell by cell, millions of years, infinity arose from nothing. And if they admit that, yes, there must have been some first cell—Where then did this first cell come from?—then they say, chemical processes. And where do these chemical processes come from? Then they break off the conversation. But when they discover an ancient bottle buried in the ground, or a fork, or a knife, then right away they say, Someone made that." I replied that my own doubt was very great, too. I could never comprehend, I said, that *that* could have happened, forty years ago, only three decades before Ilan was born. We went along without speaking, for a long while the only thing to be heard was the echo of our footsteps.

As we walked past the shunting tracks of the station my rabbi spoke. "You will be . . . I think you will be horrified at what I am feeling now. I must figure out how to . . . it's hard to find the right words. You know that the Everlasting, may His Name be praised, gave us a promise; if we keep faith with His Torah, he will protect us always and be benevolent to us and multiply our people. But if you do not obey my Commandments, says the Everlasting, then you shall be accursed among all people into whose hands I shall deliver you. He will send a people upon our heads from the ends of the earth, one which soars like an eagle—so it is written: like an *eagle*—an insolent people who take no heed of the old and do not spare the young. If we take up the customs of the alien people, HaShem will hide His face from us and deliver us into the hands of our adversaries. To be chosen does not mean to be better, it means we have to assume a greater burden of responsibility. And never since HaShem first spoke to us, never has disregard of His Commandments been so great as in this century. And where has it been worst of all, this assimilation of ours, where? In those very countries where later the Unspeakable happened. HaShem carried out His threat. That one lunatic and his henchmen—the only thing they will be known for in days to come is that it was they who wanted to obliterate us—they were the tools in HaShem's hands, they were. . ."

"Ilan," I shouted, "stop! That's enough now. The others, the ones who kept to the absolute letter of the Law, they, too, were murdered and burned in exactly the same way." I stammered, I was assailed by a shuddering chill. Who is this boy, where do these words of his come from? "The good will perish along with the others," he replied calmly. "They failed to battle with all their might against the evil, they were accomplices. HaShem wants us to *live*, we wouldn't be here otherwise. Yes, the world stood and stared at our incineration, and it would simply stare again if something like it should happen to the nation where we live now. But this time there's a difference: If Yerushalayim perishes, then the whole earth will perish. That Great War was the final warning HaShem gave man to reverse his course. And once again it was *we* who were the sign He gave, His people, chosen and raised up as His example. If the return does not take place soon, the entire earth will be burned to ashes next time. We must go on a journey, out into the fear-racked world, and admonish it to return."

A bundle of tears was forming at the roof my mouth. Exhaustion, agitation, like a child on the threshold of a separation. I wanted to shake Ilan by the shoulders, embrace him. Had I only imagined the words he spoke, had I infused my own thoughts into him, a vessel I had found? After a long march back, we passed by the city theater, shut now these twenty-four hours. Standing next to a closed café, two young men with their long-haired and luminous girl friend, probably just passing through, I could hear them cursing the strict observance of the holy day, one of the boys pressed his mouth against the girl's lips; the other part of me, that other half, entered his bones, seized and lifted the shining girl in a deep embrace. As if none of the thoughts and words between Ilan and me had occurred only minutes before, I suddenly longed to travel through the night with these three friends, to be naked with them, and I began to formulate a sentence in my brain to help dislodge myself from Ilan, so swiftly did my focus shift. I was already no longer at his side by the time he turned the corner into Oliphant Street; the three messengers were behind me arm in arm, and I ran to catch up with Ilan, to say goodbye to him quickly. He was standing in front of the apartment house. I didn't want to enter the building. "You will be staying the night with me, won't you?

I'm sure my parents have put an extra bed in my room." His voice sounded compressed. The words stuck like a blade between the two halves of my split nature, slashed the road before me into a path that forked. I wanted to stay with him. I decided to leave. I wanted to stay with him. "You don't know what you want," he said. "You're looking for something and trying at the same time not to find it. . . ." Was he about to cry? "But what you are really looking for you will find." Or was it I who was the one close to tears? "Where do you think you can go now in the middle of the night? Come, please, you haven't said goodbye to my parents, come. And early in the morning we'll go to the mikvah, you've never been to a mikvah yet, have you? And then afterwards to the synagogue." Ilan could see that I wasn't going to be staying with him. "You are going to ruin your Sabbath. You don't know much yet. At least swear to me that you will go on learning. Put on the tefillin, wear them. Buy them Sunday, buy them right away." I grew impatient with him; I didn't want to put on tefillin, I explained, not if I couldn't believe that HaShem spoke to us from Mount Sinai. "You're not supposed to *believe*, you're supposed to *know*, you've only forgotten. You must learn, learn, then you'll remember." I laughed sadly. "Do you want to keep running away all your life? The things you've learned since you've been here, they're things that will never leave you. Up to now, ignorance isolated you from the Law; but now you know what they mean, the Commandments, some of them." I leaned down and pressed my forehead against his shoulder, felt his hand on the back of my head, pulled away from my brother. "You have to come and get your things at the temple, you know. You'll come by tomorrow evening, promise?" I turned away, tore myself away, fork in the road, looked back once more, in the darkened stairwell he was climbing up to the home of his parents.

My steps took me through a little barren park. Not a trace of the three strangers I was looking for. A green bird dead in the gravel. I was wearing phrases, words of wisdom, over my shoulders and they hung down both sides, still untied, I could not bind their fringes. I should have spent the night with my brother; why did I not stay with him? My pockets empty. I liked being without money, without anything to write with, anything to write on. But if the world was not created in six days, why then Sabbath every seventh day? Why not six hundred million years of work and a hundred million years of Sabbath? That You rule the earth, HaShem, that You created the universe (why did You create the universe?)—was I put into this world to *comprehend* all of that? The sky clear, full of stars, to the north a storm brewing. I longed for my teacher, decided to turn back—didn't turn back. A hundred flashes of lightning in a bank of clouds. Not a sound of thunder in the cool air, too far away. Like the flickering of artillery. You are making flames, HaShem, You? On the Sabbath? This lightning, forged in the days of Creation, and released now, today, in this place? Across a narrow valley to my right, Mount Zion and the walls of the Old City, illuminated by electricity—beyond them churches, domes, battlements. The Citadel of Herod. Jaffa Gate. . . . No passport! I had forgotten that I had lost my passport. . . . Who am I? Why no brothers, no sisters, and why no friends, no wife, no children, one day no parents? To enter the Law will help me alleviate my loneliness, but I do not want to have to invent You out of my own weakness, HaShem. Where am I to go? Woe unto Yerushalayim, woe also unto me. "The voice of the Everlasting divides the flames of the fire. The voice of the Everlasting shakes the wilderness. The voice of the Everlasting makes the oaks whirl and strips the forests bare, and in His temple every one speaks of His glory." I didn't know how it went on.

Through a high revolving door into the brilliantly lit lobby of the King David Hotel. (One more proof of the fact that the earth is round, some forefather of mine is said to have declared each time he took his constitutional and returned home.) Lobby tall as a house—a home and refuge. Far away, a man sunk into a leather armchair was playing a game of chess with an invisible opponent. I looked for the night porter, could not understand how one of the grandest hotels in the city could be left with no

guard at its entrance, until I saw that little camera high over-
head, oscillating from side to side, secured to a gilded beam. An
elevator door snapped open with a loud sound, no one had rung
for it. The hand on a clock face jumped one marker to one-forty-
four. I entered the elevator; even before I could push a floor
button the door closed, the cabin whooshed to the second floor.
The door opened, closed by itself, the elevator went up to the
third floor. Without my touching a single button I ascended floor
by floor to the top. I was in a Sabbath elevator that conducted
its passenger from floor to floor without his having to complete
the electric circuit, without his having so much as a hand in the
making of the future. (And even with this, the true observants
walked the staircase up to their rooms on this holy day.) I ran
back down the carpeted steps to the ground floor, met on the
fourth floor one of the ladies to whom I had loaned my newspaper that afternoon; she was wearing a silk nightgown that
hung down to her ankles, leaned against the elaborately curved
stair railing, it looked like a scene in the belly of an old ocean
liner.

The night porter, a balding man with the bushiest eyebrows
I had ever seen, was drying his hands on the entire contents of
a packet of Kleenex. When I told him about my lost passport he
looked at me with a combination of gentle concern and glee at
my loss. He disappeared behind a column, made metallic clink-
ing noises with his bunch of keys, didn't reemerge for a long
time. The seconds seemed as immense and endless as the corridors of the hotel. Then he leaned over the reception desk, his
face close to mine, holding the open passport in his hand,
compared photograph with fact. "Well—hmm. Good. Just one
thing though—this country you call your own country up there,
it's like a wife, yes? You're married but you don't know if it's
forever, right? Will she cheat on you, will you cheat on her? But
if you belong to *our* country, then she's like a mother to you.
No escaping, nix. And cheating on her? You couldn't, even if
you should happen to try." His loud laugh lasted only a second.
The elevator arrived at the ground floor, doors snapped open

automatically. In the far background the chess player. The night porter handed me my Diaspora pass. The elevator doors snapped shut. The night porter winked. I wanted to give him a reward for finding it, remembered that I had no money with me, blushed, broke out in perspiration, made a pretense of going through all my pockets, stammered some excuse or other and something about the Sabbath, whereupon the night porter exploded once again with his laugh, so loud, so brief, turned his back on me, vanished behind a column. I wanted to call out something to him and didn't do it. Out onto the street. Longing for my brother Ilan. I jogged off in the direction of Zion Square—over there not far away, the apartment house where Rachel lived.

LEO SUCHAREWICZ

The Girl and the Children

1.

"**D**ON'T GO," she said softly.

"I have to." We were silent for a while, then she put her hand on my cheek.

"Don't go. If you go, I'll die of fear."

"I have to go, and you're too pretty to die. Try to understand."

I removed her hand from my face, but kept it in mine. Strange, how much she had changed in the last few hours.

"The thing is, I don't understand you! No, I just don't understand you," she said obstinately. That was a little better. I wished she would get really angry. Anger works wonders as a sedative. Anger is a bridge that will take you across any abyss of fear, despair, or disappointment. And anger produces clarity. But she remained calm.

"They can't force you to go," she said softly. I wanted to stroke her hair, but she turned her head away. She was sitting on the mattress, her knees drawn up to her chin. She had been sitting this way when I first met her at the university. She sat in the lecture hall with her knees drawn up, and later she sat on the floor with her arms around her knees when our study group met in my student digs in Schwabing. She was a contented doe, pretty and calm and clever, with fragile legs.

We were working under tremendous pressure, preparing for

a major exam in political theory; we often stayed up all night talking things through. She made coffee and raided her parents' icebox to provide us with food. All semester everything went without a hitch, thanks to her. When summer vacation came, I thought I would have to manage without her marvelous coffee: she was going to Cannes with her parents, while I would be staying in Munich and driving a taxi, mostly at night. After two weeks I got a postcard from her, with only one sentence: "Don't forget to go to the cafeteria at noon; you're much too skinny."

And two days later she phoned: "Can you pick me up at the airport tomorrow? I don't feel like staying here anymore."

The next day I raced through the city in my taxi and got to the terminal just in the nick of time. She ran up to me and gave me the kind of matter-of-fact airport hug a wife gives a husband coming in on a commuter flight.

I was going to drive her to her house, but she said, "Let's go to your place first. I have to make sure everything's all right there. After all, I've been gone two weeks."

She whisked through my apartment with wrinkled brow, laughed at the new bookcase I had made out of bricks and boards, peered into the refrigerator, and summed up her inspection with comic gestures of despair: "Now I know why you're so thin. Your refrigerator is empty, just as I feared. It's positively depressing."

We spent an inconsequential afternoon strolling through Schwabing. She told me about Cannes and its gigolos. In the evening I drove her to her apartment and then went out on my night shift.

2.

She woke me the next morning with a very tentative ring of the doorbell. I wrapped my old army blanket around my waist and staggered to the door. There she was, holding out a Little Red Riding Hood basket with fresh rolls, milk, ham, and eggs. Too tired to greet her properly, I stumbled back to my mattress and immediately fell asleep again.

The aroma of her marvelous coffee woke me. She was sitting on my mattress, observing me with amused curiosity, as if I were an experimental subject. On a stool nearby she had placed a carefully arranged breakfast. It was delicious, and I found myself falling a little in love with her.

That was the beginning of our breakfast ritual. Every morning she would wake me by ringing the doorbell. After teasing me about my old blanket, she would come in and prepare breakfast quietly while I went back to sleep. When it was ready, she would sit on the edge of my mattress with her knees drawn up until I woke up by myself, or wake me gently. She always insisted that I eat every crumb.

"Give me a key so I don't always have to wake you," she said after a week.

"A key is a very symbolic piece of metal. Is it only the key you're after?"

She laughed artlessly. "No, of course not. But it's your own fault if you haven't noticed anything." She was in love. "I'm too old for you," I said. She laughed. "Too old at twenty-four? Too bad for you: I happen to like older men."

"You know any other older men?"

"No, you're my first."

"Then you have no way of knowing whether you like them."

"Look here, are you going to give me the key or not, old man? You could doze in the morning until I have your gruel

ready. Just think: an extra half hour of sleep—that's very important at your age."

I gave her the key because she was pretty, because I liked
her, and because I still made mistakes.

The next morning she floated into my apartment and woke
me gently. "Let me sleep," I grumbled. "I was out driving till
six; I'm beat."

She kneeled on my mattress and said nothing.

"I'll have breakfast later," I murmured, and turned over onto
my stomach.

"No breakfast today," she whispered.

I was wide awake then; the touch of nervousness in her voice
took me by surprise, and I felt her breasts pressing against my
back.

"I'm too old for you," I said into my pillow. She was trying
to turn me over. I sighed. "And you're too pretty."

"That's true," she said contentedly, "and too clever."

We stayed in bed until evening. I missed my night shift, and
the next morning we went for a walk in the English Garden. We
had breakfast at a café in the park, and she sliced my rolls for
me. From then on we had breakfast almost daily at this café, and
in the evening she made all sorts of interesting salads. My
apartment became our island, and occasionally we swam to
neighboring islands, the cafés and bars of Schwabing. An additional link to the outside world was the perpetually upbeat
blaring of the American Armed Forces Network, AFN.

"So, are you happy, old man?"

"Yes."

"Because you've never met a girl like me?"

"Yes."

"Because I'm pretty?"

"Yes, because you're pretty."

"Because I'm smart?"

"No, not for that reason. If you were smart, you wouldn't
have fallen for me."

"Idiot."

"I'm serious. I'm too old for you."

Every time we reached this point in the discussion she would hurl herself at me, crowing with joy, and give me a big hug to cheer me up.

Our love was lighthearted and easy, as far from Romeo and Juliet as we were in years from Shakespeare. When we went walking in the English Garden, we seemed to hover effortlessly a few inches above the puddles, and sometimes, when we hugged each other tight, we would lift off and float the rest of the way home.

3.

"No milk today. . . ," AFN played nostalgically, and then the news came on and we heard that war had broken out in Israel. She sensed how disturbed I was. She was puzzled; she brooded, but said nothing. In the evening I told her.

"I'm going to be on the next plane to Israel."

"What? When? *What* did you say you're going to do?"

"Tomorrow morning. The plane leaves around nine."

"But why, for God's sake? Have you gone out of your mind?" She opened her eyes very wide.

"I'm going to report for duty."

"You're going to *what*? You want to go there? Report for combat duty? On which side? And why? Don't drive me crazy—explain!"

"Well, first of all on the Israeli side, and second because the situation is very serious. The Syrians are involved and. . . "

She interrupted me breathlessly: "Would you please tell me what you have to do with that damned war down there?"

"A lot. I have a lot to do with that war. It certainly is damned. But for me it's not somewhere 'down there' but at the

top of my list. Maybe I should have told you earlier . . ." I
looked past her and was not sure *what* I should have told her.

"Damn! Can you please explain this to me somehow, quick,
before I lose my mind!"

I thought hard. I could sense her anxiety and did not want
to leave her waiting, but my mind was blank. Where to begin?
Suddenly I was confronting a mountain of explanations. I looked
up, but its peak was lost in a hazy sky. Impossible to pull out
just one explanation—they were all interconnected. The establishment of the State of Israel in 1948 came to mind. A good
beginning for a school composition. You can never go wrong
starting with a brief historical sketch. Or should I tell her about
the book. It was called *The Uprising in the Warsaw Ghetto*, and as
a child I had stumbled upon it among my parents' books. Should
I tell her I was only twelve at the time? And that it's best not
to read books about the Warsaw Ghetto when you're only
twelve? No, she wouldn't understand that. But I could try
another tack. In a flash I prepared a disquisition on the problems
of minorities in general. The Indians in black Africa, the Chinese
in Indochina, the Pakistanis in England, the Druse in Arabia, the
Kurds in Iran, the Armenians in Turkey, the Huguenots in
France, the Christians in Rome, the Jews in Germany, and the
Germans in Romania. It might be a good idea to tell her about
the exciting transformation of the old underdog, who one day
got sick of playing that role and decided to defend himself. Or
should I try to explain why history itself can make you furious,
and why Jewish history in particular can put me in a white heat?

"There's nothing to explain," I said. "It's very simple: six
years ago I was in the Israeli army and fought in the Six Day
War."

It sounded like a confession, and I was annoyed that it came
out that way. She paced back and forth and lectured me. This
hour transformed us both. She wanted answers, but I shook my
head because I didn't know where to begin and because I was
gradually and very quietly beginning to feel the fear I had

forgotten over the last five years. As it spread through me, I was
actually glad to meet this old acquaintance again.

"Stop!" I said. "There's no point arguing. I have to get to the
airport very early tomorrow; they may take off ahead of schedule. Be a good girl and come to bed."

I crawled under the blanket and she followed with an
exhausted sigh. We lay there in silence next to each other. I was
wishing she would reach out her hand to me, touch me with her
knee or brush me with her breath, and I knew I would not get
to sleep without her. I refuse to arrive tired, I said to myself, as
if wishing could make it so, and I felt fear stretching out under
the blanket like a sick dog. No, I could not arrive tired. This
time I would start out rested and always make sure to get
enough sleep. This time I would be more careful, no matter
what.

Sleep is the most important thing when you're at war. Why was
everything in Israel always connected in my mind with being
tired? I thought of the endless nights spent on guard duty in
Syria, and of the days that were too hot for sleeping, thinking,
forgetting, even too hot for staying awake.

The greatest miracle in the Holy Land is that you can live
without sleep. At the kibbutz we would get up at four in the
morning during the cotton harvest, work until three in the afternoon, go to the swimming pool, do our laps at dusk, and in the
evening we had our parties, back at the swimming pool. We
danced and horsed around until one or two in the morning, and
at four we got up again. At the kibbutz, fatigue produced a sort
of intoxication. In the military, during basic training, it became
a barrier that we had to scale anew with each step, but during
the Six Day War it put us in a dangerously unreal, shadowy
state of mind. The first days of the war passed without the
slightest prospect of sleep. We drove to the Syrian front, scaled
the Golan Heights by night, and didn't sleep. At four in the
morning we attacked the village of Baniyas until the last intact

Syrian tanks retreated, and we didn't sleep. We advanced on Kuneitra—a company of hollow-cheeked eighteen-year-old ghosts with enormous, bloodshot eyes, for whom the fight against exhaustion became more important than the fight against the Syrian army.

*   *   *

I couldn't afford to be tired when I arrived. Not the first day. The first day was crucial. I tried to get to sleep, but the curtain to the world of dreams refused to open, because she was lying beside me awake, and because we weren't touching each other. If I could take her in my arms, or at least put an arm under her neck, I would go to sleep. I felt her crying quietly and reached out my hand to her, felt her firm belly and stroked her breasts. But she was already filled with the rage of one betrayed. Why do people who love each other always get furious at the worst possible time? She pushed my hand away and sat up in bed.

"You should have told me you were an adventurer, an irresponsible adventurer who pretends to be the experienced older man."

"That's precisely what I'm not," I said wearily, and lost all hope of going to sleep with her in my arms.

What image did she have of an adventurer? Was it from Camel ads? She didn't know a thing about adventurers. The founding of the State of Israel was an adventure. Jewish history was adventurous and could make you so furious that you lost interest in any other adventure. In a single day in Israel more happened than she could see in an entire year of movie previews. But I was no adventurer. There she was wrong. An adventurer seeks out risks voluntarily, but I was being involuntarily sought out by the adventurous history of the Jews.

She took a deep breath.

"You should have told me you were Jewish," she suddenly said with defiance.

"Well, I am, in case there's any doubt," I said, and finally felt the first wave of tiredness sweep over me. Should I say more, or just try to ride the wave and go to sleep? "Yes. I should have told you. No doubt about it. But when? After your first breakfast, or before we slept with each other? But no, that would have been far too late already. Let me think: the best time would have been when you spilled fruit salad on my pants in the cafeteria. Yes, damn it, that would have been the right moment. I should have said to you: Just so you know whose jeans you're ruining with your clumsiness, I'm Jewish, and please don't place any hopes in me."

I had sat up and was waiting for her reaction, but she said nothing.

"But whether I'm Jewish or not, I have to get some sleep. And the only thing you can do for your Semitic lover at this particular moment is make sure he gets on the plane tomorrow halfway rested. But for that he has to get to sleep, and in order to do that he first has to put his hand on your breasts. If people knew what a fantastic sleeping aid your breasts are, the stock of Hoffmann-La Roche would crash. No one would be buying Valium anymore."

I slid back under the covers. She still did not react, and I was afraid she had already got sucked into the game of *the-one-who-makes-the-first-move-loses*. So I rolled over to the edge of the mattress and tried to picture sheep. But the shepherd had stuck helmets on their heads that slid back and forth grotesquely, and the sheep were jumping over barbed-wire barricades. Many of them hurt their slim legs and limped away.

As I was falling asleep I finally felt her hand on my shoulder, and she whispered, "Don't go. Please don't go. If you go, I'll die of fear." She was still sitting up, and I answered her without knowing what I was saying. She wouldn't die of fear. Fear itself sees to it that its victims survive, in its own interest. Maybe many people aren't even cut out to be victims of fear; maybe fear has to treat its good victims, the ones who are really afraid, with tender consideration?

No, she certainly didn't know what fear was; presumably she was acquainted with only one, or at most two, forms of fear, but there are many, many more. There is the fear that comes over you unexpectedly and grabs you in the throat, or sometimes in the joints. Both of those types usually ebb fairly quickly. In contrast there is the stomach variety, like a painful burr that you get rid of only after many hours. There is fear of choking and fear of silence, fear of hate and fear of noise. Why hasn't anyone written a fear thesaurus yet? It could be called "Roget's International Thesaurus of Fear." I would be happy to sign on as editor, making sure the volume was as comprehensive as possible. I had been introduced to a whole series of interesting fears, so I knew how hard it is to die of fear. All you have to do is come up with the right response to each fear, but for that you have to have experienced them.

In 1967, by the time the war was over, I had developed my defensive strategies quite well. But there was one time, just one, when fear attacked me in a new form, bored its way into my brain like a nasty virus, shot through my entire nervous system in a matter of seconds, and after that nothing was ever the same. That was when Samir rejoined us, a few days after the ceasefire. He sneaked in among us one morning, with an embarrassed grin and an endless stream of nonsensical jabber that kept us constantly on edge. He shuffled through our camp and with grand gestures lectured us: "Why didn't you advance to Damascus, you assholes? If I'd been there, we'd be in Damascus today, and not in this dump Kuneitra. Ah, Damascus, Damascus . . ."

He crossed his froggy eyes, wiggled his hips in a ridiculous dance step, and sighed as if he were an expert on Damascene belly dancers who was graciously calling our attention to the irreplaceable experience we were missing.

We had orders to collect any materiel left behind by the Syrians. This included Czech trucks and Russian jeeps, which we lined up in an area the size of a soccer field. There were also artillery pieces from Poland, bandaging materials from East Germany, and K-rations from China. We stacked up crates of munitions, puffing and panting with the effort as we patiently bore Samir's reproaches. He chattered incessantly, sometimes groaning as he strained, eyes bugging out, under the preposterous load of an empty munitions crate. He kept dreaming up new strategies for bold military operations that would have brought us to Damascus.

During the lunch break, postcards were handed out and everyone had to write home. We called them "survival cards." Samir read us his text as he was writing it, syllable by syllable: "Dear Mother, Can't come home at the mo-ment, am in-dis-pen-sable to the gener-al staff. Food is good, ser-vice first class. Only problem, champagne is served much too warm in Syria."

The cards were collected and the Tiger, our squad leader, pushed us to get back to work. Until evening Samir entertained us with detailed descriptions of making out with the nurses in the field hospital. Then each of us headed off for a brief rest before supper. Suddenly the Tiger leaped forward with giant steps yelling, "No! Samir, no!" Did he really yell his name? I didn't remember, but I could feel that fear again, a fear that demonstrated the full dimensions of its power.

She was shaking my shoulder. "Hey, old man, are you asleep? Are you listening to me?"

No, I wasn't listening to her. I couldn't hear anything, for my ears were deafened by the detonation. The earth rumbled and the sky rained stones. And shredded bodies. And one of them was Samir. Slowly we stood up. We looked around us and counted to ourselves. No one dared to count out loud. Eleven lay there shredded, and one of them was Samir. They were still with us, but torn to bits. No one said so, but we all knew. It was Samir. Samir had stepped on a mine. Samir, that dark-skinned unhappy mixture of clown and devil. Samir, that clumsy Pinocchio, had pulled the pegs out of his own joints, and ten others from our company had stumbled over his parts. It was like a cautionary tale by Wilhelm Busch.

Samir, our transistor. But he wasn't light enough for the mine. Samir, you damned idiot. The Tiger yelled "No!" but you can't give orders to a brown-skinned, froggy-eyed Yemenite klutz. It was his last order to Samir, but it came too late for Samir to obey. His shredded limbs would not go back together. Why didn't the Tiger have more power? Why wasn't he God?

I stood next to him and said, "Bring him back to life."

"I can't," said the Tiger, and his powerful chest expanded and expanded. He was breathing hard. "I know he was your friend."

"I'm not sure *he* knew it."

"Yes, he knew."

"No. He knew I thought of him as a little brown clown. And now he doesn't know anything anymore."

I didn't answer her and still couldn't hear anything, but I felt her nestle against me, I felt her whispering, and I knew I would go to sleep now.

4.

Schwabing woke up first and mercilessly roused us with its racket. She was still lying pressed against me, her face buried in my neck, and I felt her eyelashes move. She said to my neck, "Listen, legionnaire, I have a suggestion for you. This time you stay here, but if I've had enough of you in six months or more, then you can go off and take part in any war you please, if you think it can't be won without you: Vietnam, the Basque separatist movement, the Third World War. . ."

She ticked off the possibilities like the varieties of vegetables available at the open-air market.

I sat up and checked cautiously to see whether I was tired. I noted with satisfaction that I felt rested, and had to grin with relief.

"Will you drive me to the airport? The plane leaves in two hours."

Her outburst took me by surprise.

"Are you completely out of your mind? Don't you see that what you do is completely irrelevant? One soldier more or less has never made the difference in a war. If something really depended on you, maybe I could understand it, but this is pure lunacy. Or an Israeli form of voodoo, with some medicine man pulling you across the Mediterranean on invisible strings! I wish I could understand what's going on here!"

"You can't understand because you live in Schwabing, and Schwabing quite simply has nothing to do with the Warsaw Ghetto. But that's my second legal residence. I'm registered here in Munich, and there as well. You can't understand because the Isar isn't the Jordan and the kindergarten kids in Bogenhausen don't play 'bunker' because they don't have Katyusha rockets crashing down in their playground all the time."

"But we're in Munich now, and Munich isn't Haifa, so no one can force you to go. Do you want me to drop a bomb on the Marienplatz to give you a reason to stay? Must people die here, too? Or do you think maybe too few people died in Germany? You should be happy that things are finally halfway peaceful here. Our country's suffered enough. I know, it was our own crazies who were mostly responsible, that doesn't change things. I don't find wars original at all, and I don't find you original in the slightest. What's the point of studying political science if you're going to go rallying round the flag like the most idiotic German footsoldiers in history?"

"It's not the same. I'm not rallying round the flag; this is something that has to be done. In Israel it's different."

Again I was confronting a mountain of explanations. Maybe Masada? Yes, Masada was good. She must have heard in history class about the battle of Masada. The last Jewish mountain fortification in the desert that resisted the Roman legions. The suicide of the last defenders, so as not to become slaves. But she would refuse to understand—that was just history to her.

"Nothing's different!" she shouted. "It's always the same, it has been since the first Neanderthals! If I see a truck full of German soldiers, it makes me sick—that's how stupid the whole thing is!"

"ZAHAL isn't the German Army. You don't understand."

"Then please explain to me what the difference is!"

"No one's ever attacked Germany, and no one ever wanted to kill off the Germans just because they were German. That's probably the most important difference."

"The Allies came close, and the Huns too, and more than once Germany almost ceased to exist as a nation. And damn it all, I wouldn't have cared!"

"And damn it all, I do care! Israel has to survive, if only to be available as an exile for anyone who urgently needs one."

"I suppose you mean for every Jew?"

"Yes, primarily. If the Germans in Romania are harassed, or in Ecuador or somewhere else they are subjected to a nice little pogrom, they usually go to Germany. Pardon: I mean West Germany, of course."

"Ahhh . . . I'm so angry I could kill you. What's supposed to be different about Israel? What do you people think you are? The chosen people? Still? What has to happen before you come down off your high horse? Another six million? Israel isn't the center of the world, and certainly not the only place where there are decent people. Do you think we have only robots in Germany? Am I one? Do you think there's no love and friendship in Germany? Do you think recruits in Israel look any smarter than those in West Germany when they're marching around in a circle? Every soldier marching looks just as dumb as the rest!"

It was pointless; she couldn't grasp it. Maybe the first day for recruits in the West German Army was really no different than for recruits in the ZAHAL, but the last day certainly was. It's the last day that counts when you compare these things. The way two people who have split up go their separate ways, the way a prisoner is released, the way a soldier is allowed to go home: the last day is the decisive one.

I picked up my discharge papers at an office where two officers were laughing and flirting with the woman soldiers going in and out. The girls were all wearing short, close-fitting uniform skirts, provocatively hip-hugging wide military belts, and sandals.

"What are your plans?" the older officer asked me.

"I'm heading back to Munich. I want to study political science."

It sounded like a confession, and I was annoyed with myself.

"You can study here, too," the younger one remarked.

"No, I can't. I can hardly decipher the street signs."

"Israel is a country of immigrants," he said. "Most of them bring their own street signs with them."

"When I'm back in Munich, I'll miss this gentle Israeli sarcasm. If I live in Israel some day, *that* will be the first thing I'll get used to."

They fell silent and exchanged brief glances. The older one bent forward slightly over his desk and said in a soft, neutral voice, "You're going back, but your friends are staying here. Three times a day you'll be able to stretch your legs out under your mother's dining room table, but your friends' mothers have to tremble three times a year when the reserves are called up."

"I'm going back because I have to. Munich is the only place I can study, and if I don't get started now, I may never do it."

"Do you know how many young men in Israel will never get to study because they're cripples now? Do you know how many men here will never do anything at all? Their wives are the only ones still doing something: crying. Well, maybe you're just scared—it's all right to admit it. But if your arms and legs are more important to you—case closed, you can go."

"That's not the reason, and you know it." There was no point in explaining further. He would say: Many people here have lost a friend, that's the price we pay for our country. He wouldn't say: Many here have lost their hopes. Of course not. Either you come to Israel without any hope, or you are born in Israel full of irrepressible hope, which you never lose. No. It was pointless to argue with him. He didn't know Samir, and he wasn't the Tiger. I wished the Tiger were in his place. I wished I could have one good, long talk with the Tiger. But he was drilling recruits in the desert. Why couldn't that bastard talk properly for a change, instead of always giving orders! The officers in the discharge office wanted to talk, even though I didn't feel like talking with them. Give me my discharge papers or give me an order, I demanded silently.

Now the other one bent forward: "What are you going to do if there's war again? Have you given any thought to that?"

"No, I haven't given it any thought. What do you think I'll do?"

"You'll come back, just like the others."

"How do you know? When I'm in Munich, no one can force me."

They exchanged glances again.

"We don't have to force you. It's enough if you promise. Where do your parents come from?"

"From Poland."

He paused a moment, then said reflectively, "Do you know about the Warsaw Ghetto?"

"Yes, damn it, I know."

I remembered the book. Somewhere in the middle was a photograph of a boy of ten, maybe twelve. He was looking fearfully at the barrel of the gun that an SS-man was pointing at him, and he had his hands up. A child surrendering.

I was twelve when I came upon that picture. I stared at it for a whole hour. That child could have been me if I had been born earlier. No matter how I held the book, from every angle the boy was looking directly at me. His visored cap was on crooked, and he was wearing an odd jacket-like article of clothing, and his eyes were full of SS-fear. I had often heard of fear of the SS, but I didn't know it firsthand. SS-fear must be included in the thesaurus, just in case.

Had the boy survived the ghetto? He was too little to grab the SS-man's gun from his hand and smash it down on his head. But perhaps he had thought of that in a moment of madness? Perhaps for one fatal second his muscles had actually tensed to hit the SS-man or kick him in the shin? Strike and die, or suffer fear and live? One blow in self-defense—and then nothing more—never to sleep with a girl, never to have children. The boy stared at me and demanded a decision. I held the book far from me, turned it sideways to escape his gaze. Strike him! I thought, but I couldn't speak the words. I clapped the book shut.

"I promise," I said.

Again they exchanged glances.

"Massadah lo tipol." Masada will not fall again, they said.

"Massadah lo tipol," I said.

They shook my hand and gave me a brown envelope containing my discharge papers.

"Answer me!" she shouted. "What's supposed to be different?"

"I've forgotten. Really, I'm sorry. I know it's different, and I know you'll think I'm a complete idiot, but at the moment I've completely forgotten."

I stood up and wrapped my army blanket around my hips.

"Will you drive me to the airport?"

She reached for her jeans. Slowly she climbed into them, pulled the waistband up over her hips, and chose a hole for her belt buckle. She reached for her bra and slipped it up over her arms. I felt a longing for her skin and wished she would put her arms around me before she was completely dressed. She looked at me, and I discovered in her eyes, just in time before she answered my question, the extinguished curiosity that comes when a social experiment is ending.

"Fine," she said. "I'll take you. But if you come back, I won't be here anymore."

5.

"When I go back, she won't be there anymore," I told the others. We were sitting in the sand, exhausted, passing pictures around. The other soldiers whistled the internationally recognized whistle of appreciation and envy. Did the Egyptians on the other side of the front use that same whistle?

"Is she German?"

"Yes."

"Not bad-looking."

"Nope, not bad-looking."

"Why won't she be there anymore when you go back?"

"Because she doesn't believe that Israel is a special country, and because it's none of your business."

"Maybe you won't be going back, and then it won't matter to you whether she's waiting for you or not. Come on, give us her phone number. One of us is sure to come out of this alive. Let him bring her greetings from you. Oh, boy . . . if I get the chance . . . she won't forget my greetings for the rest of her life."

"Well, just in case, give me *your* girlfriend's number," I said. "So far I've survived the craziest things, and in Germany I work as a professional survivor, in addition to my graduate studies. Besides, I'm lucky Hans."

"Who's that?"

"That's someone who always has terrible luck but never bites the dust."

"If you have bad luck now, you've only yourself to blame. Why did you come here, anyway? Weren't things going well enough for you in Europe, or was this war something you needed in order to be happy?"

A group of reservists with shovels marched by. Most of them still in T-shirts and jeans. They were chanting, "Tnu lanu rowim!" Give us guns!

Our non-com shook his head, "They're all nuts. Just as nutty as you. Tens of thousands of them come from America and Europe and God knows where, abandon their jobs or their studies, jam the airports, mess up the supply lines, and are bound and determined to get to the front." He scrambled to his feet. "Come on, we've got to get to work." He laid his hand on my shoulder. "You see those tanks? They're yours."

I looked at the six Russian tanks lined up at a safe distance in the desert, like elephant pearls.

"You're going to empty them out, pile the munitions and whatever else is inside them neatly next to each tank, make an inventory of everything, and in double time."

I trotted off, but he called after me, "And watch it! Sometimes they leave mines inside. The nastiest ones are the Chinese baby mines. They'll rip your hand off. The other kind will blow up your tank, and leave you standing there in the open. If you want to grab your German girlfriend's tits again, watch out for those baby mines!"

I climbed into the first tank and sat down on the floor. The heat was unbearable, and in seconds I was drenched in sweat. I tried to stand up again, but suddenly I could hardly move for fear. I forced myself to push my head out the hatch and look around. If a mine was going to go off, this time there wouldn't be ten other soldiers torn to bits. An Egyptian tank would be destroyed, and five others would presumably be found to have slight or moderate damage to their paint jobs, and one of those nuts from abroad would be dead. No point to being foolhardy. The whole thing in double time? To hell with the non-com! I would check over every centimeter with German thoroughness. I tried to give my face an expression of German thoroughness. No Yemenite foolhardy grin would heighten the risk I was taking. Who would get word to my mother?

*

"You go tell his family. You were his friend," the Tiger had said. "That's not an order, that's a request."

"I can't. I can't do it. I can't tell his mother."

"There's no one better than you. Please, go!"

His request was an order.

I rang the bell and heard her shuffling to the door. Even before she opened it, I knew that she would look old and brown and wrinkled. I took my gun off my shoulder and looked past her.

Suddenly she was breathing hard.

"Mah im ha ben sheli?" she asked in a guttural, expressionless voice. Something with my son?

I couldn't say a word. I merely shook my head to indicate to her that she shouldn't ask any more questions.

"Atah ha chawer shelo?" Are you his friend?

I nodded.

"Atah ha Germani?" Are you the German?

I nodded again.

"Hu met?" Is he dead?

I didn't move. She shook her head energetically, reached into the pocket of her worn housedress, and held out a card to me. I hung my gun over my shoulder again so I could hold the card in both hands. I recognized the "survival card" and Samir's spidery handwriting: "The war is over, I'm fine. I was in the field hospital the whole time, but now I'm better. Soon we'll be furloughed. I'm longing for you all. Samir." Why had he read us only that other idiotic text? Why could he never be serious?

"Hu met?" she asked again.

I nodded, and before I heard her wail, my brain switched off. In literature and screenplays it always says in such situations, "He stood there as if paralyzed," but that doesn't explain a thing. You hear a question, but at that moment your brain decides to take a siesta. It simply fails in its duty to make the voicebox and the tongue speak. Meanwhile your knees shake, and your heart experiments with new rhythms.

I sat in the Egyptian tank from Russia and stared at my hands, which with German thoroughness were groping around on their own for Chinese baby mines. When I got back, she would not be there anymore, and my hands would never touch her firm belly or her wonderful breasts. But the boy in the Warsaw Ghetto would still be there, and the other children who were slaughtered. Why was I so afraid of a mine? Why had my hands gone off on their own? Screenplays that use phrases like "He stood as if paralyzed" describe only a side effect. Something much more important than the paralysis of the brain is a new self-awareness of the body's individual parts.

KATJA BEHRENS

Crows of God

I AM ALONE IN THE CROWD, it is afternoon, the light already a little dim: winter in Jerusalem, it gets dark early. A touristy area. Cafés and souvenir shops. Shabbes goblets, Shabbes lights, menorahs, Hanukkah lights, piles of yarmulkes, piles of talliths, and a little fellow who bobs up in the crowd and then disappears, a black-coated Rumpelstiltskin: earlocks bouncing on his shoulders, dignity conferred by a high-crowned hat and the pious garb, womanish like a priest's cassock but not so full, his legs barely have room to move; perhaps he has lived in this caftan for a long time, poor little fellow, he probably grew up in it, and now it is too tight. The thin material reveals the shape of his little butt. When I stop, he stops too; when I move on, he scurries after me . . .

hungry crow has spotted flesh. I have no idea how long he has been following me, this odd bird; I turn around and see a glitter in his dark eyes. Why are birds' eyes so cold? I feel no fear—a little fellow, a yingele, a Yeshiva student, should stick his nose in The Book . . . a crow with payess, hopping through the crowd,

and I really used to think the men of God were beyond the flesh, at least until that evening in Tel Aviv: Dizengoff, the main boulevard, loud and stinking of exhaust fumes. Restaurant, neon-lit, white-tiled.

I was waiting for friends. It was loud, it was evening, summer and warm, doors and windows open everywhere. I was eating something the menu called *spaghetti Bolognese*, eating it and feeling annoyed, noodles with ketchup and rock music, when this old man laden down with shopping bags came in. Black suit, black hat, snow-white hair, biblical beard.

With a hand that trembled gently like a leaf in the wind he placed a ten-agorot coin on the table.

I understood at once. He was showing me what he wanted of me, but the ten agorot were to be understood symbolically; of course it was supposed to be more.

A poor old man, I thought, and I sit here and eat expensive spaghetti, I have to give him something.

I put down my fork, reached for my pocketbook, and dug out my change purse.

He put down his bags and waited patiently.

My change purse was empty.

I stared at the plate with the limp spaghetti, now getting cold, and tried to recall when and where I had spent all my change. The roar of traffic, the rumble of buses passing, and the accelerated heartbeat of the music. The old man was waiting. I looked up at him: good black eyes in a face marked with dark furrows in those parts the white thicket did not cover, and a beard like GodtheFather in the Land of the White Mountains, where HisServant had taken us in, although we had been the ones who had nailed OurLordJesusChrist to the Cross, even though it was all long ago and we really could not do anything about it, it was still our fault, somehow, we knew that, somehow, I knew that and fetched Reverend-Father his slippers even though it could never be made good, nevermore, poor Lord-Jesus, repentantly I fetched our benefactor's slippers, He liked that, and once I pulled up my skirt to show Him what was underneath, *new panties*, He didn't like that, the women dragged me away, horrified, the Lord'sServant in the Land of the White Mountains bathed in his shirt, Saturday evening in the kitchen he climbed into the washtub in his shirt, so chaste or so careful to avoid the sight of his naked body, terrible when the bird in this cage spreads its wings, sin, the women said, one mustn't, on that they agreed, the women hovering over him and the women hovering over me, agreed, even if they had never seen themselves down there and never would, *down there* was shame! no matter what was there, it was shame on you! and the boy who wanted to become a ReverendFather understood and was disgusted by his own flesh and lived in his body as though it were a prison cell in the Land of the White Mountains. It was there that I first heard the expression *to gas* and asked what it meant, and learned that it had to do with breathing and with the country on the other side of the border where we came from, we must be grateful, the women said, so I learned to breathe unobtrusively, for one's breath was dangerous and could betray one, *we* can't afford that, Lord have mercy, said the women, if it comes out, and I did not know what *out* meant, or where *down there* or *up above* were, and I turn around and see that the yingele is still following me, slinking like a beast of prey, ducking down when I turn my head, I have an eye on him even when I do not look directly at him, he must be crazy the way he hops and scurries after me and the earlocks bounce on his shoulders when he hops and leaps and takes cover behind people and trees, as though all would be lost if he were caught, he must be crazy, but what is crazy? the yingele, that Rumpelstiltskin must have his reasons, although Adonai is not as petty as OurLadyof-Sorrows, who turns away shuddering when the spirit escapes from the bottle and, once outside, stands erect and grows to twice its size until, trembling with strength, it juts out into the world, then she says For shame! but she has nothing to say to the yingele, she is not responsible for him, but nevertheless he hides, I allowed myself to be fooled by the black garb, he is not a crow, he is a yingele, even if he hops and eyes me and comes closer and closer—crows eat carrion, they dip their beaks into dead flesh, but this little Talmud student is hunting something living, or at least so he imagines, *at be-emet chaticha*, as they say here when they want to pay you a compliment, *you're a real piece*, and lick their lips like a cat in a butcher shop, I allowed myself to be deceived by the pious garb, again, black, the color of mourning and of men of God, that is probably why I am picturing the old man, black suit, black hat, and the beard reminiscent of God, as white as eternity, standing without humility, without impatience by my table in the neon-lit restaurant, where a serving of spaghetti cost exactly a hundred times as much as the value of the coin he had silently placed beside my plate, to make clear to me what he wanted.

I said, or tried to say, that I had no change, only German money left. He nodded with dignity and did not budge from the spot.

I wanted to go on eating my spaghetti, reached for my fork. The old man stood there as though he had put down roots, an old tree, dignified in posture, but visibly marked by long, hard winters. I put my fork down again and pulled out the hundred-shekel note. The old man stirred, said he could give me change, reached into his pantspocket, and brought out a thick bundle of banknotes. I was surprised, felt distrust rising in me, looked up at the flowing beard and the lined face, and was ashamed. What an ugly thought!

The old man was collecting for a pious cause, that was it, that had to be it, and he did not really look decrepit, only a little grubby. That is how pious men are, I thought. Have no idea where the thought came from, or rather I do, I was thinking of the starets, or some other holy man: it was only the sinful body—that a person could feel free to neglect, OurBlessed-Mother would never have turned up her nose at someone who reeked, the main thing was that the soul be pure—on that she placed great value, VirginandMotherofGod, invented by men in the place where I come from, except that she is not responsible for him, and Adonai does not claim that the devil sits in a woman's hollow place. Have no idea why I am suddenly so furious at the Rumpelstiltskin, such hate, or rather, I know I should feel pity, a little man stands in the woods, still and silent, must wear a woman's robe, a tight black ridiculous thing, in which he thanks his Creator every morning that He did not make him a woman. I have a rage in my belly and a desolate cry for justice, and now I buy myself an ice cream cone, maybe it is not true at all, perhaps I only imagined it, maybe he is not following me at all, the little rat the crow of God, that remains to be seen, Malaga Torrone Stracciatella, neon light and rock music pounding like an overeager heart, is in such a hurry, will never arrive anywhere, an enraged heart strikes, again and again, mercilessly,

had I known, I would not have gone into this restaurant. The old man seemed to lower his head involuntarily, while the gnarled hands leafed through the packet of money and the silently counting lips made his beard tremble on his chest.

He could not change a hundred after all.

I asked for the check, paid, and gave him the coins I received as change.

Now he was sitting at my table, uninvited—the dignity of age had given him the right to stow his bags and bundles under the table, to sit down and ask where I came from.

Whenever I am asked that, I cringe for a moment. I know how the word sounds here, *Germania*, in Germany just the name of a kind of beer, but here the pounding of boots, the rattling of trains, and the smell of gas and smoke, *Germánia* I say, and sense them pulling back, establishing their distance, a *Germaniá, better not to breathe the same air.*

The old man was called Ariel and had survived in Hungary—how, he did not say, and I did not ask. In 1946 he had come here from Romania. His wife had died two years ago. He had twelve grandchildren. He got up and went to the other tables to beg. He was very small. The black, somewhat grubby figure with the solemn hat, the deliberate movements that did not speed up with the music; I looked away. Now that I knew him I felt a bit ashamed. He had left his bags and bundles with me. I quickly ate the last of the spaghetti.

He came back and took his place at the table the way a person comes home. Did he want anything to drink, I asked. He shook his head.

Only talk, he said. Do you have children?

Everywhere in the world the same question when people

meet, the Indio on the riverbank by night with the cicadas chirping, the waiter in the old fortified city of Galle, and the hair-
dresser in Hanover, New Hampshire, all ask the same thing.
They would ask the same thing in Baghdad or Beirut: parents,
siblings, children, how many, what ages, boys or girls? And they
must have asked thus in earlier times. Two sons, I said, and
because I had just arrived in the country and had forgotten the
word for twenty, I said thirty.

He looked at me kindly and asked how old I was, and
nodded when I told him.

Good, very good.

I imagined he meant I looked good for my age. We talked,
Ariel and I, somehow, I had come back poor in words, with the
remnants of a limited vocabulary I had scraped together many
years ago, which my memory now seemed reluctant to cough
up. So I grasped only a word here and there of what Ariel was
saying, and each word stood out like a marker in a desolate
landscape, a shrub in the steppe that helped me find my way in
the vast expanse of the foreign language, and sometimes it
turned out to be a mirage. When Ariel noticed that I was not
following, he would try an English word, which, spoken with a
Hungarian accent, sounded even stranger than the language in
which we were trying to communicate. But I nodded, out of
politeness and because I already knew that even patient repeti-
tion would not put me in a state of understanding. Ariel nodded
likewise in response to everything I tried to say, looked at me
with his kind eyes and said tov or *tov meod*, and once he placed
his hand on mine, left it there for a bit, in a fatherly or grand-
fatherly way, next to my empty spaghetti plate, from which a
faint smell of ketchup still rose. At some point he asked whether
I was coming with him. I did not understand all of it, only *bench*
and *sit* and a gesture with his head indicating outdoors. I assumed that this place with the rock music and the sparsely clad
people was too worldly for him, that he felt out of place, and it
really was not the right setting for a pious man, unthinkable for
ReverendFather in the Land of the White Mountains, where the

little church, the cemetery, and the rectory formed the seemingly peaceful center of the village, in which at dusk the mooing of the cows blended with the sonorous pealing of the church bells, and in the house the stove crackled, and on the wall hung OurLordJesusChrist, who was bleeding because they had nailed him up, as some kind of punishment, he must have done something, certainly he regretted it, he held his head bowed and was ashamed, but he should have thought of that earlier, now it was too late, and it was probably my Mama who had nailed him up there, maybe he had run away or made so much noise that it disturbed ReverendFather, and he had to write his sermon, but the stove was crackling, and now and then it opened its mouth and wanted to be fed, and I saw its red throat and knew that this was the entrance to hell, where the poor souls were simmering in purgatory, what wailing and gnashing of teeth!

But we needed the stove; without a fire it was cold.

Out gathering wood we came to a crossroads, and there stood OurBlessedLady, who had red cheeks from all the fresh air, sometimes she reached out her hands and wanted to be given something, and sometimes she held OurSavior on her lap, he was naked, BabyJesus, was terribly cold, but OurLordinHeaven had his reasons, He knows best, Lisi said, she was Reverend-Father's sister and her name was probably Elisabeth, and she certainly never guessed who we really were, for later, when ReverendFather was dead and we were back where gas was now used only for cooking, she said, It wasn't right to endanger ReverendFather that way, you shouldn't have done that. But she certainly was pious, was Lisi.

"Kumm," the old man said.

I nodded and got up at once. He remained seated for a moment, then he bent down for his bags. Only then did I see that one was filled to the top with potatoes.

It was noisy on the street. Many people were hurrying along. We walked slowly side by side. He was so small that I could gaze down on his black hat.

He did not live in Tel Aviv, he said.

Well, where then?

He murmured something that was drowned out by a bus rumbling by and sounded like *Bnei Brak* or *Bnei Brith*, I had heard of that somewhere, somehow, something especially pious.

We walked very slowly, past neon-lit shops, acrylic pullovers, silk scarves, a movie house, a bus stop, we pushed our way through the crowd, and then the old man wanted to turn in at a side street.

Away from the noise, I thought. The noise was getting on my nerves, too, especially the buses. But it was very dark in the alley, quiet and dark, and not a soul to be seen.

I stood still like an animal that senses something.

No, I do not want to go in there.

The words *no* and *do not want* are things one never forgets when once one has spoken a language, yet for a moment, when the old man took my hand and tried to pull me, I was not sure whether he had understood me.

"Kumm," he said.

He tugged at my hand. I stood still, feeling like a stubborn mule, but I stood stockstill without really knowing why.

The old man said something I did not understand.

"Pardon me?" I asked.

He repeated what he had said, and I still did not understand.

The furrowed face took on a roguish expression, and the hand that still grasped mine tightly tried to pull me down to his toothless mouth, which had opened like a small entry to hell in the white thicket.

"A kiss," he said in English.

The shock made me resort to German: *Auf Wiedersehen.*

I hurried away, but not without tossing a *Shalom* over my shoulder, along Tel Aviv's main boulevard, back to the restaurant we had left and to the table where I had been sitting, which now appeared to me a refuge, a familiar spot in a hostile world—my empty plate was still there.

At the next table someone said, "That was fast."

At least I think that's what he said.

HENRYK M. BRODER

Our Kampf

ONCE MORE THE GERMANS have been betrayed by history, this time in a particularly perfidious fashion. They've lost a war in which they didn't even really take part. Like the beaten Iraqi army, the "noble souls" of the German peace movement slunk away from the battlefield.

How remarkable: while all over the world people were breathing a sigh of relief, while the Iraqi soldiers were gratefully hugging the American GIs who'd captured them, in Germany a secret feeling of disappointment began to spread. What had happened in the Gulf War was bad, but not bad enough. The expected apocalypse hadn't occurred; in spite of all the hopes and fears, a third world war had been averted, and even the predicted environmental catastrophe had failed to materialize. And above all: the oil slick on the Gulf had been blocked long before it reached the Baltic island of Sylt, famous for its nude beaches.

Normal conditions returned. Bedsheet banners, now gray with grime, were hauled in from balconies. The obituaries for "our beloved Mother Earth," printed but never distributed, landed in the green recycling bin. The question "When will *we* be the desert?" disappeared from the main entrance to Humboldt University, and the demand "Honk if you're against the war!" suddenly lost its meaning. Yet the German peace movement had achieved its most important war objective: from the first day of the war to the last, the movement had remained morally pure. Those who'd settled in for a longer war felt cheated out of any reward for their efforts by the sudden end of hostilities. Among them were "male and female judges, male and female attorneys, and other male and female legal experts," 1118 of them to be precise, who'd taken out full-page ads demanding "An End to the War in the Gulf!" and calling for a "Peace Forum of Legal Experts." Suddenly one day they found themselves forced to turn their attention once more to the civil and criminal justice system. The overwrought women of "Operation Scheherazade" could no longer pursue their goal of a "World Plebiscite Now!" in which "every single person in the world would be heard on this life-and-death issue." Instead, two Scheherazade women traveled to New York to bring U.N. Secretary General Pérez de Cuéllar a petition with forty thousand signatures.

But the package containing the petitions got "lost in the shuffle," and the Secretary General deputized his press secretary to receive the women. They presented their proposal to him: an "extraparliamentary women's world security council" should be established and have the right "to block all resolutions of the U.N. Security Council directed against human and women's rights or against peaceful means of conflict resolution." The U.N. press secretary, according to one of the women after her return from New York, seemed "visibly impressed" by the proposal.

When the main actors withdrew from the international arena to the domestic sandbox, the time seemed to have come to close the chapter "The War in the Gulf and the German Peace Movement." There remained just a few particularly valuable utterances from the period between January 15 and February 28, 1991 to be preserved for posterity, footnotes to history, so to speak. So let us hear a few contemporaries speak their parts, in their own inimitable styles. Gerhard Schröder, for instance, a Social Democratic politician, at that time prime minister of Lower Saxony.

Shortly after Saddam Hussein had threatened to turn Israel

into one big crematorium, Gerhard Schröder refused to participate in a demonstration of solidarity with Israel, since the call
to the demonstration contained no demand for a ceasefire. On
February 3, 1991 Gerhard Schröder took the opportunity to
explain his carefully worked-out position on a television talk
show. Among other things he said, "I refused because they were
demanding that I simultaneously show solidarity with Israel and
support for the war. And I do not support the war and cannot
support it. . . . I think anyone who embraces the logic of the war
must face up to what it implies. It implies that if Saddam
Hussein uses poison gas, the other side, the Western allies, will
be discussing atomic weapons, and if you follow that out, the
use of atomic weapons cannot be ruled out. This war scenario
would destroy everything in the Middle East, including Israel,
and us, and the basis of life for our young people . . ." Asked
what he felt about the British position on the war, Gerhard
Schröder said, "It's quite a country, and when I was there,
because the pubs close at 10:30, I watched a whole bunch of
stupid movies on TV, and it upset me to see how for forty years
we've been portrayed as so warlike and just panting for war,
and I never felt that was right and also not an accurate image
of the Germans. But now, now the majority of Germans are saying 'We're against war,' and now that's not right either. You
know what, this British campaign annoys me, and I find it
undignified the way we're reacting to it in Germany, I mean
knuckling under and saying, They're right to see it that way.
They're not right; the British are working through not just this
conflict but also a couple of other things, and it's really time to
tell them, and I'd be glad to tell them myself: Get going and
organize a reasonable, socially responsible society, and then we
can engage each other on these problems as Europeans on an
equal footing, even critically . . ."

Well, all right, the Social Democratic Party is still struggling
to live down the fact that its deputies voted for war credits in
the First World War and subsequently made sure the kaiser got
his pension in exile. The party doesn't want to repeat its earlier

mistakes, and that speaks in its favor. But must it go so far as to let Gerhard Schröder take a position on moral and political questions? One should handle Saddam Hussein with care, Schröder opined, so as to keep him from using poison gas, which in turn would keep the Americans from using atomic weapons, which in turn would keep the atomic fallout away from his electoral district. That would be the real catastrophe! And if the pacifist Schröder, who doesn't want to demonstrate for Israel, represents national interests, it must disturb him, of course, to see the Germans react in such an "undignified" way and "knuckle under" to the "British campaign" against Germany. How lucky that the Germans no longer have the option of sending over a couple of V-2 rockets to give the British a notion of dignity, since one simply cannot talk with them on an equal footing, primitive as they are. The German schoolmaster is peace-loving these days and confines himself to exporting scientific know-how for the manufacture of biological and chemical weapons, then letting others do the dirty work. This is how German social democracy comes to terms not only with history but also with any conflict between Baghdad and Buxtehude.

Another spokesperson for the new German pacifism who bears an unresolved grudge toward the old and the new allies is Alice Schwarzer, editor of the feminist magazine *Emma*. In a television interview with Günther Jauch on January 23, 1991 she said, among other things, "Generations of Arab peoples were humiliated and enslaved by white masters, and they've had it up to here [hand at nose level]; they're not taking it anymore. Then came the period when the two blocs, east and west, divided up this entire area, and now, as we know, all that's begun to erupt, and so the Third World and the Arab world have begun to erupt . . . And the march into Kuwait is certainly problematic but not entirely absurd. The country's existed for only thirty years, it really belonged to Iraq at one time. Be that as it may, it's a conflict. But I'm of the opinion that the Americans would have done better to stay home. In the last few decades—I have a good memory—they've given us a whole slew of conflicts where they thought they had a right to intervene, for whatever reasons, and millions were killed on both sides . . ."

Asked about the missile attacks on Israel, Alice Schwarzer said, "They're very dramatic, they're dramatic just in themselves, I mean, people in danger and getting killed, that's always bad, and especially painful for us Germans, because the fact that Israel exists, and thank God exists, has something to do with the Holocaust and fascism, after all. But I think the safest thing for Israel in the long run would be peaceful coexistence with its neighbors; anything else won't help Israel much."

Anyone familiar with the eloquence with which the editor of *Emma* usually expresses herself cannot help being surprised to hear her stuttering and stammering this way. If we leave aside the embarrassed fillers, one statement stands out. The missile attacks on Israel are "especially painful for us Germans." Once more the Jews have had preferential treatment! While they merely had to contend with the Scuds, "we Germans" were forced to choke on the Holocaust again.

If this spokesperson suffers from certain inhibitions where Israel and the Jews are concerned, she has no compunctions at all about expressing herself on other matters. According to her, it's not just the Third World that's beginning to erupt. The march into Kuwait, so we hear, was "certainly problematic but not entirely absurd," analogous to the rape of a woman who resists an admirer's overtures and then is simply taken by force. Problematic but not entirely absurd. That Kuwait has existed as a country "for only about thirty years" is a similarly fetching argument.

For one thing, the Federal Republic of Germany has existed only ten years longer than that, and for another thing, we have a succession of countries of even more recent date. The Americans, she thinks, would have done better to stay home, and the reference to a "whole slew of conflicts" and "millions killed" makes one suspect that she's thinking not only of the most recent intervention but also of one that ended about forty-five years ago. If she were active back then, Alice Schwarzer would not be editing *Emma* but at best the magazine of the Nazi women's organization. As far as the details are concerned, for example the condemnation of United States imperialism, there wouldn't be much difference. Her view of the world is untarnished by any thoughts of where she would be and what she would be doing today if the Americans had stayed home in 1941—even though she has such a good memory. Alice Schwarzer leans back contentedly and says with perfect equanimity, "I'm so glad the Americans have no reason to help us over here."

This new German innocence, the leftist version of that blessing of having been born later of which Helmut Kohl speaks, also inspired Hans Christian Ströbele to make a statement that he still considers just fine in content; he apologizes only for the infelicitous formulation: "The Iraqi missile attacks on Israel are the logical, almost unavoidable outcome of Israel's policies."

Only a few days earlier he had said in a telephone conversation with Christian Vogt-Moykopf, the Greens' regional council member in Tübingen, "If I could prevent an escalation of the war by having a million Jews die, I'd accept that price." The occasion for the telephone call and this utterance, which Vogt-Moykopf swears was really made, was a letter that some Greens from Baden-Württemberg, Vogt-Moykopf among them, sent the Israeli ambassador in Bonn, saying they supported deliveries of Patriot missiles to Israel. "After our letter was made public, Ströbele phoned me at the Landtag. He said I'd always been 'such a reasonable person' in the past, and he didn't understand how I could advocate delivery of Patriots and in certain cases the deployment of troops to 'that country' . . . Any weapons delivery to Israel would result in 'an escalation of the war and of the conflict in the Middle East in general' . . . I asked him whether the lives of thousands of people meant nothing to him, whereupon he answered, 'If I could prevent an escalation of the war by having a million Jews die, I'd accept that price.'"

After this utterance became known, Vogt-Moykopf received a

letter from Ströbele's lawyer, warning him to "refrain in the future from claiming that Herr Ströbele said . . . " The lawyer's letter noted, among other things: "Herr Ströbele made no such statement. Additionally, you are reporting publicly on a conversation that was conducted in confidence between the two of you . . . Herr Ströbele did not authorize you to disseminate alleged details of this confidential conversation."

Was it a question of a confidential conversation with alleged details, or of an alleged conversation with confidential details? Is it correct to interpret the lawyer's letter as suggesting that a conversation took place in private, with Ströbele relying on the other person's keeping the contents to himself? "When it's a case of anti-Semitic statements, one cannot hide behind confidentiality," Christian Vogt-Moykopf says, "especially not when these statements are made by politicians, who otherwise always want to make everything a matter of public record."

Whether Ströbele expressed his opinion confidentially or by mistake, or presented views that did not reflect his actual opinion, must be left for later investigation. What can be established is that he was reflecting the opinion of at least part of the Greens' grass-roots supporters. After he resigned, citing the best interests of the party, expressions of support came in, not only from the Communist balladeer Franz Josef Degenhardt, who began a letter to the editor with "Dear Ströbele, I congratulate you warmly . . . ," but also from less well-known friends of peace who could identify with Ströbele: "The first prominent German and Green politician to counter the intolerably black-and-white picture with a few clear words on Israel's policies," wrote a reader of the Green paper *Tageszeitung*. "Ströbele is absolutely correct when he talks about the necessity of consistency," wrote another. "Ströbele is right! Without the Israeli policies of the past, there would probably be no Iraqi attacks," a third affirmed.

Many letters to the editor of this newspaper read exactly like the editorials in the right-wing *Nationalzeitung*. And some were of precisely the type that once provided Horkheimer and

Adorno with the insight that the problem in Germany was not the Nazis but those who opposed them. For example: "The hypocritical posturing of Joschka Fischer, elements of the so-called peace movement, and others can no longer be tolerated. When are we finally going to shake off the heavy hand of a past that no longer allows us to reach our own conclusions? It is precisely the protest movement in Germany that shows that 'we Germans' have learned something from the past, but that does not suit the brothers-in-war Shamir and Bush." The right-wing call for Germans to step out of the "shadow of Auschwitz" was thus adapted to the needs of the left. If at one time the slogan had been "The Jews are our misfortune," this time the peace movement came together around the slogan "The Jews are to blame for their own misfortune."

That Saddam Hussein had long ago announced his intention of pursuing the total destruction of Israel was either ignored or made light of. There hadn't been time to call attention to the threat to Israel, explained Brigitte Erler the evening before the big peace demonstration in Bonn. By the time the first Iraqi missiles landed on Tel Aviv, the calls to the rally had already been printed . . . And if during the Nazi period every decent German had hidden at least one Jew for a time, now almost every German friend of peace had at least one Israeli or Jewish friend to whom he had to write an open letter conveying how things should be understood. "In the long run it is not the missiles that pose the greatest threat to Israel's right to live in peace but the unresolved problem of the Palestinians, the enmity of Israel's Arab neighbors," a friend of peace exclaimed in *Die Zeit* to an Israeli woman, who must have taken great comfort in these mature, clever statements as she and her children, wearing their gas masks, waited in a sealed room for the next missile to land.

And when the real danger could no longer be denied, even with the best will in the world, at least cause and effect could be reversed. "Doesn't the threat to Israel stem precisely from the U.S. military response to the Iraqi occupation of Kuwait?"

Andreas Buro asked at the peace demonstration in Bonn. A rhetorical question, as the following sentence confirmed: "Since then the Scud missiles have been landing, and the fear of poison gas is abroad in the land." Following the same logic, one could claim that in a bank robbery involving the taking of hostages it was the intervention of the police that endangered the hostages; until then, everything had been fairly harmless. This attitude led to the logical, almost unavoidable question: What was the cost of preserving the peace, or who should pay the price? "Not even Hussein's unabashed aggression, not even his willingness to commit further genocide, especially on Israel, justifies a war," said Ako Haarbek, superintendent of the Lippe Protestant church.

And his East German brother, the bishop of Berlin-Brandenburg, Gottfried Forck, used an example from daily life to illustrate how one could get the best of Saddam Hussein: "This madman is standing on a roof with a bomb in his hand that could kill not only him but many innocent people as well. My goal must thus be to coax him down from the roof with friendly, cleverly chosen words, so that I can then disarm him."

Bishop Forck had another recommendation for depriving the Iraqi dictator of his power: "The people in Iraq should be encouraged by us to resist this violent regime . . . Let me remind you of the resistance to the government here in the GDR. When we took to the streets, no one thought the system would dissolve so quickly. In the end we were all amazed and taken by surprise when we proved successful. This success is a sign to me that in fact one should place even more faith in non-violence."

Bishop Forck was not the only one whom the impact of Iraqi aggression inspired to think about the advantages of non-violent resistance. The political scientist Ekkehart Krippendorff used an essay on Gandhi and Martin Buber as the occasion to outline how the Third Reich could have been derailed—through passive resistance against the Nazis by the Jews. "Imagine the following scenario: no German Jew complies with the discriminatory measures imposed by the German authorities (the Star of David, separate park benches, limited shopping hours, etc.): could those measures have been implemented in the face of hundreds of thousands? Imagine if not one German Jew had obeyed the order to report to collecting points—the German police would have dragged a few dozen, a few hundred, perhaps even a few thousand one by one from their apartments (passive resistance) and loaded them onto trucks, but hundreds of thousands? . . . Or imagine if the columns of hundreds and thousands on their way to the freight stations had simply sat down—had staged what we call a sit-in today—would the police, the SA, the Wehrmacht, and the SS have dared, with all the Germans watching, to beat up these people of every age and gender and load them, body after body, unresisting yet powerful, onto trucks? . . . It is at least legitimate to speculate whether the regime would not have collapsed in the face of such massive passive resistance."

Yes, it's legitimate to speculate, and the response is also legitimate: Anyone who asks himself something like that is a total idiot who understands just enough about the nature of totalitarianism to merit a professorship at the Otto Suhr Institute. We're left with the bizarre notion that the Nazi regime failed to collapse merely because the Jews failed to stage a sit-in at the loading ramp.

The ink on this meta-nonsense was not yet dry when Krippendorff stepped up for the next round in the academic sack race. I'd written an article in which I suggested that the best way to avoid a war would be to have the Pope go to Baghdad and a high-level German delegation to Tel Aviv; in reply, he offered another scenario: "What if Israel withdrew unconditionally this very day from the occupied territories, accepted the relevant U.N. resolutions, and gave the Palestinians in Israel the right to elect their own representatives and form a self-determined Palestinian state: That would be the heaviest blow and in the long run the most decisive defeat for Saddam Hussein." With that, the finger of blame had been pointed again. The Jews had not only failed to undermine the Third Reich by passive resistance; they had also brought about the war against Hussein through their absurd refusal to "withdraw unconditionally from the occupied territories." Even before Ströbele called out to the Israelis, "All your fault!" Krippendorff commented that the strikes by Iraqi missiles on Israeli cities and the rejoicing of the Palestinians was the "storm for which Israel's policies provided the wind."

Yet Krippendorff considers himself a friend of Israel, as Walter Jens considers himself a friend of the Jewish people, something he is fond of proving by quoting Albert Einstein, Yeshayahu Leibowitz, and Martin Buber. Jens in his own words: "It is precisely the friends of the Jewish people who are the first to be willing to ponder the thesis put forward by the novelist Yoram Kaniuk—namely that the Germans love the Jews only as victims, not as strong and active . . . we are precisely the ones, I meant to say, who have been charged for years by militant right-wingers with crude philo-Semitism; we are the ones, I believe, who should be careful not to rush to formulate expressions of solidarity that are least appropriate for those who rightly refrained from manifesting time and again their disgust for the misdeeds of the RAF."

Is there anyone in the Federal Republic of Germany, including the five new states, who can explain to me, Henryk Modest Broder from Polish Katowice, what in the world Professor Walter Jens means by that? That he doesn't want to be charged with crude philo-Semitism, certainly not by militant right-wingers, with whom he is usually so concerned? That anyone who manifested his disgust for the misdeeds of RAF, or refrained from doing so, should remain silent on the subject of Israel? And does Walter Jens mean the Red Army Faction or the Royal Air Force? I really don't know; all I know is this: anyone who has friends like this has no need for enemies.

I guess I prefer those who say what's on their minds and don't try to disguise themselves as friends of Israel. Deputy Vera Wollenberger, for example (Alliance 90/Greens), who, after returning from a fact-finding trip to Syria and Jordan, announced that sending weapons to Israel was "very dangerous, because that will cause greater bitterness in the Arab world." One would

like to thank Deputy Wollenberger for her contribution to the
political Ash Wednesday; she simply but clearly pointed out a
causal connection: the better Israel's chances of survival, the
worse the mood in the Arab world. That should make it clear
to even the most unassuming friend of peace in Radebeul how
one could cure the Arabs' bitterness.

A similar sentiment, though worded differently, was expressed by the Party of German Socialists' honorary chairman,
Hans Modrow. He stated: "The only real protection for Israel is
not to deliver any weapons." That was spoken by a Party of
German Socialists/Socialist Unity Party functionary who was
one of those responsible for the GDR's sending instructors to
teach the Iraqi army the proper way to handle chemical weapons.

What can we learn from all this? In normal human relations
we consider someone who fails to aid a person in danger an
accessory to a crime. If a person is being threatened by his
neighbor, and one doesn't help him but instead lectures him
about trying to establish good neighborly relations; if a person
is drowning and one launches into a discussion of whether one
should throw him a life preserver, since he's to blame for his
situation because he didn't learn to swim when he should
have—anyone who behaves this way should at least not pretend
to be a well-meaning friend. Shame sets a limit on every form
of hypocrisy. And anyone who behaves this way should ask
himself whether he isn't secretly hoping for the misfortune that
he conjures up with all his so-called rational deliberations.

After the first Iraqi missiles landed on Tel Aviv, Joschka
Fischer commented that the attacks on Tel Aviv did not have
"the status they should in people's minds;" the slogan "Hands
Off Israel!" should be as powerful a demand as "Stop the War
Immediately!" But Joschka Fischer was way off. The Iraqi attacks
on Israel had exactly the status in the minds of the peace-
movement folks that they were supposed to. There was a simple
reason why the attacks did not produce the shock and horror
Fischer hoped for. The possible destruction of Israel was not
only accepted approvingly as the logical, almost unavoidable

(i.e., deserved) consequence of Israeli policy; it was this option that earned Saddam Hussein the sympathy bonus that he could not have achieved with his anti-imperialist fulminations alone.

To make sure I'm misunderstood correctly: I don't mean that the majority of Germans want to see Israel destroyed. I mean that in a quantitatively and qualitatively substantial segment of the peace movement, the unconscious but very pressing desire was at work to see Saddam Hussein exploit the historic opportunity to finish the job the Nazis had been prevented from bringing to a conclusion. Then certain restrictions would finally disappear, and no German would have to refrain from saying things about German history that he wants to say but isn't permitted to. We, that is to say, the better Germans, would finally be rid of a past that no longer allows us to judge freely. In other words, with the second final solution of the Jewish question, in Palestine, the first final solution would disappear behind the scenes of history. And coincidentally, proof would be supplied that no one can live in peace with the Jews, not even the Arabs, who after all are also Semites.

Krippendorff would call such notions a "scenario." I consider it a logical, almost unavoidable consequence of the insights that have been forced upon one by the weeks just past. One must calmly face up to the fact that at the same time as Saddam Hussein's promise to destroy Israel was not being taken seriously or was being made light of, the scenario of a "third world war" was being developed, a war that would cost "several million lives" (Vera Wollenberger).

Young Germans who settle in for vigils under the slogans "When will *we* be the desert?" and "This time the Gulf—and tomorrow?" and hand out obituaries for "our beloved Mother Earth" and at the same time urge Israel not to get all worked up over a few rockets but instead to withdraw from the occupied territories—they may be confused souls, objectively speaking, yet they know exactly what they're doing. If one reproaches them for practicing their pacifism on the backs of third parties, they respond that they've simply learned a lesson from German history: Force should never again be used as a political tool. They remind me of a thoroughly rehabilitated violent criminal who watches calmly while a mugger attacks a passerby, and doesn't intervene because he's sworn off violence and is determined not to suffer a relapse.

The peace movement's resolute silence in the face of the massacre of Kurds and Shiites by Iraqi troops, just like its silence at the beginning of the Gulf War when Kuwait was attacked, should be disturbing only to those who believe the leaders of the movement when they say they're not motivated by anti-American resentment.

On April 13, 1991 a letter appeared in the *Frankfurter Rundschau* in response to an article by *FR* editor Reifenrath. The author of the letter was a Dr. Andreas Buro, spokesman for the Committee for Basic Rights and Democracy, headquartered in Bonn-Beuel. He was searching for an answer to the question many people were asking themselves: Why doesn't the peace movement take to the streets en masse to protest the murder of the Kurds? This couldn't be expected of the peace movement, Buro explained, for "What kind of super-humans are these demonstrators expected to be; are they supposed to be on the streets constantly, and at the same time hold down jobs, and also live the good life and have lots of hobbies like every other man and woman?" After all, there are "on average ten to twenty wars going on at the same time in the world," and "in many countries torture goes on all the time, and human rights are trampled on . . ."

That makes sense. Even the most committed fighters for peace have to earn their daily bread, and it wouldn't be fair to expect them to miss their belly-dancing and Ikebana courses for some war or other. Let's be generous and give them a chance to relax with their hobbies and gather new strength. Next time it's a question of protesting U.S. imperialism or Zionist aggression, they'll be back out in force.

BENJAMIN KORN

Witching Hour
Images of Germany
—Sixty Years Later

> *One often has the impression that the Hitler boil has not yet*
> *burst. The pus is pulsating, but it does not come out.*
> —Norbert Elias, "Studies on the Germans," 1989

ON FRENCH TELEVISION HELMUT KOHL always used to appear at the side of François Mitterand when the two of them, like Laurel and Hardy, solemnly reviewed an honor guard. Now he appears more often alone, expressing his dismay after fire-bombings and racially motivated murders, such as that of three Turkish women in Mölln. Yet when the German chancellor steps up to the microphone, he does not give the impression of a man determined to put an end to this new brand of terrorism. He seems more like a perplexed, deeply hurt father no longer able to defend his incorrigible son who, in a drunken state, sets fire to cars, houses, and people, a father who, with heavy heart, is turning his son over to the courts.

Anyone who remembers the set jaws, the toughness, the ruthlessness with which German politicians, police chiefs, and prosecutors smashed the Red Army Faction's terrorism at the end of the seventies, anyone who remembers all the police road-blocks and house searches, the hounding of BMW drivers (the RAF drove BMWs in those days), one of whom was shot by mistake while trying to get away, anyone who has not forgotten that it was almost impossible to take a nap on the edge of certain forests without awakening to find the muzzle of a submachine gun in your face, anyone who remembers all that must be wondering what is really going on in Germany and whether the old distinction between the leftist "fellow without a Fatherland" and the gung-ho nationalist, whose heart is in the right place and who occasionally just gets carried away, is not still alive and well in the new German state. That would certainly seem to be the case.

The comparison people are fond of drawing between left- and right-wing terrorism makes a mockery of German reality and masks the *life-threatening* problem that the German people has with itself. For the right-wing terrorist is like a fish in water, a far cry from the leftist who appears on Wanted posters, whom the average citizen hates and happily turns in to the authorities. If, as *Der Spiegel* claims, up to 25 percent of all Germans agree with the slogan "Foreigners get out," and a third of the population believes that "we're at the point when Germans must defend themselves in their own country against foreigners," the simple arithmetic suggests that more than the 10 percent usually mentioned are potential sympathizers for the fascist gangs. To smoke out this popular movement, which has thus far remained rather quiet, would require far more than the creation of a special police commission. But those responsible are neither willing nor able to offer a political response, and they are incapable of a humane one. As a result Germany is lurching and sliding, via nocturnal murders, beatings, and arson, back into its murderous past. The impressive counterdemonstrations seem not to make a dent. The witching hour.

We are offered metaphors aplenty: the wave of terror has been compared with old "vipers' eggs" now hatching everywhere, with a "forest fire," an "epidemic," a "virus"—and indeed the incredible rapidity and force with which fascism is welling up in Germany, as if through a system of underground communicating tubes, does resemble an epidemic, except that this virus was not buzzing around in the air! The Nazi slogans the young men have mastered so perfectly were not picked up by the side of the road; the young men did not invent them themselves or hear them only yesterday. It's all been handed down; it goes way back. It would be wrong to say that the old demons are returning, for they were here all the time, frozen into the Wall, kept down by our protective forces, which, we now realize, were aptly named: they protected us from ourselves, and others from us.

Handed down from whom? From grandparents to parents to grandchildren, as always. There's something like an irresistible underground current in the German people which secretly swept Hitlerism along in both east and west, despite all the communist and western propaganda campaigns, all the slogans and lip service; now this current is shooting to the surface. It's uniting the Germans. And if I speak here of *the* Germans, of course I don't mean *all* Germans. I mean the widespread subservient type and the petty-bourgeois type, who fears and hates foreigners, a type all of us have a bit of in ourselves and which unfortunately also exists in England, France, Italy, Spain, Russia, and among the Jews.

The so-called innocent bystanders who applauded as houses burned in Rostock and other cities are not abstract adults from another planet; they were the fathers and mothers of the fire-bombers, cheering their sons and daughters on for having the courage to do what the parents hardly dare to dream of: undo Germany's defeat in 1945. A defeat festers in a people's consciousness for a long time; after a defeat every people thirsts for revenge—the Germans started the Second World War because they had lost the first, among other reasons. 1945 is a central date in German history; here we find the bitter pill that the Germans never quite got down and must now swallow; if they fail to do so, they will race headlong toward their next unavoidable catastrophe. What kind of pill is it? Smashed by the Allies but never comprehended, digested, or excreted by the losers—national socialism. Perhaps the fiasco was too enormous, the fear of its consequences too great, the awareness of having commited one of the most barbarous crimes in the history of the human race too crushing; at any rate, the Germans have never really discussed the psychic consequences of their defeat. They have simply denied that it was a defeat, declaring it a victory instead, on both sides of the Spree River (victory of democracy or victory of socialist progress)—yet it was a devastating, unforgettably humiliating defeat. It cries out for revenge, now as then.

The enormous psychic energy that propelled Germany into a murderous war of destruction against half the western world (and not only that world) must have gone somewhere. It did not disappear from the face of the earth overnight, blasted out of people's souls, just because the victorious powers issued orders to that effect.

The Waterloo of this illusion had to come sooner or later, and those who thought it had come on November 9, 1989, when the two divided hemispheres of Germany's brain grew together on the map, seem to have been proven right, and I, who thought it might turn out differently (a more amicable, cordial, relaxed society), seem to have been sorely mistaken.

I am not speaking of the obvious Waterloo of the Stalinist system; I am speaking of the invisible but no less devastating Waterloo of the system of representative democracy that the western powers imported and which now, in the souls of the Germans left behind, reveals itself to be a poorly constructed house of cards.

When the writer Ralph Giordano announced two weeks ago that from now on Jews would arm themselves and undertake their own defense, I at first thought he'd gone mad. I thought he wanted to send the last little band of Jews who had survived genocide into a heroic final battle against their merciless enemies. No! It was a cry for help! The Jews still want to stay in Germany; even now they don't want to leave. Giordano is defending his right to live in his homeland! And because that's the case, the Germans must protect their Jews, their gypsies, their Turks and Moroccans, their Albanians and Iranians; for these people cannot protect themselves. Germans must protect them from Germans! Away with the primitive concept of blood relationship! Since the French Revolution, the *citoyen* has been a citizen of the world, a freeborn human being, related at most by shared ideas, never by blood.

In this country blood is still seething, and in an ancient authoritarian reflex, the Germans, when they hear the blood seething and see their old, powerful, tradition-laden racist and anti-Semitic right wing resorting to violence, are struck to the core, to the very center of their democratic nerve; they seem about to lose all their strength, the whites of their eyes show; their thinking comes to a standstill; they give in, grow weak, and trot along obediently. . . .

There are times when the undigested remains of an entire century lie before a people, and it no longer helps to shut one's eyes and hold one's nose to what one has been spewing out. If German unification does not come about through love, through understanding, through talking with one another, it will come about through hate. And because the hate cannot be directed at other Germans, because every society needs something to glue it together, the hate will be directed at others; this hate bears the names racism, anti-Semitism, xenophobia. The hundreds of thousands who have been taking to the streets for weeks now to express their opposition and to hold up an image of brotherhood to counter the images of hatred—in them resides the hope that things may turn out differently.

About the Authors

Katja Behrens was born in Berlin in 1942. She survived the war with her mother and grandmother in a Catholic parish in Austria. She has worked as a translator of American literature into German, and as a fiction editor. She is the author of a novel and of several collections of short stories, and is writing her second novel. She lives near Darmstadt (formerly West Germany).

Maxim Biller was born in 1960 in Prague and emigrated with his family to Hamburg in 1970. He studied German literature and journalism in Munich, where he now lives. He contributes regularly to *Tempo*, a monthly magazine, and is the author of two collections of short stories. He is currently working on his second collection of essays.

Henryk M. Broder was born in 1946 in Katowice, Poland and lived in Cologne, West Germany from 1958 to 1980. Since 1981 he has lived in both Jerusalem and Berlin. He is a frequent contributor to German newspapers, magazines, and radio programs. He has published numerous books of political essays.

Esther Dischereit was born in 1952 in Heppenheim, West Germany. After working as a typesetter, she has written political nonfiction, children's books, and radio plays, as well as two novels. She lives in Berlin.

Thomas Feibel was born in 1962 in Santiago de Chile to German-Jewish parents. He has lived in Mannheim (formerly West Germany) since 1968. He is a journalist, and his first novel was recently published.

Matthias Hermann was born in 1958 in Bitterfeld, East Germany, and now lives in Grossumstadt/Odenwald (formerly West Germany). He is the author of one collection of poetry.

Barbara Honigmann was born in 1949 in East Berlin, where her parents chose to live after returning from exile in England. She was a theater producer and director before becoming a writer and artist. She now lives in Strasbourg, France.

Peter Stephan Jungk was born in 1952 in Santa Monica, California. He grew up in Vienna, Berlin, and Salzburg. He studied film at UCLA, and has lived in Basel, Vienna, and Jerusalem, where he spent a year at a yeshiva. Since 1988 he has lived in Paris. He is the author of three novels, a biography, and numerous radio plays and screenplays. The biography and one of his novels have been published in English.

Benjamin Korn was born in 1942 in Lublin, Poland and grew up in Frankfurt. Since completing his degree in sociology, he has become a prolific theater director, bringing his productions to all the major German stages. He moved to Paris in 1982 and now divides his theater work between France and Germany. He also writes for German newspapers and periodicals.

Robert Menasse was born in 1954 in Vienna. He taught Austrian literature at the University of São Paulo, Brazil from 1981 to 1986. He is the author of two novels and a book on social aesthetics, as well as much literary criticism. He lives in Vienna.

Chaim Noll was born in 1954 in East Berlin. His parents were high-ranking members of the Communist Party. He studied mathematics and art. After refusing to join the army, he was sent to a psychiatric hospital, and in 1984 he was allowed to emigrate to West Berlin. He is the author of four books, and lives in Rome.

Robert Schindel was born in 1944 in Bad Hall, Austria. His parents, disguised as alien laborers from Alsatia, were sent by the illegal Communist Party to set up a network in Linz. They were apprehended four months after his birth and sent to Auschwitz. An Austrian nurse saved Schindel by transferring him under a false name to a Nazi-run home in Vienna. He was reunited with his mother after the war. Schindel is the author of several books of poems, and one novel. He lives in Vienna.

Rafael Seligmann was born in 1947 in Israel. His parents, German Jews, decided to return to Munich in 1957. He studied political science and history in Munich and Tel Aviv, and worked as a political consultant, journalist, and lecturer at Munich University. He has published two novels and a political analysis of the German-Jewish problem. He lives in Munich.

Leo Sucharewicz was born in 1948 in Lodz, Poland. He grew up in Munich, where he still lives. After studying political science and psychology, he turned to writing and has published a book of short stories and a collection of aphorisms. He is also director of a computer company.

Acknowledgments

MAXIM BILLER: "Finkelstein's Fingers" by permission of the author, © 1991 Maxim Biller, Munich. "See Auschwitz and Die" from *Die Tempojahre*, © 1991 Deutscher Taschenbuch Verlag GmbH & Co. KG, Munich.

HENRYK BRODER: "Heimat? No, Thanks!" by permission of the author, © 1987 Henryk Broder. "Our Kampf" by permission of the author, © 1991 Henryk Broder.

ESTHER DISCHEREIT: From *Joemis Tisch,* Copyright © 1988 Suhrkamp Verlag, Frankfurt am Main.

THOMAS FEIBEL: By permission of the author, © 1991 Thomas Feibel.

MATTHIAS HERMANN: From *72 Buchstaben,* Copyright © 1989 Suhrkamp Verlag, Frankfurt am Main.

PETER STEPHAN JUNGK: From *Shabbat* by Peter Stephan Jungk. Copyright © 1985 by Peter Stephan Jungk. Reprinted by permission of Times Books, a division of Random House, Inc.

BARBARA HONIGMANN: "A Love Out of Nothing" excerpted from *Eine Liebe aus Nichts,* Copyright © 1991 Rowohlt Berlin Verlag GmbH, Berlin. Translated and reprinted with permission. "Novel of a Child" from *Roman von einem Kinde,* © 1989 Luchterhand Literaturverlag GmbH, by permission of the publisher.

BENJAMIN KORN: "Shock and Aftershock" © 1988 Benjamin Korn. "Witching Hour" © 1993 Benjamin Korn. Both by permission of the author.

ROBERT MENASSE: Excerpted from *Selige Zeiten, Brüchige Welt,* © 1991 Residenz Verlag, Salzburg und Wien, by permission of the publisher.

CHAIM NOLL: Translated and reprinted with permission. Chaim Noll, from *Nachtgedanken über Deutschland,* Copyright © 1992 Rowohlt Taschenbuch Verlag GmbH, Reinbek bei Hamburg.

ROBERT SCHINDEL: "The Two-Headed Lamb" excerpted from *Gebürtig,* © 1992 Suhrkamp Verlag, Frankfurt am Main. "Memories of Prometheus" excerpted from *Im Herzen die Krätze,* © 1988 Suhrkamp Verlag, Frankfurt am Main.

RAFAEL SELIGMANN: From *Rubinsteins Versteigerung,* Eichborn-Verlag, © 1989 by permission of the publisher.

LEO SUCHAREWICZ: From *Israelische Geschichten,* © 1992 Roman Kovar Verlag, Munich, by permission of the publisher.